Microsoft Office 2016 Explained

Books by the Same Author

BP757	Windows 10 Explained
BP747	Windows 8.1 Explained
BP743	Kindle Fire HDX Explained
BP741	Microsoft Office 2013 Explained
BP738	Google for the Older Generation
BP735	Windows 8 Explained
BP284	Programming in QuickBASIC
BP259	A Concise Introduction to UNIX
BP258	Learning to Program in C
BP250	Programming in Fortran 77

Books Written with Phil Oliver

BP726	Microsoft Excel 2010 Explained
BP719	Microsoft Office 2010 Explained
BP718	Windows 7 Explained
BP710	An Introduction to Windows Live Essentials
BP706	An Introduction to Windows 7
BP703	An Introduction to Windows Vista
BP595	Google Explored
BP590	Microsoft Access 2007 Explained
BP585	Microsoft Excel 2007 Explained
BP584	Microsoft Word 2007 Explained
BP583	Microsoft Office 2007 Explained
BP581	Windows Vista Explained
BP580	Windows Vista for Beginners
BP563	Using Windows XP's Accessories
BP557	How Did I Do That ... in Windows XP
BP555	Using PDF Files
BP550	Advanced Guide to Windows XP
BP545	Paint Shop Pro 8 Explained
BP538	Windows XP for Beginners
BP525	Controlling Windows XP the Easy Way
BP514	Windows XP Explained
BP509	Microsoft Office XP Explained
BP498	Using Visual Basic
BP341	MS-DOS Explained

Microsoft Office 2016 Explained

by

Noel Kantaris

Bernard Babani (publishing) Ltd
The Grampians
Shepherds Bush Road
London W6 7NF
England

www.babanibooks.com

Please Note

Although every care has been taken with the production of this book to ensure that all information is correct at the time of writing and that any projects, designs, modifications and/or programs, etc., contained herewith, operate in a correct and safe manner and also that any components specified are normally available in Great Britain, the Publishers and Author(s) do not accept responsibility in any way for the failure (including fault in design) of any project, design, modification or program to work correctly or to cause damage to any equipment that it may be connected to or used in conjunction with, or in respect of any other damage or injury that may be so caused, nor do the Publishers accept responsibility in any way for the failure to obtain specified components.

Notice is also given that if equipment that is still under warranty is modified in any way or used or connected with home-built equipment then that warranty may be void.

First Published - March 2016

British Library Cataloguing in Publication Data:

A catalogue record for this book is available from the British Library

ISBN 978 0 85934 762 4

Cover Design by Gregor Arthur

Printed and bound in Great Britain for Bernard Babani (publishing) Ltd

About this Book

Microsoft Office 2016 Explained has been written to help users to get to grips with the integrated components of this package, namely, *Word*; the word processor, *Excel*; the spreadsheet, *PowerPoint*; the presentation graphics, *Notes;* the application that allows you to capture and organise notes you gathered on your PC and *Outlook*; the e-mail and desktop manager. The latter is only bundled with the *Home and Business Edition* of *Microsoft Office 2016* and those above it, although it can be integrated with all other editions if bought separately. All these components are specifically discussed within the *Windows 10* environment. Users of *Office 365* should also find all parts of this book relevant as at the time of writing *Office 2016* and *Office 365* are identical.

Microsoft Office 2016 is an exciting new Office suite that will help with the new demands and challenges to individuals and business. It offers additional tools on earlier versions of the package that use Web technology to provide enhanced single user or workgroup productivity and the ability to access and analyse important business data more efficiently. It also offers real-time collaboration, and the ability to easily connect to various social networks.

This book introduces each application within the *Home and Business Edition* of *Microsoft Office 2016* by itself, with sufficient detail to get you working. No prior knowledge of these applications is assumed, but the aim is to present the package in the shortest and most effective way.

To get maximum benefit from this book, it is recommended that you follow explanations and exercises on screen. Enjoy!

About the Author

Noel Kantaris graduated in Electrical Engineering at Bristol University and after spending three years in the Electronics Industry in London, took up a Tutorship in Physics at the University of Queensland. Research interests in Ionospheric Physics, led to the degrees of M.E. in Electronics and Ph.D. in Physics. On return to the UK, he took up a Post-Doctoral Research Fellowship in Radio Physics at the University of Leicester, and then a lecturing position in Engineering at the Camborne School of Mines, Cornwall, (part of Exeter University), where he was also the CSM Computing Manager. Lately he also served as IT Director of FFC Ltd.

Trademarks

Microsoft, **Windows**, **Windows 10**, **Windows 8.1**, **Windows 8**, **Windows 7** and **Microsoft Office 2010**, **2013**, **2016** and **Office 365** are either registered trademarks or trademarks of Microsoft Corporation.

Wi-Fi is a trademark of the Wi-Fi Alliance

All other brand and product names used in the book are recognised as trademarks, or registered trademarks, of their respective companies.

Contents

1

Package Overview

Microsoft Office Editions

Office 2016 and *Office 365* are an integrated collection of powerful, full-featured programs with the same look and feel. They were specifically designed to allow you to work with your data, either by yourself or to share or collaborate with others and come in five editions, each with a different mixture of applications (for what these Apps can do, see page 3).

Office Stand Alone Editions & Volume Licensing	Word	Excel	PowerPoint	OneNote	Outlook	Publisher	Access	Price (rounded up)
Stand Alone 2016								
Home and Student	✓	✓	✓					**£120**
Home and Business	✓	✓	✓	✓	✓			**£230**
Professional	✓	✓	✓	✓	✓	✓	✓	**£390**
Volume Licensing								
Office 365 Home	✓	✓	✓	✓	✓	✓	✓	**£80**
Office 365 Personal	✓	✓	✓	✓	✓	✓	✓	**£60**

Office 365 Home can be used by up to five PCs or tablets in a single home with 1 TB OneDrive data capacity for an annual fee or £80 (or a monthly fee of £8), while the Personal version's annual fee is £60 (or a monthly fee is £6). Students can use it for 4 years on 2 PCs or tablets for £60.

There are additional versions of *Office 365*, such as *Office Server* versions, but these are more suitable for organisations with a very large number of users, but it also comes with an increased monthly subscription.

If you need extra enterprise features in Outlook or you like the ability to import data from a variety of databases into Excel, then you need to either purchase the Professional edition of *Office 2016*, which also comes with Publisher and Access or subscribe to *Office 365*.

The difference between *Office 365* and *Office 2016* is that with the former major upgrades are carried out frequently, but the moment you stop your subscription you lose the ability to use the programs, while with the later you'll have to wait for the next version release before you get such major updates and you'll have to pay again, but at least the programs are on your computer or tablet and you can continue using them if you don't want to upgrade.

Microsoft Office Across Devices

Apart from *Office 2016* for Windows 7 or higher on desktops, laptops and tablets with Windows 8 or higher, the same suite of applications is also available on the Mac OS X and iPad running iOS 7 or higher.

Also available is a version of Office for iPhone running iOS 6 or higher, Office Mobile for Android phones running OS 4 or higher and Office for Android tablets running KitKat 4.4. However, on the non-Windows operating systems, Office only includes Word, Excel, PowerPoint and OneNote. If you want Outlook for the Mac you'll have to subscribe to *Office 365* which also includes Publisher and Access 2016.

There are also free *Office Online* versions of Word, Excel, PowerPoint and OneNote, for your Smartphone (Windows phone, Android phone and iPhone), but these don't have all the features of *Office 2016* or *Office 365*, but include full, touch-based versions of the programs. These online versions of Office allow you to view and edit documents created in *Office 2016* or *Office* 365 which are on the cloud and store them back on the cloud after you finished.

Applications in both ***Microsoft Office 365*** and ***Microsoft Office 2016*** have the following main functions:

Word	A Word processor that offers almost every imaginable feature, including background spelling and grammar checking, integrated drawing tools, basic picture editing within a document, Smart Tags and Task Panes.
Excel	An electronic spreadsheet that allows the depiction of colourful graphs, the creation of 3D super-spreadsheets by using multi-page workbooks which support 3D *drill-through* formulae, and includes a long list of 'goal-seeking', 'what-if?' type analysis tools and an excellent set of database capabilities.
PowerPoint	A presentation graphics application that allows the creation of slide shows for training, sales, etc., and includes such facilities as object animation, speaker notes, and recorded voice-overs.
OneNote	An application that enables you to capture, organise and reuse notes you gathered on your computer. It stores all your notes in one place and gives you the freedom to work with them later on.
Outlook	An e-mail and Personal Information Manager (PIM) that provides a full set of multi-user, group-scheduling functions, including Calendar, Contacts, Notes and Folder List.
Publisher*	An application that allows the design and creation of printed documents with the help of publication templates. It can auto-fit text to frame sizes, provide inter-frame text flow options, and auto-wrap text around irregular images.

Access* A database management system (DBMS) that includes a full set of WYSIWYG design tools for database, forms, queries and reports, plus a full Visual Basic derived programming language for developing specific applications.

SharePoint* A collaboration program that helps teams work together dynamically, even if team members work for different organisations, work remotely, or work offline.

Built-in Consistency

All **Office** applications have a built-in consistency which makes them easier to use. For example, all applications, including **Outlook**, use a simplified **Ribbon** which makes it easier to find and use the full range of features that they provide. If you have not used a previous version of **Office** (2010 or 2013) then you might find this somewhat daunting at first, but once you start using this interface, you will very rapidly get used to it.

On the next page, I use Word 2016 running on a touch-sensitive screen laptop under Windows 10, to demonstrate the **Ribbon** as it is similar in functionality to all the other applications that make up ***Office 2016*** or ***Office 365***.

Another feature which is common to all applications is the **Office Backpage File** view which will be discussed after the installation of **Office 2016**.

* This book is based on the contents of *Office 2016 Home and Business* edition, so applications shown in the above list with an asterisk are not covered.

The Ribbon

The **Ribbon** is a device that presents commands organised into a set of tabs, as shown in Fig.1.1. The **Ribbon** was first adopted in **Word**, **Excel**, **PowerPoint** and **Access** of **Office** 2007 and then in **Outlook** 2010.

The tabs on the **Ribbon** display the commands that are most relevant for each of the task areas (in this case), as shown below for **Word**.

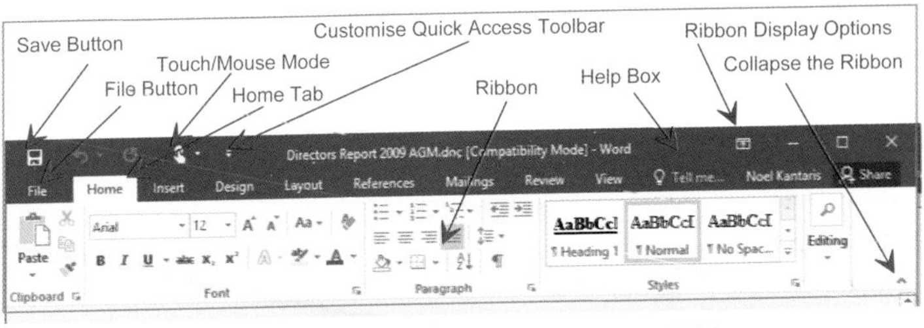

Fig. 1.1 The Home Tab of Word 2016 Ribbon.

Note the **Collapse the Ribbon** ^ button which you tap or click to gain more space on your screen. To display the **Ribbon** again, tap or click the **Ribbon Display Options** button (see Fig. 1.1 above) and select the **Show Tabs and Commands** option from the displayed drop-down menu of choices, as shown in Fig. 1.2.

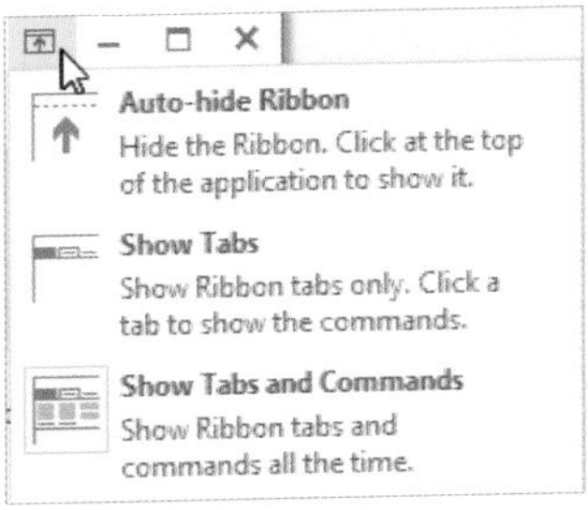

Fig. 1.2 The Ribbon Display Options.

> **Note:** A quick way of collapsing the Ribbon is to double-tap or double-click on any of Word's tabs. To display the Ribbon again, double-tap or double-click on any of Word's tabs.

There are four basic components to the **Ribbon**, as shown in Fig. 1.3 below. These are:

Tabs There are several basic tabs across the top, each representing an activity area.

Groups Each tab has several groups that show related items together.

Commands A command is a button, a box to enter information or a menu.

Quick Step Manager – Many groups have an arrow icon in the lower-right corner to open an 'old style' dialogue box.

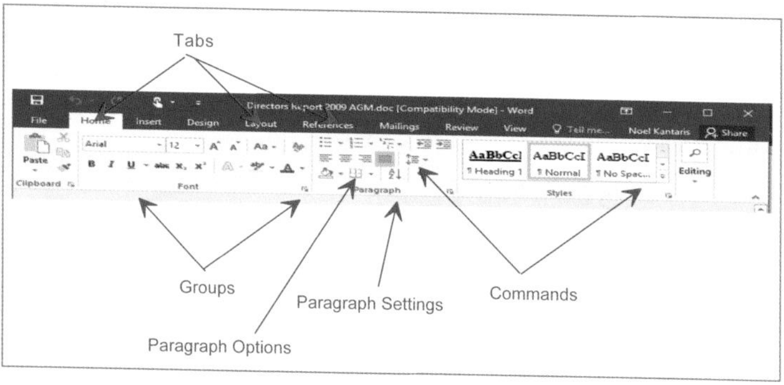

Fig. 1.3 The Components of a Ribbon.

For each activity in all **Office** applications the **Home** tab contains all the things you use most often. In **Word** these include the creation of **Styles**, selection of **Paragraph** options and use of commands that allow you to **Cut** and **Paste**, **Format** text, etc. Tapping or clicking a new tab opens a new series of groups, each with its relevant command buttons.

If you were to use, say **Outlook**, the **Home** tab would include commands to create **New Mail**, **Delete** selected mail, or **Reply** to an e-mail.

Contextual tabs also appear when they are needed so that you can very easily find and use the commands needed for the current operation, such as **Drawing Tools**, etc.

Installing Microsoft Office 2016

To install **Office** 2016 on your computer's hard disc, you must first purchase the version of the product that best suits you. What you get is a product key, but no disc, with four instructions:

- Go to www.office.com/setup.
- Enter the 25-character Product key and follow the on-screen instructions.
- Sign in with or create your Microsoft account.
- Download Office to your PC.

If, on the other hand, you already have a previous version of **Office** installed on your PC, then it will be removed and installation will take place automatically with a 32-bit version of **Office** whether or not your system is a 32-bit or 64-bit computer. While the software is being installed, a screen similar to the one in Fig. 1.4 is displayed.

Fig. 1.4 The Office Installation Window.

Installing **Office** took approximately 20 minutes, at least on my PC. Once completed, the screen in Fig. 1.5 is displayed.

Fig. 1.5 The Completed Office Installation Window.

To find the individual applications of the package in Windows 10, tap or click the **Start** button, followed by **All Apps** and swipe up or scroll down to the individual **Office** components which are displayed in alphabetical order.

To make life easier for yourself, touch and hold or right-click each application in turn and select **Pin to Taskbar** from the displayed menu. In Fig. 1.6, I show the process for **Excel**.

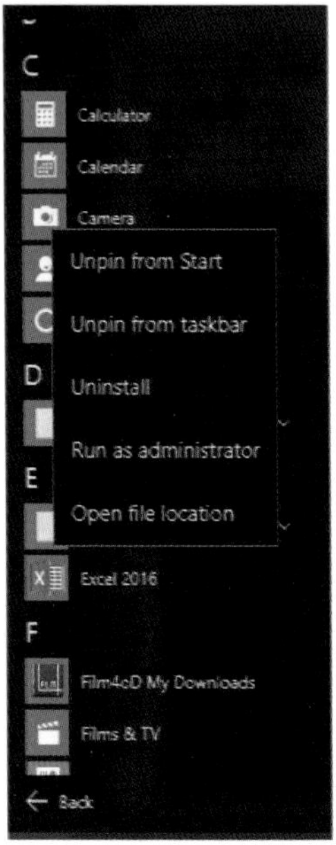

Fig. 1.6 The Touch and Hold or Right-click Menu.

The result of doing this to all the **Office** applications should result in a **Taskbar** similar to that in Fig. 1.7 below.

Fig. 1.7 Part of the Taskbar.

To rearrange the order of appearance of the individual icons on the **Taskbar**, either double-tap and move the application image where you want it to be, or point with the mouse and while holding the left mouse key down move the pointer to the new position which also moves the icon.

Starting an Office Application

To start any one of these Apps, simply tap or click on its image on the **Taskbar**. For example, tapping or clicking on the **Word** icon, opens a screen similar to the one shown in Fig. 1.8 below.

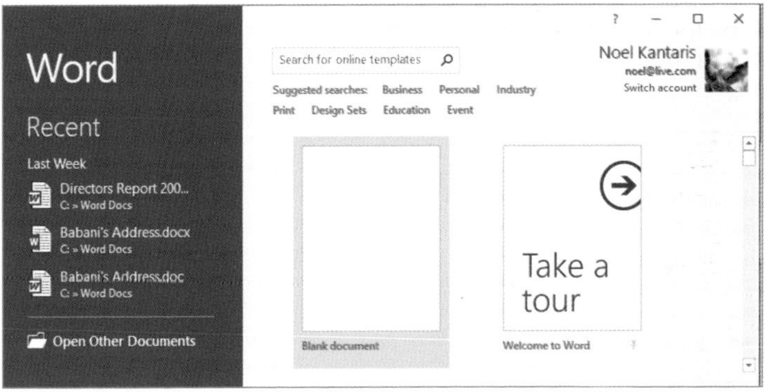

Fig. 1.8 The Opening Screen of Word.

We shall examine **Word** in more detail in the next chapter, but for now just tap or click on the **Blank Document** to open the screen below.

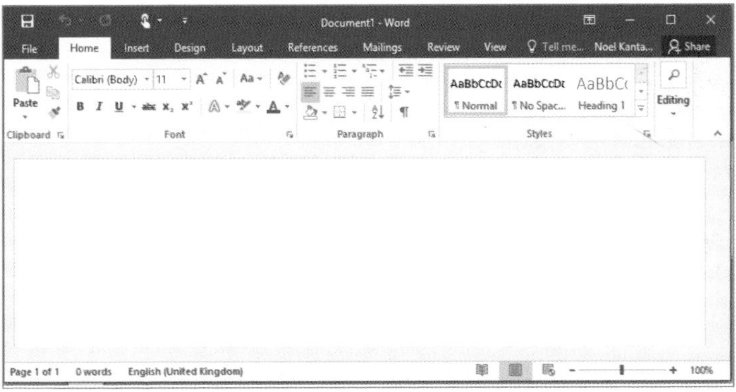

Fig. 1.9 A Word New Document Window.

At the top of the opened **Word** document is the familiar **Ribbon**, discussed earlier. To see the other common feature, the **Office Backstage File** view, tap or click the File button.

The Office Backstage File View

The File command button replaces the old **File** menu across all the pre-2010 **Office** applications with an interface for accessing all of the options relating to the application itself and the current document, as shown in Fig. 1.10 below.

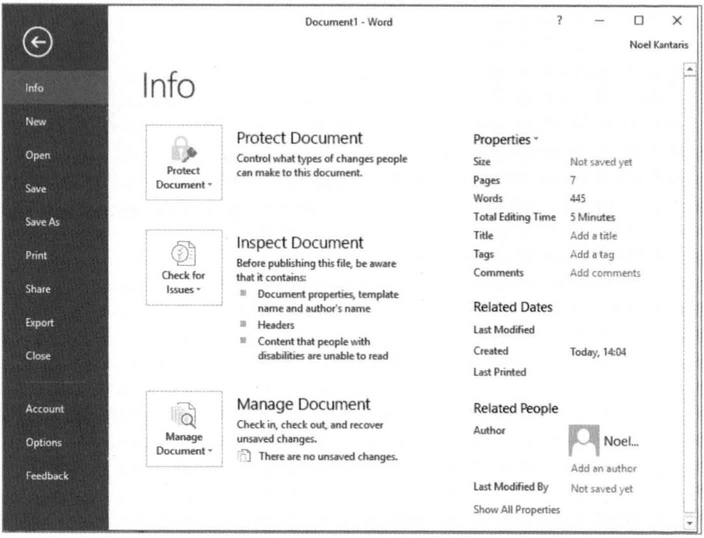

Fig. 1.10 The Office Backstage File View.

As you can see at the left of the display, you find many **Word** settings that are not directly related to creating or managing **Word** documents, such as the **Save**, **Open**, **Print** and **Share** commands.

From here you can manage your documents, protect your documents, prepare documents for sharing, and find other behind-the-scenes choices such as user interface options and personalising your copy of **Office**. These latter options can be accessed by clicking the **Options** button near the bottom of the **Backstage** screen.

The **Export** option, allows you to create a **PDF** or **XPS** file of your document and change the file type from say **.doc** to **.docx** – more about all this in the next chapter.

Getting Help in Office 2016

No matter how experienced you are, there will always be times when you need help to find out how to do something in the various **Office** applications. **Office** 2016 is a very large and powerful suite of programs with a multitude of features. There are several ways to get help.

Help Using a Device with a Keyboard

No matter which module of **Office** 2016 you use, pressing the **F1** function key on the keyboard displays a screen similar to that of Fig. 1.11, but what displays depends, of course, on which **Office** application you are using and what question you typed in the search box.

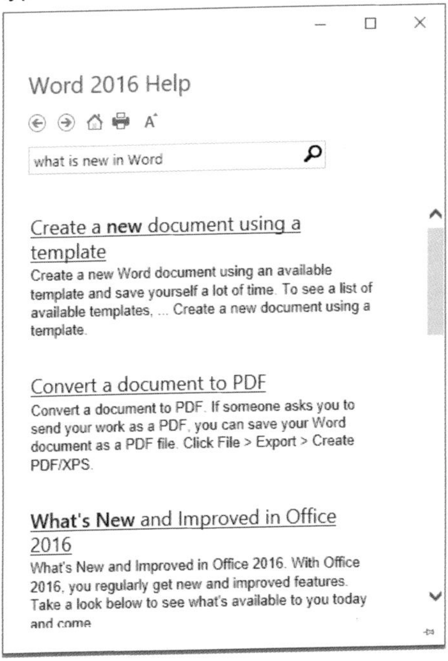

Fig. 1.11 The Microsoft Word Help Window.

Office 2016's **Help** system expects you to be 'online' (connected to the Internet). If you are not, it will inform you and ask you to connect.

Alternative Help on All Devices

Whether your device has a keyboard or not, you can use an alternative way of getting help when using **Office** 2016. This method involves the use of the **Tell me** tab to be found near the right hand side of **Word**'s tabs, as shown in Fig. 1.12.

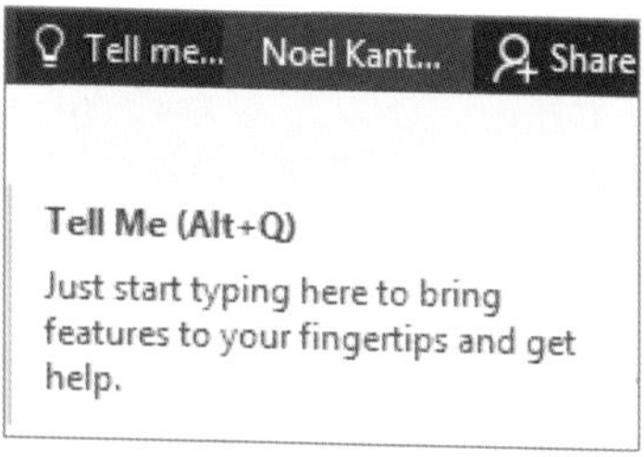

Fig. 1.12 The Tell me Tab.

Tapping or clicking the **Tell me** tab, allows you to start typing a question. If your device does not have a keyboard, you'll need to activate the virtual keyboard before tapping the **Tell me** tab. The virtual keyboard for Windows 10 is to be found at the extreme right of the **Taskbar**, near the **Date** & **Time** area.

Typing a question in the **Tell me** search box, such as 'what is new in Word' displays the screen in Fig. 1.13. Amongst the display options is the **Get Help on "what is new in Word"** which you access if you want to find out the answer to your question.

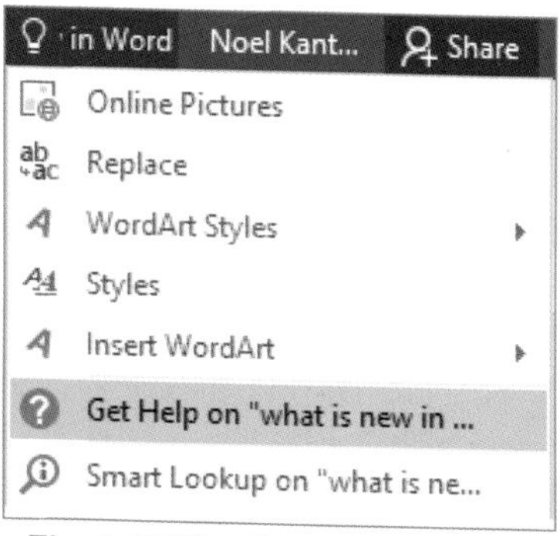

Fig. 1.13 The Tell me Help Menu.

In this case, the result for the question asked is displayed in Fig. 1.14 on the next page.

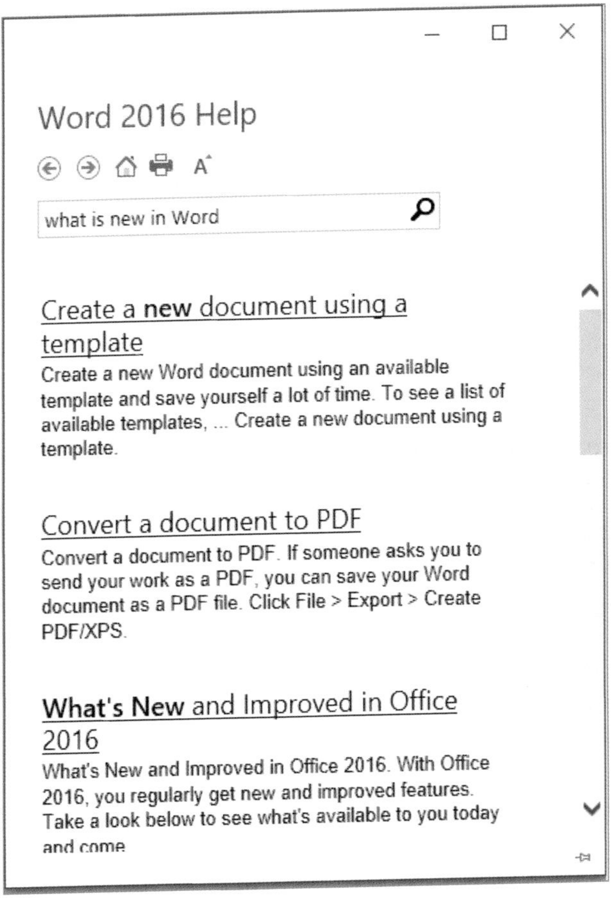

Fig. 1.14 The Tell me Help Screen.

The Help Toolbar

Above the **Search** box, you'll find the **Help Toolbar** with buttons that can be used to control the **Help** window as follows:

Back – Opens the last Help page viewed in the current session list.

Forward – Opens the previous Help page viewed in the current session list.

Home – Opens the first (or Home) Help page for the open application.

Print – Opens the Print dialogue box to let you print all, or a selection, of the current Help topic.

Use Larger Text – Increases the size of text in the Help window.

Note: It might be a good idea when you start each Office 2016 application, to spend some time working your way through the **Help** system of each, to find out how it works. You can find amongst other things, 'What's New' in each application, 'How to use a Template', 'How to convert a document to a PDF file', etc. Time spent on this now will be time saved later!

Using OneDrive to Store Documents

To use the **OneDrive** facility (with **Word**, **Excel**, **PowerPoint** and **OneNote** documents), you must set up a **Windows Live ID**, which is very easy to do and is free! If you already use **Hotmail**, **Messenger**, or **Xbox Live**, then you already have a **Windows Live ID**. If not, use your **Internet Explorer** or **Microsoft Edge** and go to the **www.live.com** Website, tap or click the **Sign up** link, fill in the required information, then tap or click the **I accept** button.

Saving documents on **OneDrive**, allows you to access them from anywhere you happen to be, on any of your devices provided, of course, you are online. All you have to do is **Sign in**, so it is really worth using the facility.

2

Microsoft Word 2016 Basics

In the previous chapter I discussed **Word**'s **Ribbon** and how to get help using the **Tell me what you want to do** text box where you enter your queries. This latter feature is unique to this version of **Word** and allows you to quickly get answers on actions you want to take or what options are available to use.

Undoubtedly, you'll find **Word** 2016 the best Windows word processor so far, easier and more intuitive to use than earlier versions with added features, particularly for mobile users. As in previous versions of **Word**, the **Ribbon**, which groups tools by task and commands you most frequently use, has been improved. Also, as with previous versions of **Word**, you get a live visual preview of the formatting in your document before you actually make any changes.

You can use **Word** 2016 to share and collaborate with colleagues by storing documents on **OneDrive**, then by tapping or clicking **Share**, generate a link or an e-mail invitation. Such documents can be accessed by those who have **Word** 2016 or **Word Online** (a free, but reduced in functionality App that allows you to read, change and comment on such documents).

Another new feature of **Word** is the **Smart Lookup** which is a touch and hold or right-click option on a selected word or phase, which opens an **Insights** pane giving you definitions, Wikipedia articles and results of Web searches.

If you have mathematical leanings, there is an easier way of creating a complex equation. Simply write it with a stylus or finger on a touch-sensitive screen and **Word** 2016 converts it into text – it can't get any better! But don't worry, I will start with the simpler features of **Word** before delving into the more advanced ones.

Starting Word 2016

I have already discussed in the previous chapter how to pin shortcuts on the **Taskbar** (see page 8) of all the applications that make up **Office** 2016. This makes it easier to access the individual Applications.

So, to start **Word** 2016, tap or click its icon on the **Taskbar**, shown here on the left, which opens a screen similar to that in Fig. 2.1.

Fig. 2.1 Word 2016's Opening Screen.

Whether you have used a previous version of **Word** or not, the first time you use the program it might be a good idea to refer to the **Help System** as discussed at the end of Chapter 1 or 'Take a tour' as suggested above, before you start experimenting with anything else. Note the number of templates available to you on the opening screen.

The Word Screen

Word follows the usual Windows and **Office** conventions and if you are familiar with these you can skip parts of this section, but even so, a few minutes might be well spent here.

As seen in Fig. 2.1, the opening screen includes a variety of templates for you to choose from, but it is worth looking at the **Blank Document** first which, when selected, displays the screen shown in Fig. 2.2 below.

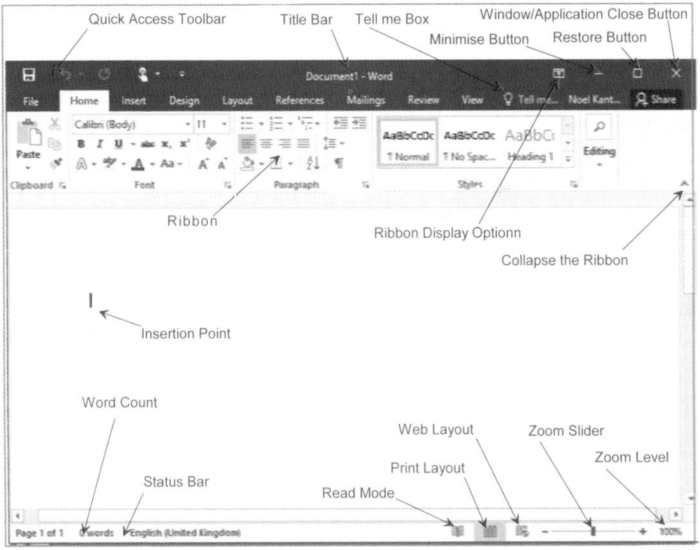

Fig. 2.2 Word 2016's New Document Window.

It is perhaps worth spending some time looking at the various parts that make up this screen.

Note that in Fig. 2.2, the **Word** window displays an empty document with the name **Document1** in the **Title** bar. The **Title** bar appears darker in colour, indicating that it is the active application window. Although multiple windows can be displayed simultaneously, you can only enter data into the active window (which will always be displayed on top, unless you view them on a split screen). Title names of non-active windows appear in a lighter shade than that of the active one.

The Word Ribbon Tabs

If you have used **Word** 2007-2013, then you will be familiar with the **Ribbon** and you can skip this section. If not, then please read on.

In **Word** 2016, the **Ribbon** has eight tabs, one **Tell me what you want to do** search box and a **File Backstage** view. Each tab displays the most used control commands grouped on it. You can have a quick look at the **Home** tab discussed in Chapter 1 (page 5), also shown in Fig. 2.3.

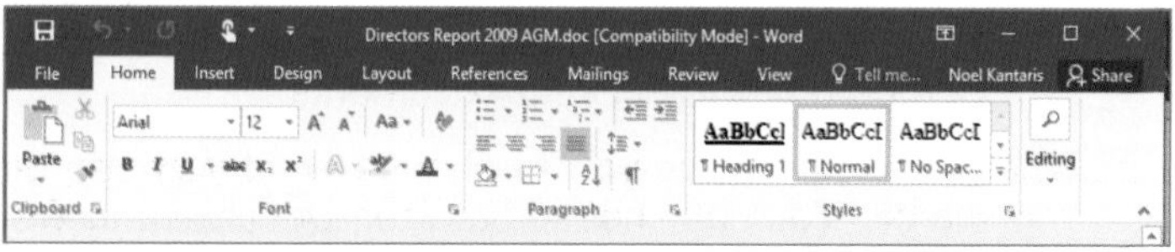

Fig. 2.3 The Home Tab of the Word 2016 Ribbon.

The **Home** tab contains all the things you use most often, such as the **Cut** and **Paste** commands and those used for formatting text, paragraphs and styles, such as changing text font, size, bold, italic and so on.

Tapping or clicking a new tab opens a new series of groups, each with its relevant command buttons. The content of the other tabs allow you to do the following:

- The **Insert** tab displays groupings to enable you to immediately insert Pages, Tables, Illustrations, Links, Headers and Footers, Text, and Symbols.
- The **Design** tab allows Document Formatting such as changing Style, Colour, Font size and Paragraph spacing, while the Page Background allows you to change Page colour, Page borders, etc.
- The **Layout** tab groups controls for you to set your Themes, Page Setup, Page Background, Paragraph and to Arrange graphic content.
- The **References** tab is used mostly with large documents and reports; to add and control a Table of Contents, Footnotes, Citations and Bibliography, Captions, an Index and a Table of Authorities.

- The **Mailings** tab groups all the actions involved in sending your personal and office correspondence. These include: Creating envelopes and labels, Starting a Mail Merge, Writing and Inserting Fields to control a mail merge, letting you Preview Results and then Finish a merge operation.
- The **Review** tab groups controls for Proofing your documents and to initiate and track document review and approval processes in an organisation, for instance. It lets you handle Comments, document Tracking, any Changes made to a document and lets you Compare or Protect your documents.
- The **View** tab allows you to change what you see on the screen. You can choose between Document Views, Show or Hide screen features, Zoom to different magnifications, control Document windows and record and run Macros.

That is the content of the fixed **Tabs**, but there are still others that only appear when they are actually needed. These contextual tabs contain tools that are only active when an object such as a picture or chart is selected in a document. These will be covered later as and when they crop up.

Quick Access Toolbar

The **Quick Access Toolbar** is the small area to the upper left of the **Ribbon** (Fig. 2.2), and enlarged here in Fig. 2.4.

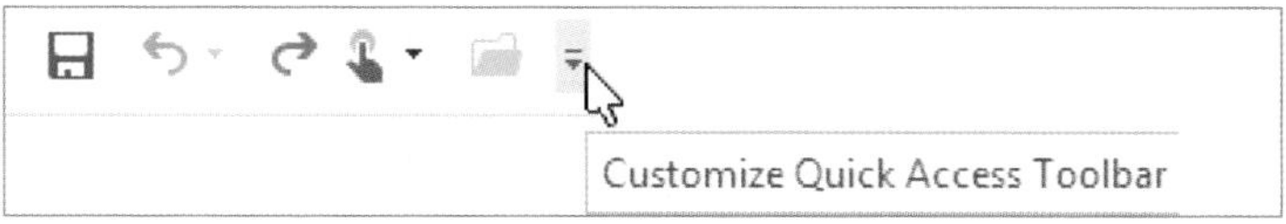

Fig. 2.4 The Quick Access Toolbar.

This is one of the most useful features of **Office** 2016. It contains buttons for the things that you use over and over every day, such as **Save**, **Undo**, **Redo, Repeat Clear**, **Touch/Mouse Mode** and **Open** by default. The bar is always available, whatever you are doing in a program, and it is very easy to add buttons for your most used commands.

Selecting the **Customize Quick Access Toolbar** button, pointed to in Fig. 2.4, displays a menu of suggested items for the toolbar. You can select the **More Commands** option in Fig. 2.5, to add others or even easier, just touch and hold or right-click on the **Ribbon** control and select **Add to Quick Access Toolbar**.

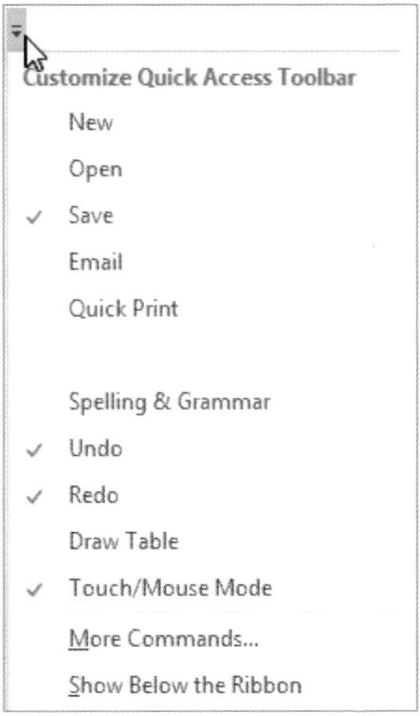

Fig. 2.5 Quick Access Options.

The Status Bar

This is located at the bottom of the **Word** screen and is used to display statistics about the active document.

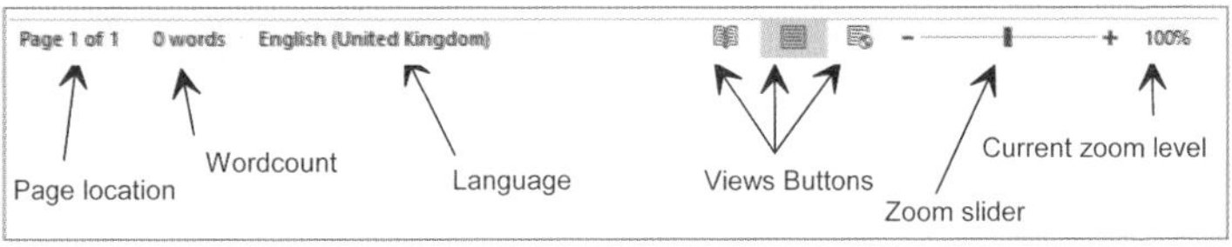

Fig. 2.6 The Word 2016 Status Bar.

When a document is being opened, the **Wordcount** on the **Status** bar starts counting the words in the document and displays the result. Once a document is opened, an additional icon appears on the **Status** bar which displays any **Proofing Errors** when tapped or clicked. This extra icon appears between the **Wordcount** and the **Language** icons. Tapping or clicking the **Language** icon, allows you to change the language from English (US) to English (UK).

You can control what appears on the **Status** bar by touching and holding or right-clicking it and making selections in the **Customize Status Bar** box that opens, as shown in Fig. 2.7 on the next page.

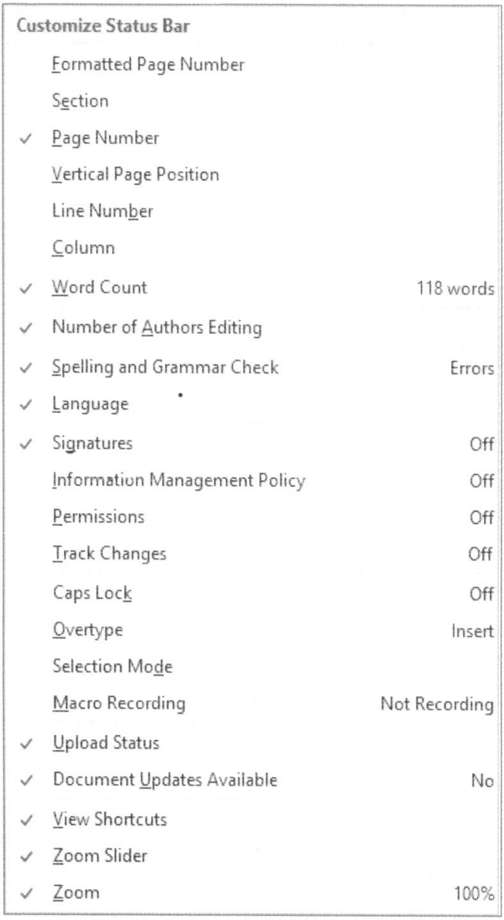

Fig. 2.7 The Customize Status Bar Screen.

Creating Word Documents

When the program is first used, all **Word**'s features default to those shown in Fig. 2.2. It is quite possible to use **Word** in this mode, without changing any main settings, but obviously it is possible to customise the package to your needs, as we shall see later.

If you are familiar with entering text in **Word**, or navigating around a document, you can easily skip the next few sections of this chapter.

Entering Text in Word

In order to illustrate some of **Word**'s capabilities, you need to have a short text at hand. I suggest you type the memo below into a new document. At this stage, don't worry if the length of the lines below differs from those on your display. The important thing here is to have text with headings, subheadings and numbered paragraphs, so I can show you how to make this simple text more appealing.

As you type in text, any time you want to force a new line, or paragraph, just press the **Enter** key. While typing within a paragraph, **Word** sorts out line lengths automatically (known as 'word wrap'), without you having to press any keys to move to a new line.

MEMO TO PC USERS
Data Processing Computers
The computers in the Data Processing room are a mixture of IBM compatible PCs with Intel Core i5 and i7 processors running at various speeds. These PCs are connected to various printers, including a couple of colour Laser printers via a network.

Structuring of Hard Disc
Each computer has at least a 500 GB capacity hard disc on which a number of software programs, including the latest version of Microsoft Windows and Microsoft Office, have been installed. To make life easier, your data is kept in separate folders (Documents, Pictures, Music and Videos) from that of the programs.

Finding Data Folders
In Windows 10 you can navigate to your data folders in two ways:
Method 1. Use the This PC tile on the Start menu to navigate via Documents to the appropriate folder holding your data.
Method 2. Use the File Explorer on the Taskbar to navigate via Documents to the folder holding your particular data.

Fig. 2.8 A Short Memo to Illustrate Some of Word's Capabilities.

Moving Around a Document

You can move the cursor around a document with the normal direction keys or with the listed key combinations.

To move	***Press***
Left one character	←
Right one character	→
Up one line	↑
Down one line	↓
Left one word	Ctrl+←
Right one word	Ctrl+→
To beginning of line	Home
To end of line	End
To paragraph beginning	Ctrl+↑
To paragraph end	Ctrl+↓
Up one screen	PgUp
Down one screen	PgDn
To top of previous page	Ctrl+PgUp
To top of next page	Ctrl+PgDn
To beginning of file	Ctrl+Home
To end of file	Ctrl+End

To move to a specified page in a multi-page document, use the **Ctrl+H** keyboard shortcut or use the **Replace** menu option which displays when the **Editing** group on the **Home** tab is selected. Both of these display the window in Fig. 2.9.

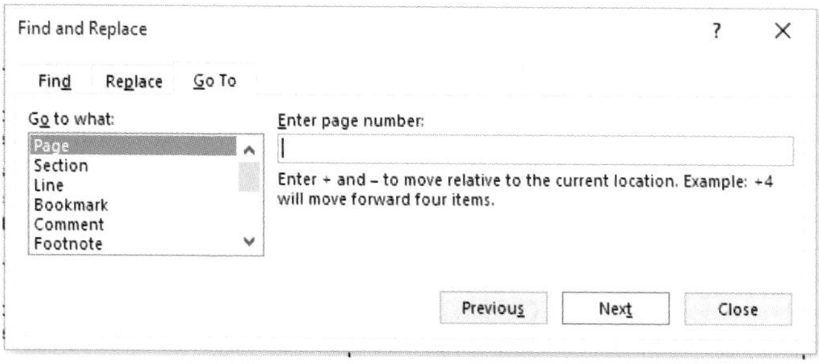

Fig. 2.9 The Find and Replace Dialogue Box.

An alternative method of navigating to a specific page in a multiple page document is by using the **Navigation** pane to be discussed next.

The Navigation Pane

Sometimes it is useful to open the **Navigation** pane to help with multiple page documents. I use the text of the **Memo to PC Users** to illustrate this facility. With the memo opened in **Word**, use the **View** tab and select **Navigation Pane** from the **Show** group of commands to display the composite (the action to be taken and its effect) screen in Fig. 2.10.

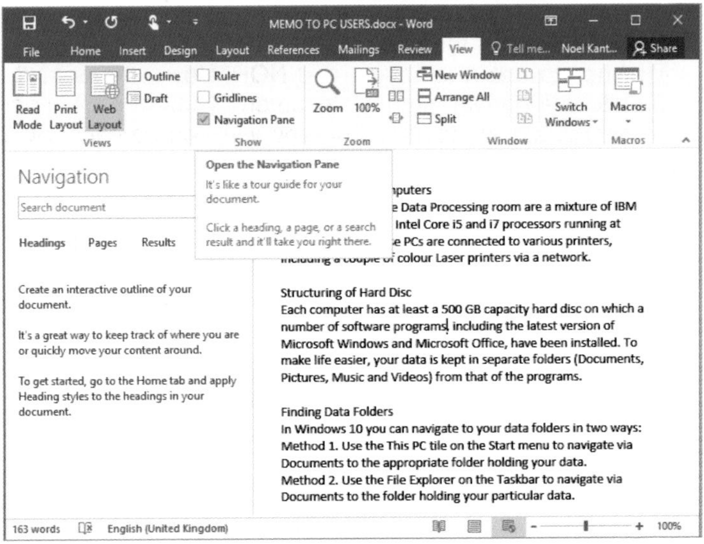

Fig. 2.10 The Navigation Pane.

It is best to work in an enlarged **Word** window, otherwise as the window shrinks, the various commands are compressed within each **Group** and are not displayed in full. Instead, they are to be found within a drop-down menu created for the purpose, as shown opened here in Fig. 2.11.

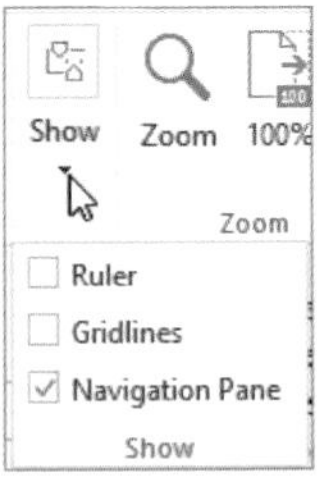

Fig. 2.11 The Drop-down Menu of Compressed Group Commands.

Styles, Templates and Themes

Fig. 2.12 The Styles Gallery on the Home Tab.

When you start **Word**, it opens with a new empty document and defaults to the 'Normal' style in the **Styles** gallery shown in Fig. 2.12. This means that any text you enter is shown in the 'Normal' style which is one of the styles available in the **NORMAL** template. Every document produced by **Word** has to use a template, and **NORMAL** is the default. A template is a special "starter" document type. When you open a template, a new document opens with the content, layout, formatting, styles and the theme from that template.

To change the style of a paragraph, place the cursor in the paragraph in question, the title line in our example, then move the pointer through the options in the **Style** gallery – you might need to click the **More** button to display additional styles. Each one is instantly previewed, as shown in Fig. 2.13.

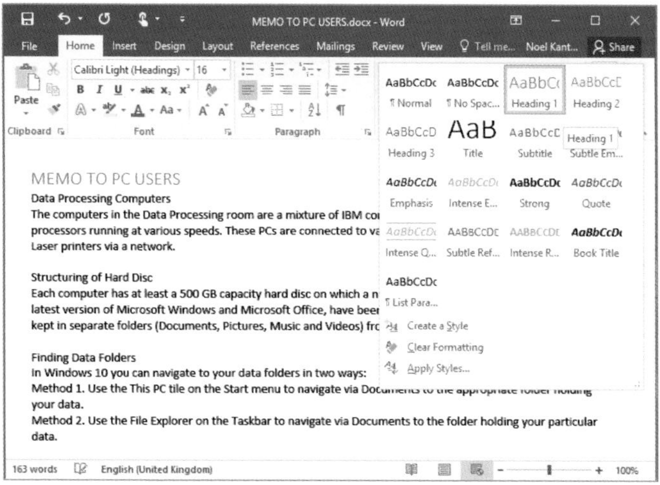

Fig. 2.13 Using the Styles Gallery.

You can tap or click on the **Title** style to select it and the paragraph reformats to **Calibri Light (Headings)** typeface at point size 16. Very clever.

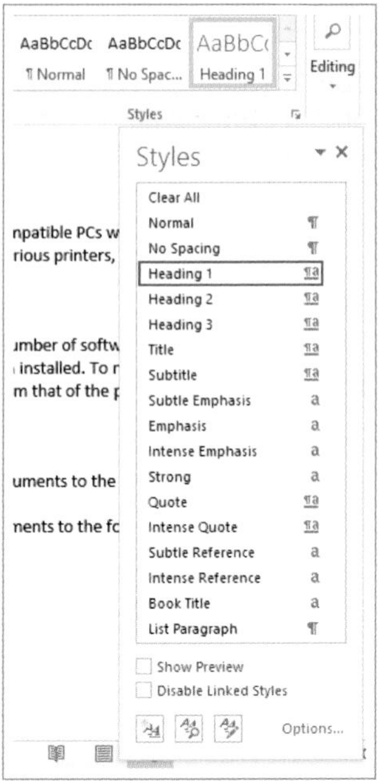

Another way of setting a style is from the floating **Styles Task Pane** which is opened by tapping or clicking the dialogue box **Launcher** on the **Styles** group of the **Home** tab, as pointed to here in Fig. 2.14.

Now with the cursor in the second line of text, I selected **Heading1** which reformatted the line of text to **Calibri Light (Headings)** 16 point in blue. I repeated this with the "Structuring of Hard Disc" and "Finding Data Folders" headings. Your memo should now look presentable and be similar to Fig. 2.15 below.

Fig. 2.14 The Styles Task Pane.

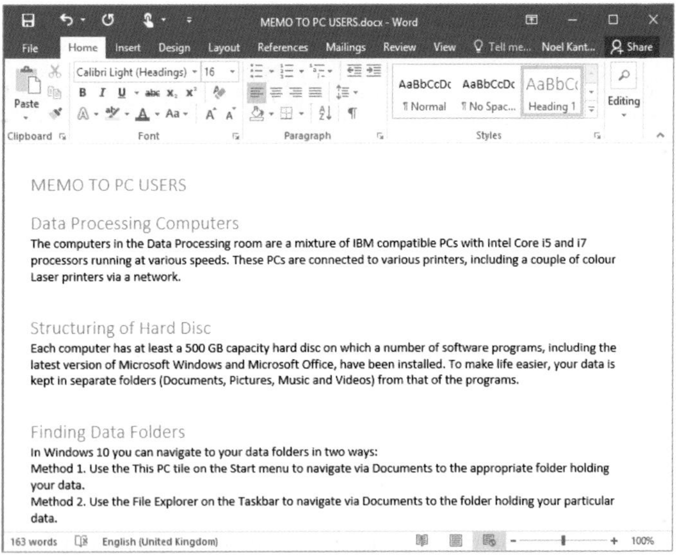

Fig. 2.15 Applying Styles to a Document.

Document Themes

Every document created in **Office** is based on a **Theme** which can be accessed from the **Ribbon**'s **Design** tab. **Themes** provide fonts, colours or effects that apply to all parts of the document, which simplifies the process of creating matching documents across all the **Office** applications.

Try pointing on a thumbnail in the **Themes** gallery and noticed how your document changes.

Fig. 2.16 The Themes Group.

Document Screen Views

Word provides five main display views, as shown in Fig. 2.17, in the **View** tab of the **Ribbon**.

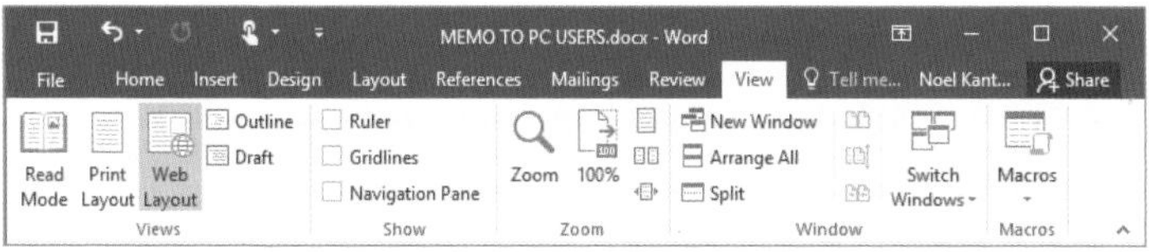

Fig. 2.17 The Document Views.

You can also view your documents in a whole range of screen enlargements with the **Zoom** controls from the **Status** bar. When a document is displayed you can switch freely between them. When first loaded, the screen displays in the default **Web Layout** view.

The main **Views** options have the following effects:

Read Mode – Provides an easy to read and very customisable view of a document. You can change the text size, edit the document, carry out commenting and reviews and see how the pages will print.

Print Layout – Provides a WYSIWYG (what you see is what you get) view of a document. The text displays in the applied typefaces and point sizes and with the selected attributes.

Web Layout – A view that optimises the layout of a document to make online reading easier. Use this layout view when you are creating a Web page or a document that is viewed on the screen. In **Web Layout** view, you can see backgrounds, text is wrapped to fit the window, and graphics are positioned just as they are in a Web browser. This is the default working view and all features appear on the screen as they will in the final printout.

Outline – Provides a collapsible view of a document, which enables you to see its organisation at a glance. You can display all the text in a file, or just the text that uses the paragraph styles you specify.

Draft – A view that simplifies the layout of the page so that you can type, edit and format text quickly. In draft view, page boundaries, headers and footers, backgrounds, drawing objects and pictures that do not have the **'In line with text'** wrapping style do not appear.

Changing Word's Default Options

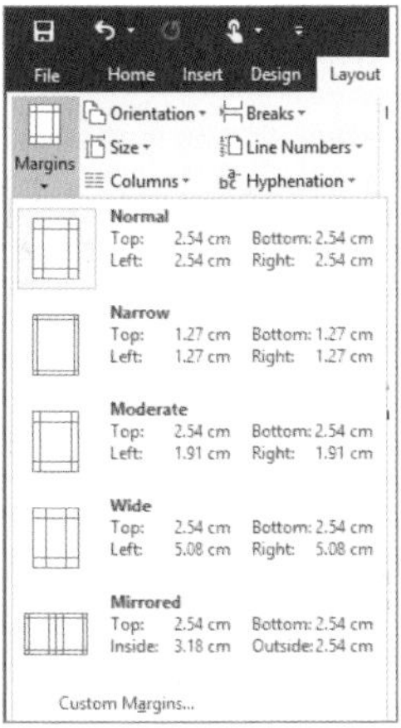

Modifying Margins

It is easy to change the standard page margins for the entire document from the cursor position onward, or for selected text.

Tab or click the **Layout** tab, then the **Margins** button on the **Page Setup** group on the **Ribbon** to display Fig. 2.18. There is a gallery of five pre-set options to select from.

Fig. 2.18 Changing Margin Settings.

Alternatively, you can tap or click the **Custom Margins** option, to be found at the bottom of Fig. 2.18, to open the **Page Setup** dialogue box shown in Fig. 2.19.

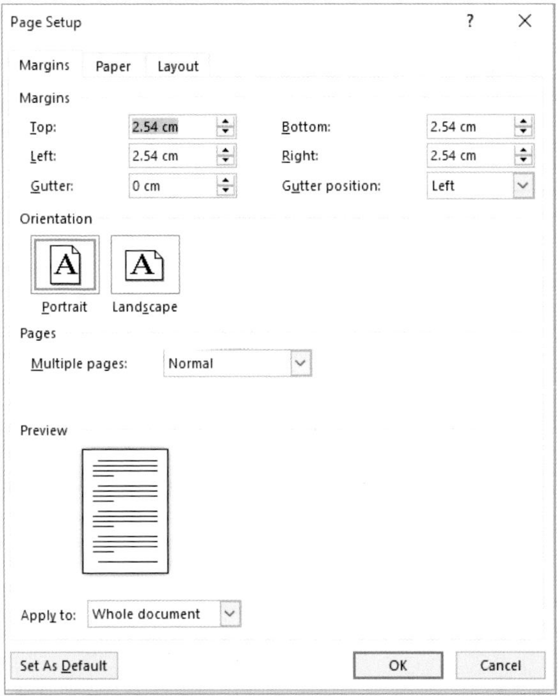

Fig. 2.19 The Margins Tab Sheet of the Page Setup Box.

On the **Margins** tab of this box you can change any of the margin or gutter settings. The **Preview** diagram at the bottom of the box shows how your changes will look on a real page. The orientation of the printed page is normally **Portrait** where text prints across the page width, but you can change this to **Landscape** which prints across the page length, if you prefer.

To make the new settings 'permanent', press the **Set As Default** button and confirm that you wish this change to affect all new documents based on the **NORMAL** template.

Changing Paper Settings

To see the default paper settings set during installation, tap or click the **Paper** tab of the **Page Setup** box (see Fig. 2.19). As you can see in Fig. 2.20, the **Paper size** is set to A4, but you could change this by using the down-arrowhead against the selected paper size to reveal a list of alternative sizes.

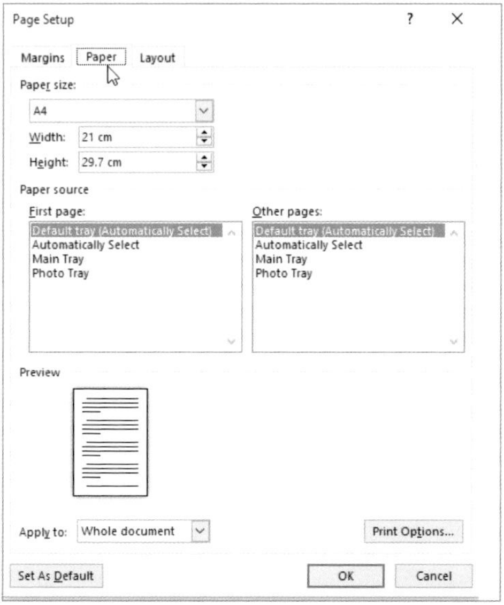

Fig. 2.20 The Paper Tab Sheet of the Page Setup Box.

Any changes you can make to your document from the **Page Setup** box can be applied to either the whole document or to the rest of the document starting from the current position of the insertion pointer. To set this, tap or click the down-arrowhead against the **Apply to** box and choose from the drop-down list. As before, click the **Set As Default** button to make your changes affect all your new documents.

The **Paper source** section of the **Page Setup** box lets you set where your printer takes its paper from. You might have a printer that holds paper in trays, in which case you might want to specify that the **First page** (headed paper perhaps), should be taken from one tray, while **Other pages** should be taken from a different tray.

Modifying the Page Layout

Clicking the **Layout** tab of the **Page Setup** box displays the sheet shown in Fig. 2.21 below, from which you can set options for headers and footers, section breaks, vertical alignment and whether to add line numbers or borders.

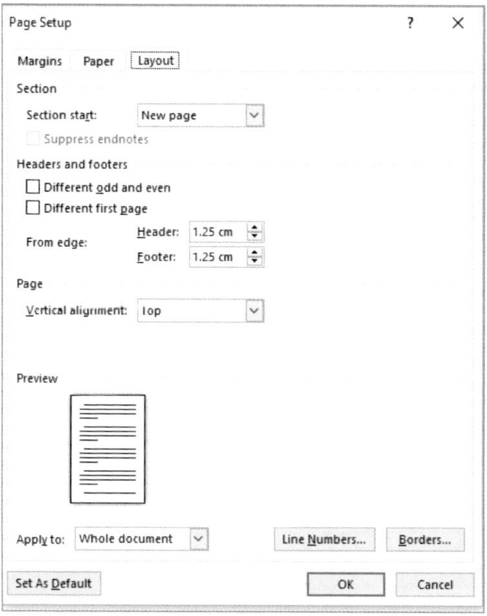

Fig. 2.21 The Layout Tab Sheet of the Page Setup Box.

The default for **Section start** is **New page** which allows the section to start at the top of the next page. Pressing the down-arrowhead against this option, allows you to change this choice.

In the **Headers and footers** section of the dialogue box, you can specify whether you want one header or footer for even-numbered pages and a different header or footer for odd-numbered pages. You can further specify if you want a different header or footer on the first page from the header or footer used for the rest of the document. **Word** aligns the top line with the 'Top' margin, but this can be changed with the **Vertical alignment** option.

Saving a Document to a File

The quickest way to save a document to disc is to click the **Save** button on the **Quick Access** toolbar. The usual way however is from the File command button which opens the **Backstage** view which gives you more control of the saving operation, as shown in Fig. 2.22.

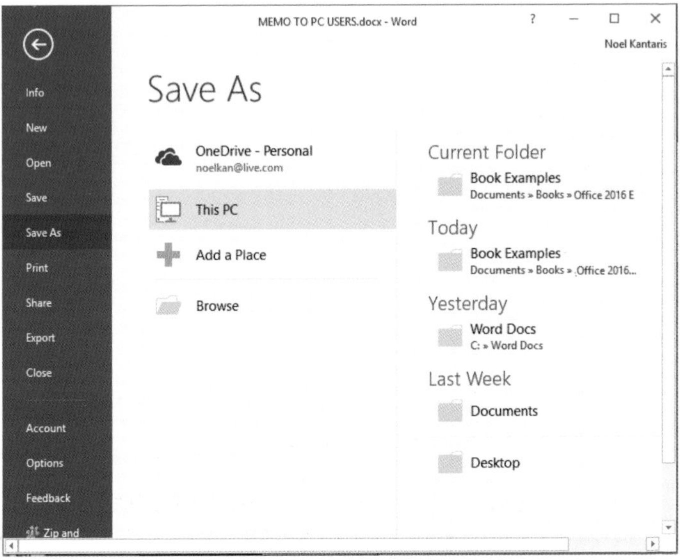

Fig. 2.22 The File Save As Box in Backstage View.

Save is used when a document has previously been saved to disc in a named file; using this command saves your work under the existing filename automatically without prompting you.

Save As is used when you want to save your document with a different name or file format, or in a different location.

There are several places where you can save a document; on your **OneDrive**, on computer's hard drive or another place, such as an external drive. If you have already saved documents on your computer, these are displayed if **This PC** is selected or you could **Browse** to a new location.

Using the **Save As** command (or the first time you use the **Save** command when a document has no name), tapping or clicking **Browse** opens the dialogue box shown in Fig. 2.23.

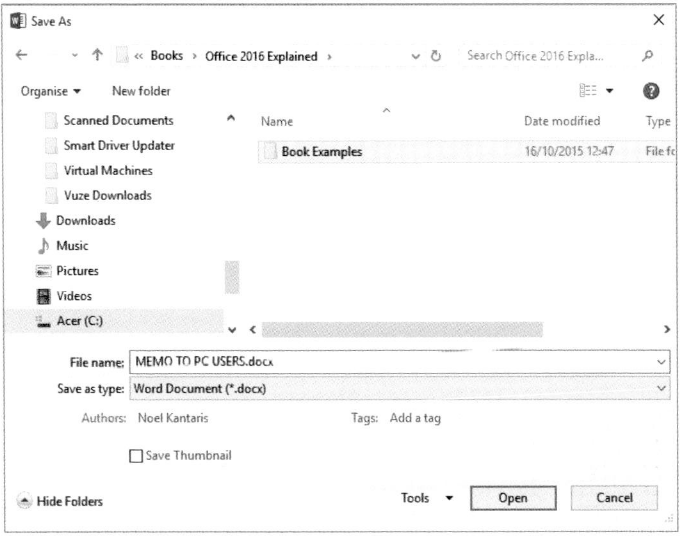

Fig. 2.23 The File Save Box.

Note that the first 255 characters of the first paragraph of a new document are placed and highlighted in the **File name** field box, with the program waiting for you to over-type a new name.

Filenames must have less than 255 characters and cannot include any of the following keyboard characters: /, \, >, <, *, ?, ", |, :, or ;. **Word** 2016 continues to support the **Word** 2010 and 2013 file extension **.docx** automatically and uses it to identify its documents.

You can select a drive other than the default **C:** drive, by tapping or clicking the down arrow on the left pane of the **File Save** box and navigating to an appropriate drive and folder.

I have used the **New Folder** button to create a folder called **Book Examples** on my **C:** drive in **Documents**, **Books**, **Office 2016 Explained**.

To save the work currently in memory, double-tap or double-click the newly created folder, then move the cursor into the **File name** box, and type **PC USER 1**.

By tapping or clicking the **Save as type** down-arrowhead at the bottom of the **File Save** dialogue box (Fig. 2.23), you can save the your document in **Word Document** type (**.docx** – the default), **Word 97-2003 Document** file type with the extension **.doc**, **Word Template**, **PDF** file type, **Rich Text** or one of two **Web Page** type options. The default is always **Word Document**, but if you want to send such a document file to a friend who does not have the latest or the previous two versions of **Word**, then you could choose the **Word 97-2003 Document** type (Fig. 2.24).

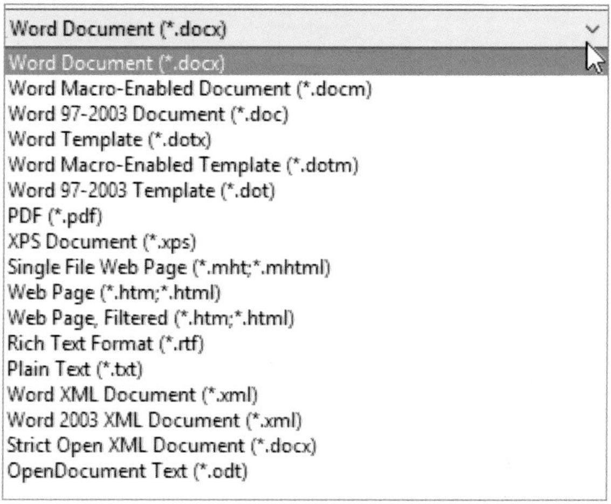

Fig. 2.24 Saving a Document as a Different Type.

Selecting a File Location

You can select where **Word** automatically looks for your document files when you first choose to open or save a document, by tapping or clicking the 

command button, then selecting the **Options** button to open the **Word Options** screen and tapping or clicking the **Save** option on the list of **Options**, to display Fig. 2.25, shown on the next page.

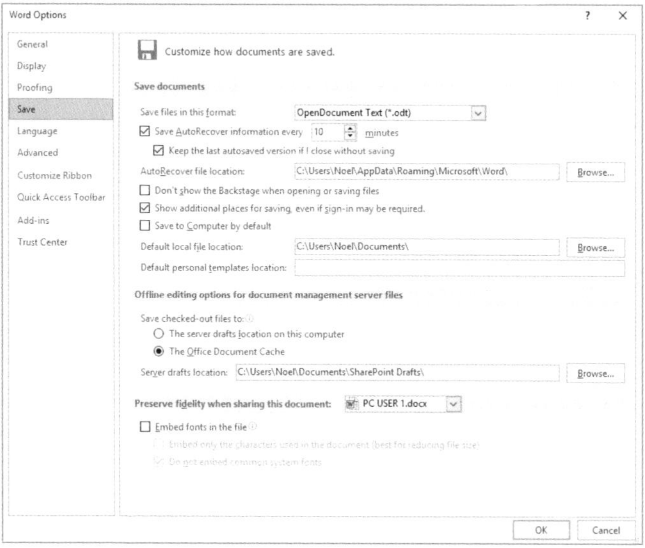

Fig. 2.25 Setting Word's File Locations.

You can store documents, worksheets, presentations, and other files either on **OneDrive**, or in your personal **Documents** folder as is the case above, which is easily accessed from Windows 10's **Start** menu **This PC** icon. This, of course, is a matter of preference, so I leave it to you to decide.

Closing a Document

There are several ways to close a document in **Word**. Once you have saved it you can tap or click its window close button which only turns red when you point to it. If you only have one document open in **Word** this will close the program, in which case it is better to use the File command button and then select the **Close** option on the **Backstage** view if you want to keep **Word** open on your desktop.

If the document (or file) has changed since the last time it was saved, you will be given the option to save it before it is removed from memory. If a document is not closed before a new document is opened, then both will be held in memory in their own **Word** windows, but only one will be active.

Restarting Word

If after saving your document you have closed down **Word**, on restarting it you'll see a screen similar to the one displayed in Fig. 2.26.

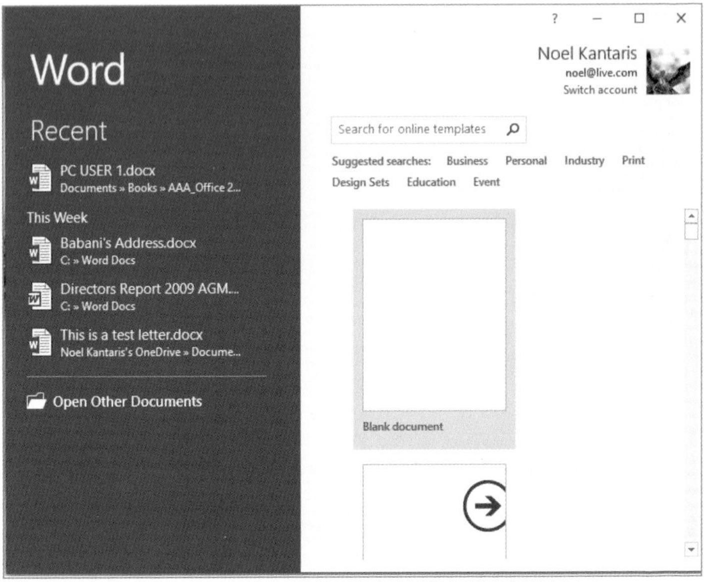

Fig. 2.26 Restarting Word.

Under **Recent** and on the first entry, you'll find the document you saved last which can be reopened by double-tapping or double-clicking it. Other documents you might have worked on previously will also be listed.

Now you could open a listed document, tap or click the **Open Other Documents** entry to display the screen shown in Fig. 2.27 on the next page or select the **This PC** icon on the **Start** menu to open **My PC** window then browse to the location of your document, also shown in Fig. 2.28 on the next page.

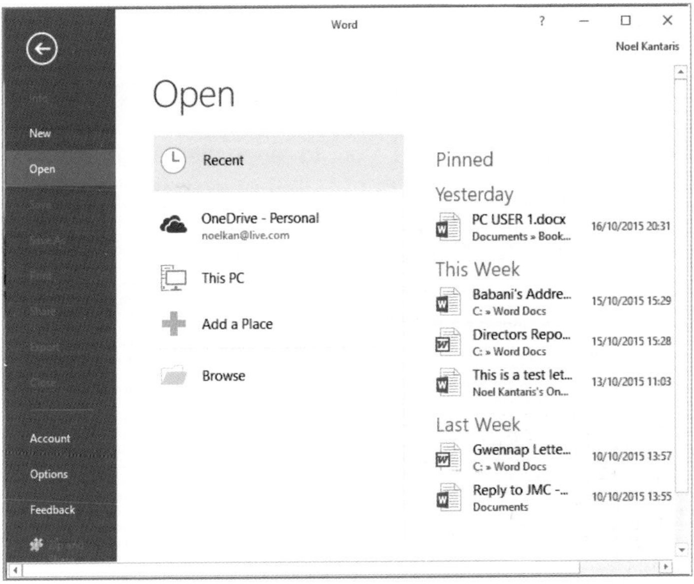

Fig. 2.27 The File Open Box.

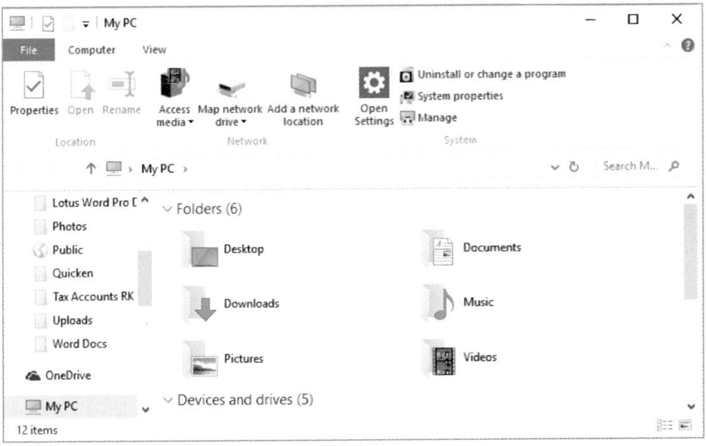

Fig. 2.28 Locating a Folder or File on your Computer.

New Documents

To open a new document into **Word** when an existing document is already opened, tap or click the File command button, and then select the **Open** option on the **Backstage** view screen. This allows you to open files that might be located at a different place from that of your default path, as shown in Fig. 2.27 on the previous page.

Alternatively, tap or click the File command button, and then select the **New** option which displays various templates, as shown in Fig. 2.29 below.

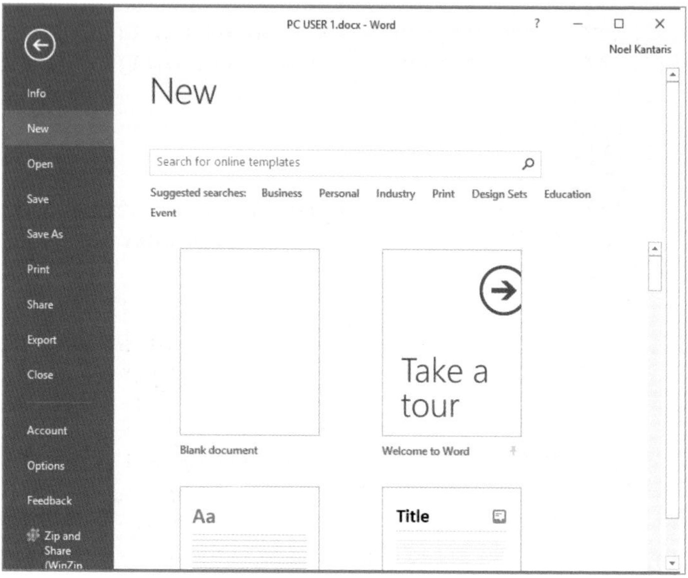

Fig. 2.29 The New Backstage Option Screen.

From here you can choose a 'Blank Document', or one of the displayed templates. On the right of the screen you can see a preview of what you'll get when choosing a particular template.

* * *

In the next Chapter I explore how to change documents by using editing and formatting techniques which can help to enhance their content.

3

Changing Word Documents

Just as in previous versions, **Word** 2016 supports some very clever editing, formatting and sharing facilities. For example, when entering text, basic errors are automatically corrected and misspelled words are unobtrusively underlined in a red wavy line, while ungrammatical phrases are underlined in green. There is no automatic formatting or sharing facilities.

The AutoCorrect Feature

To demonstrate these, start **Word** and in the displayed new document page, type the words '**teh compter is brukn**', exactly as misspelled here.

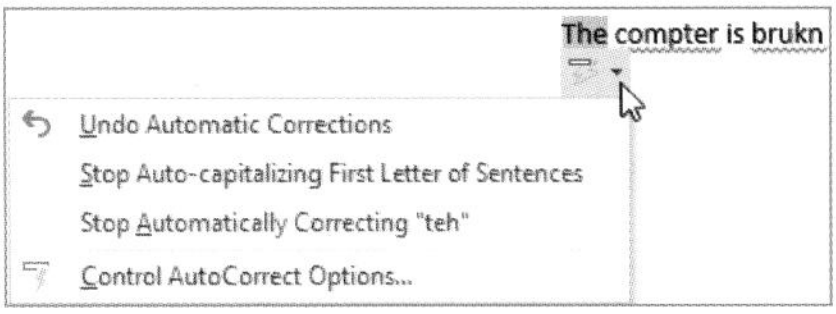

Fig. 3.1 The AutoCorrect Options Button.

As soon as you press the space bar after entering the first word 'teh', it will be changed to 'The', as shown in Fig. 3.1. This is the **AutoCorrect** feature at work, which will automatically detect and correct many typing errors, misspelled words and incorrect capitalisation. If you agree with the change made, just carry on. If not, you can move your finger or mouse pointer over the corrected word until a thin blue box appears below it. This changes to the **AutoCorrect Options** button when you point to it and tapping or clicking it opens the above menu.

Selecting the first menu option **Undo Automatic Corrections** will cancel the correction for you. The other options give you control over how the feature works in the future. It is worth experimenting a bit here to find out more.

If an error cannot be corrected automatically, it will be underlined in a red wavy line. To correct such an error you have two options depending on whether you are using a keyboard or a finger on a touch-sensitive screen.

With the keyboard – Right-clicking the misspelled word displays a list of choices from which you can select the correct word by left-clicking on it.

With a finger on a touch-sensitive screen – Tap on the misspelled word which places a cursor on the word and opens the screen keyboard as shown in Fig. 3.2.

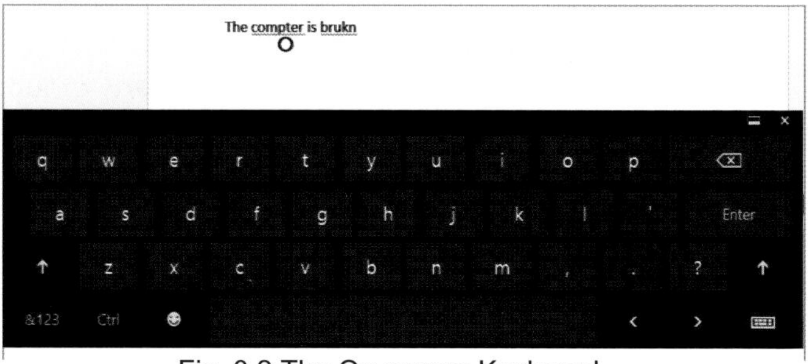

Fig. 3.2 The On-screen Keyboard.

You can now either use the on-screen keyboard to correct the word or tap again to display a list of choices from which to select the correct word by tapping on it. To remove the on-screen keyboard, tap on the ☒ icon at the top right of the virtual keyboard.

Editing Text in Word

Other editing could include deleting unwanted words or adding extra text in the document. For small deletions, such as letters or words, use the **Del** key which, however is not available on the virtual keyboard, in which case use the **Backspace** key shown here.

With the **Del** key, position the cursor on the left of the first letter you want to delete and press **Del**. With the **Backspace** key, position the cursor immediately to the right of the character to be deleted and press or tap the **Backspace** key.

Word processing is usually carried out in the **Insert** mode. Any characters typed will be inserted at the cursor location (insertion point) and the following text will be pushed to the right, and down, to make room. To start a new paragraph, press the **Enter** key, while to insert a blank line between two paragraphs, press the **Enter** key twice before starting to type text in the new paragraph. To remove a blank line, position the cursor to the left of the first character of the line below the blank line and press the **Backspace** key.

When larger-scale editing is needed you have several alternatives, but I only discuss here the simplest method. First 'select' the text to be altered (see below), then use the **Cut**, **Copy** and **Paste** **Ribbon** commands in the **Clipboard** group of the **Home** tab, as shown in Fig. 3.3.

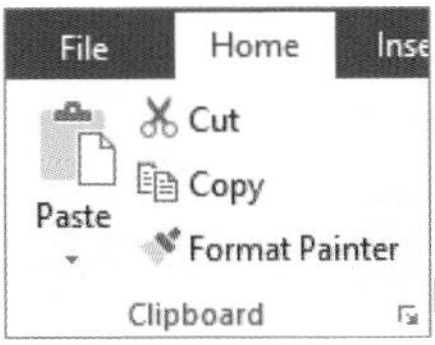

Fig. 3.3 The Clipboard Group of Home Tab.

Selecting Text

Before you can edit or format text, you must select it – use the **PC USER 1** document to experiment. Selected text is highlighted on the screen.

With either a physical or virtual keyboard: Position the cursor on the first character to be selected and hold down the **Shift** key while using the arrow keys to highlight the required text, then release the **Shift** key. To select the whole document, use the **Ctrl+A** shortcut keystroke.

With a touch-sensitive screen, tap on the first word you want to select, which is then marked with circles at the start and end of it, then drag with your finger the rightmost circle to the end of the block you are selecting, as shown in Fig. 3.4.

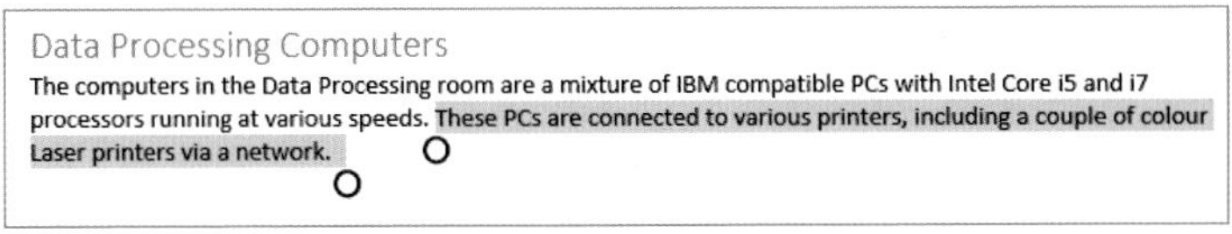

Fig. 3.4 Selecting Text on a touch sensitive Screen.

Copying Blocks of Text

As with most of the editing and formatting operations there are several alternative ways of doing this, as follows:

With the mouse or a finger on a touch-sensitive screen, first select the text, then use the **Copy** **Ribbon** button in the **Clipboard** group, move the cursor to where you want it copied and tap or click the **Paste** button.

With both types of keyboards, use the quick key combinations, **Ctrl+C** to copy and **Ctrl+V** to paste.

To copy the same text again to another location, or to any open document window or application, move the cursor to the new location and paste it there with either of these methods.

Moving Blocks of Text

Selected text can be moved to any location in the same document using either of the following methods:

Tapping or clicking the **Cut** button.

Using the **Ctrl+X** shortcut with either keyboards.

Next, move the cursor to the required new location and as described previously paste the text where you want it.

Deleting Blocks of Text

When text is 'cut' by tapping or clicking the **Cut** **Ribbon** button, it is removed from the document, but placed on the **Clipboard**. When the **Del** or **Backspace** keys are used, however, the text is deleted but not put on the **Clipboard**.

If you make a mistake with the delete command, you must act straightaway by using the **Undo** shortcut **Ctrl+Z**, on both keyboards to reverse the most recent editing or formatting command. Deeper changes can be made using the **Undo** button on the **Quick Access Toolbar**, shown in Fig. 3.5, to undo one or more editing or formatting actions, provided you haven't saved the file in the mean time.

Fig. 3.5 The Quick Access Toolbar.

Finding and Changing Text

Word allows you to search for specifically selected text, or character combinations with the **Find** and **Replace** options in the **Editing** group on the **Home** tab of the **Ribbon**.

Using the **Find** option (**Ctrl+F**), will highlight each occurrence of the text typed in the **Search** box in turn so that you can carry out some action on it. Using the **Replace** option (**Ctrl+H**), allows you to specify what replacement is to be automatically carried out. For example, in a long article you may decide to replace the word 'computer' with the word 'PC'.

To illustrate the procedure, tap or click the **Replace** button shown above, to open the **Find and Replace** dialogue box shown in Fig. 3.6.

Fig. 3.6 The Find and Replace Dialogue Box.

Tapping or clicking the More >> button, appends more choices to Fig. 3.6, as shown in Fig. 3.7 below.

Fig. 3.7 The Find and Replace Box with More Options.

Towards the bottom left of the dialogue box in Fig. 3.7, there are five check boxes; the first two can be used to match the case of letters in the search string, or a whole word, while the last three are used for wildcard, 'sounds like' or 'word forms' matching.

The two buttons, **Format** and **Special**, situated at the bottom of the dialogue box, let you control how the search is carried out. Have a look at the list of available options, when either of these buttons is pressed. You can force both the search and the replace operations to work with exact text attributes. For example, selecting:

> The **Font** option from the list under **Format**, displays a dialogue box in which you select a font (such as Arial, Times New Roman, etc.), a font-style (such as regular, bold, italic, etc.), an underline option (such as single, double, etc.) and special effects (such as strike-through, superscript, subscript, etc.).
>
> The **Paragraph** option lets you control indentation, spacing (before and after), and alignment.
>
> The **Style** option allows you to search for, or replace, different paragraph styles. This can be useful if you develop a new style and want to change all the text of another style in a document to use your preferred style.

Using the **Special** button (see in Fig. 3.7), you can search for, and replace, various specified document marks, tabs, hard returns, etc., or a combination of both these and text.

Below I list only two of the many key combinations of special characters that could be typed into the **Find what** and **Replace with** boxes when the **Use wildcards** box is checked.

Type	***To find or replace***
?	Any single character within a pattern. For example, searching for nec?, will find <u>neck</u>, con<u>nect</u>, etc.
*	Any string of characters. For example, searching for c*r, will find <u>cellar</u>, <u>chillier</u>, etc.

Page Breaks

Word automatically inserts a 'soft' page break in a document when a page of typed text is full. To force a manual, or hard,

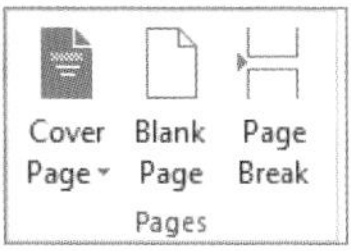

page break, either use the **Ctrl+Enter** keyboard shortcut, or click the **Insert**, **Pages**, **Blank Page** command button on the **Ribbon**. To see the **Page Break** marker, use the **Show/Hide** ¶ paragraph marker in the **Home**, **Paragraph** group.

To delete a manual page break, place the cursor at the beginning of the second page and press the **Backspace** key. Soft breaks inserted by the program cannot be deleted.

Formatting Word Documents

Formatting involves the appearance of individual words or even characters, the line spacing and alignment of paragraphs, and the overall page layout of the entire document. These are carried out in several different ways.

Primary page layout is included in a document's **Template**, text formatting in a **Template's Styles** and **Theme**. Within any document, however, you can override **Paragraph Style** formats by applying text formatting and enhancements manually to selected text. To immediately cancel manual formatting, use the **Undo** button on the **Quick Access** toolbar, or use the **Ctrl+Z** key shortcut. The text reverts to its original format. You can cancel manual formatting by selecting the text and using the **Clear All** option in the **Home**, **Styles** command to revert to the **Normal** style format.

Formatting Text

Fonts are automatically installed when you set up Windows. Originally, the title and headings of the **PC USER 1** memo, were selected from the **Style** gallery as 'Heading1', with 16 point size **Calibri Light**, while the main text was typed in 11 point size **Calibri**.

To change this memo into what appears in Fig. 3.8, do the following:

Select the title of the memo and format it to bold, italics, 20 point size **Arial** and centre it between the margins, then

Select the subtitles and format each to 16 point size bold **Arial** and finally,

Select each paragraph of the main body of the memo in turn, and format it to 12 point size **Arial**.

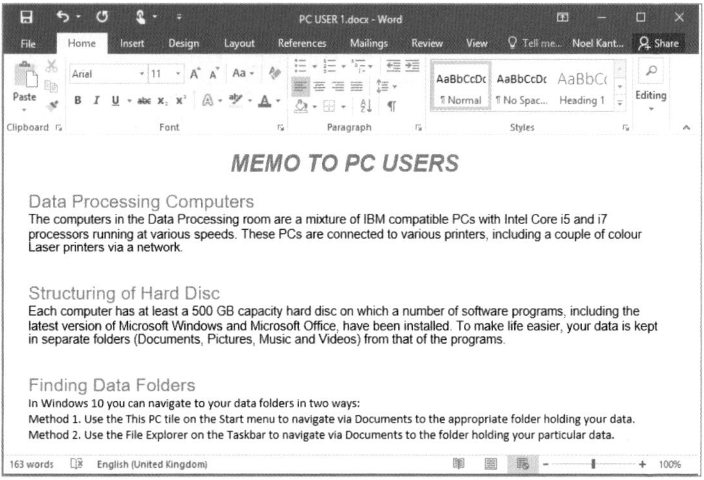

Fig. 3.8 The Reformatted Memo.

All of the formatting can be achieved by using the buttons on the **Ribbon** or by using keyboard shortcuts, some of which are listed below:

To Format	***Type***
Bold	**Ctrl+B**
Italic	**Ctrl+I**
Underline	**Ctrl+U**
Word underline	**Ctrl+Shift+W**

There are shortcuts to do almost anything, but the ones listed here are the most useful and the easiest to remember.

Paragraph Alignment

Word defines a paragraph, as any text which is followed by a paragraph mark, which is created by pressing the **Enter** key. So single-line titles, as well as sections of long typed text, can form paragraphs.

Word allows you to align a paragraph at the left margin (the default), at the right margin, centred between both margins, or justified between both margins.

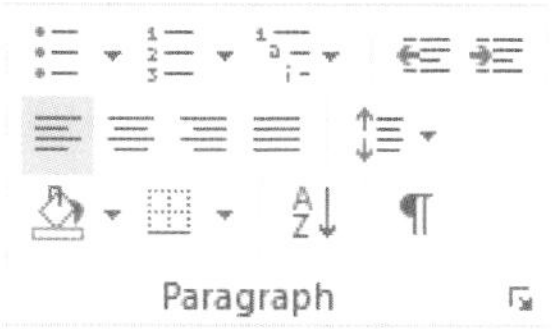

Fig. 3.9 Paragraph Group.

There are two main ways to perform alignment in Word. Using the **Ribbon**, **Home**, **Paragraph** command buttons, shown in Fig. 3.9, or using keyboard shortcuts.

Ribbon Buttons	***Alignment***	***Keystrokes***
	Left	**Ctrl+L**
	Centred	**Ctrl+E**
	Right	**Ctrl+R**
	Justified	**Ctrl+J**

Save the reformatted **Memo to PC Users** as **PC USER 2**, using the **Save As** command in the **Backstage** page.

Indenting Text

Most documents will require some form of paragraph indenting, where an indent is the space between the margin and the edge of the text in the paragraph. When an indent is set (on the left or right side of the page), any justification on that side of the page sets at the indent, not the page margin.

To illustrate indentation, open **PC USER 2**, select the first paragraph, and use the **Decrease/Increase Indent** buttons on the **Ribbon**, shown here, or open the **Paragraph** box by clicking the **Home**, **Paragraph Settings** launcher. In the **Indentation** field, select 0.5 cm for both **Left** and **Right**, as shown in Fig. 3.10 below.

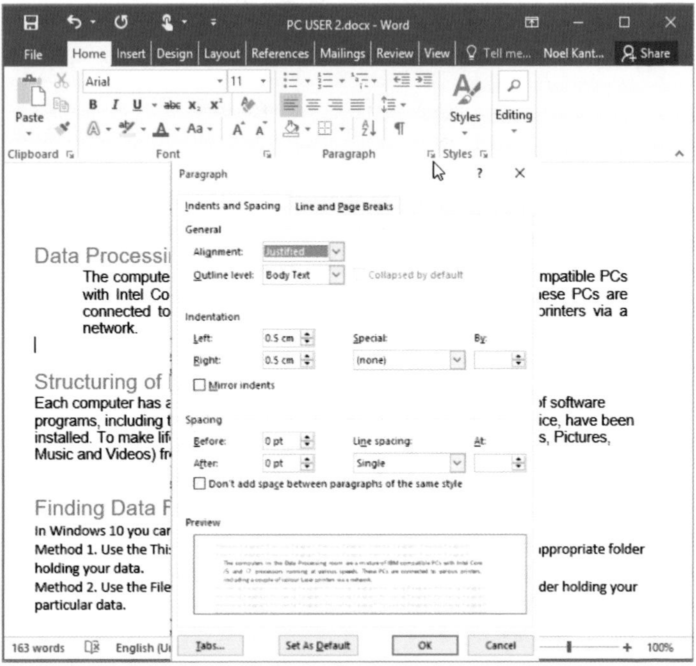

Fig. 3.10 Setting Left and Right Indentation.

In this way, the selected paragraph is displayed indented on both sides, as shown above, something you can not do just by using the **Ribbon** icon which only indents the left side. The screen above, shows the result of the indentation as well as the settings on the **Paragraph** dialogue box which caused it.

The **Indentation** option in the **Paragraph** dialogue box, can be used to create ‘hanging’ indents, where all the lines in a paragraph, including any text on the first line that follows a tab, are indented by a specified amount. This is often used in lists to emphasise certain points.

Next, highlight the text in the memo under 'Finding Data Folders', open the **Paragraph** dialogue box, and select **Hanging** under **Special** and 3 cm under **By**. When you click the **OK** button, the text formats as shown in the composite screen dump of Fig. 3.11 below, but it is still highlighted.

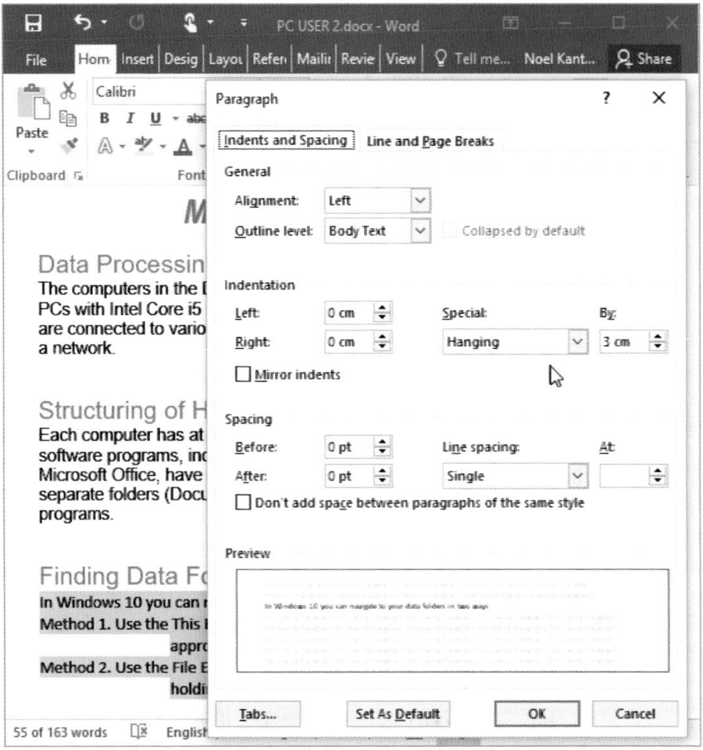

Fig. 3.11 Setting Hanging Indents Manually.

To remove the highlighting, touch or click anywhere on the page. Next, place the cursor in front of the word 'Method 1' and press **Enter**, then place the cursor in front of the word 'Use' and press the **Tab** key once. Finally repeat both operations on 'Method 2'. The result should be as shown in Fig. 3.12 on the next page.

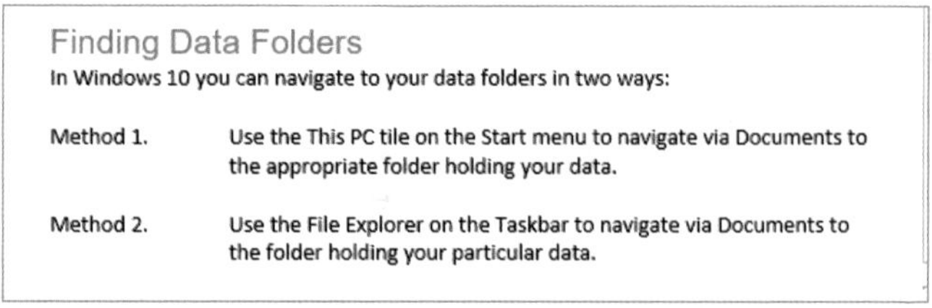
Finding Data Folders

In Windows 10 you can navigate to your data folders in two ways:

Method 1. Use the This PC tile on the Start menu to navigate via Documents to the appropriate folder holding your data.

Method 2. Use the File Explorer on the Taskbar to navigate via Documents to the folder holding your particular data.

Fig. 3.12 Text Formatted with Hanging Indents.

This may seem a bit complicated just to get hanging indents, but with **Word** you will eventually set up all your indents, etc., as styles in templates. Then all you do is tap or click in a paragraph to produce them. I will discuss this later in this chapter, but for now save your work as **PC USER 3**.

Using Bullets and Lists

Bullets are small characters you can insert in the text of your document to improve visual impact. In **Word** the main way for creating lists with bullets or numbers is from the **Ribbon**, **Home**, **Paragraph** group. Clicking the **Bullets** button, the **Numbering** button or the **Multilevel List** button will start the operation. You can change the bullet or list design used by selecting the down-arrowhead next to its button. If none of the available designs appeal to you, you can create your own by using the **Define New Bullet** option at the bottom of the box, shown in the composite in Fig. 3.13.

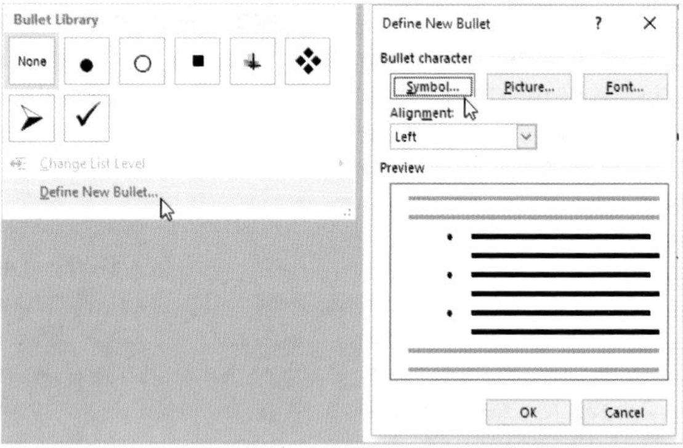

Fig. 3.13 Selecting and Defining Bullets.

There are two types of bullet you can define. The **Symbol** button in Fig. 3.13 lets you use a character from a font, whereas **Picture** bullets are just small graphic images. With the latter option you can select from an enormous number of bullet pictures. Very comprehensive indeed!

If you select the **Numbering** button or the **Multilevel List** button similar options are displayed, giving you a choice of several numbering or outline (multilevel) systems.

Once inserted, you can copy, move or cut a bulleted paragraph in the same way as any other text. However, you cannot delete a bullet with the **Del** key, but you can with the **Backspace**s key.

If you only want a simple list you can create it without using the **Ribbon** buttons. For a bullet list, just type an asterisk '*' followed by a <u>space</u>. The asterisk turns into a bullet and your list is started. To automatically create numbered lists in a similar way, type the number one and a full stop '**1.**', followed by a <u>space</u>.

When you've finished typing the first item in your list, tap or press the **Enter** key and a new bullet or number will appear on the next line. When you have finished entering your list, tapping or pressing the **Enter** key <u>twice</u> will close the list.

Inserting Date and Time

You can insert today's date (the date the current document was created or was last revised) or a date or time that reflects the current system date and time. Therefore, the date can be a date that changes, or a date that always stays the same. In either case, the date is inserted in a date field.

To insert a date field in your document, place the cursor where you want to insert it, make some room for it by pressing the **Enter** then press the **Tab** key to position it correctly within the document, then tap or click the **Insert**, **Text**, **Date & Time** command button and choose one of the displayed date formats shown in Fig. 3.14 on the next page. Fig. 3.14 is a composite of the operation required and the result of that operation.

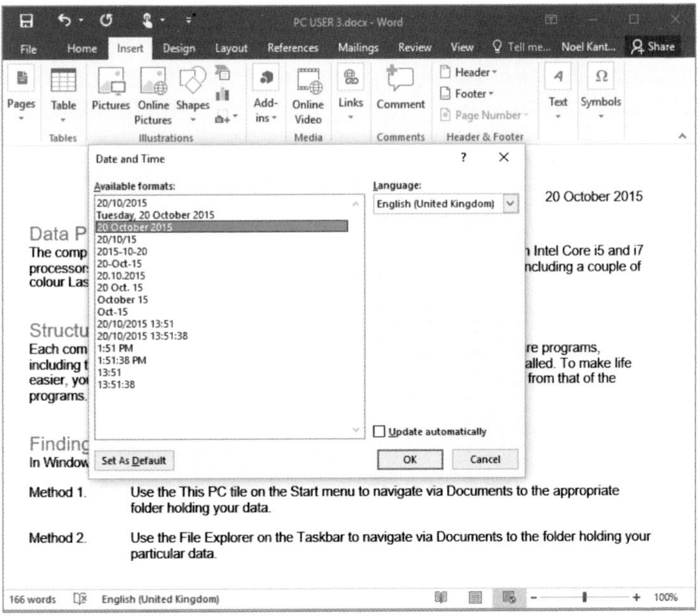

Fig. 3.14 Inserting Dates and Times in a Document.

Furthermore, as you can see on the above figure, the date font type, its size and colour was changed to be the same as that of the text in the main part of the document. Also note that the paragraph below 'Data Processing Computers' has been returned to the format it was prior to indenting it. Try doing this by yourself.

If you save a document with a date field in it and you open it a few days later, the date shown on it will be the original date the document was created. Most of the time this will probably be what you want.

However, should you want the displayed date to always update to the current date whenever the document is opened, then check the **Update automatically** box in the **Date and Time** dialogue box, and then tap or click the **OK** button.

Symbols and Special Characters

Word 2016 lets you easily add symbols to your documents. Using the **Insert**, **Symbols** command button shown below, opens a small gallery of common and recently used symbols for you to choose from. Tapping or clicking the **More Symbols** option opens the **Symbol** dialogue box shown in Fig. 3.15 below. From this you can select characters and symbols and insert them into your document.

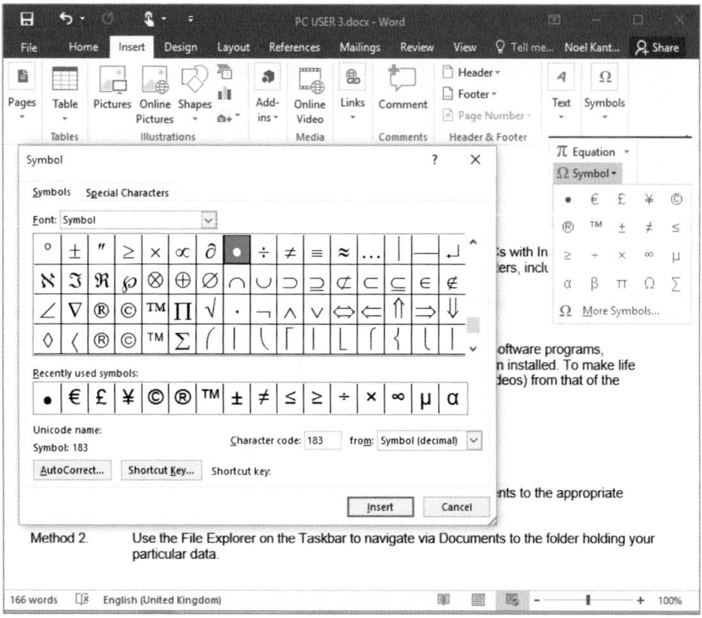

Fig. 3.15 Inserting Symbols in a Document.

You should be able to find just about any symbol you require in the **Symbol** font box shown above. But if not, pressing the down-arrowhead button next to the **Font** box, will reveal the other available character sets.

If you double-tap or double-click on a character, it transfers it to your document at the insertion point, making it extremely easy to use.

Inserting Other Special Characters

You can include other special characters in a document, such as optional hyphens, which remain invisible until they are needed to hyphenate a word at the end of a line; non-breaking hyphens, which prevent unwanted hyphenation; non-breaking spaces, which prevent two words from splitting at the end of a line; or opening and closing single quotes.

There are two ways to insert these special characters in your document. One is to click the **Special Characters** tab of the **Symbol** dialogue box which reveals a long list of these special characters, as shown in Fig. 3.16 below. You then select one of them and click the **Insert** button.

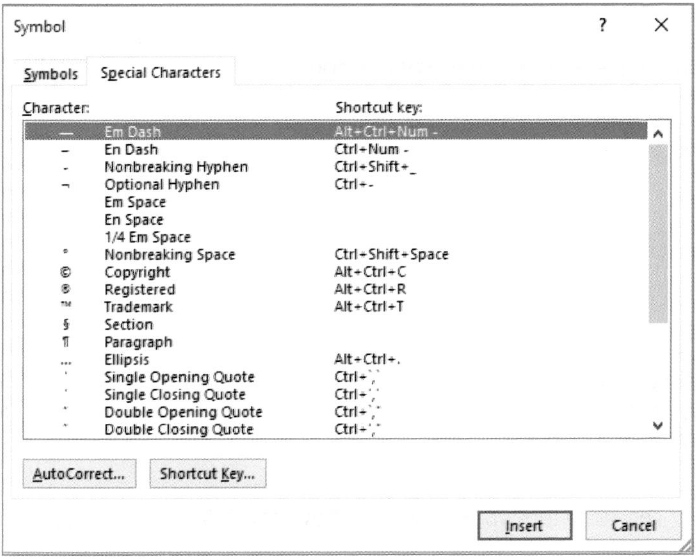

Fig. 3.16 Entering Special Characters.

The other way is to use the keyboard shortcut key combinations listed above, which does not require you to open the dialogue box, but requires you to have a very good memory!

4

Formatting Word Documents

Formatting with Page Tabs

You can format text in columns by using tab stops placed on the **Ruler**, opened by tapping or clicking the **View**, **Show**, **Ruler** button. Although they are not shown on the **Ruler**, but as small marks below it, **Word** has default left tab stops at 1.27 cm intervals. The symbol for a left tab appears in the tab type button at the left edge of the ruler pointed to in Fig. 4.1 below when **Views**, **Print Layout** is selected.

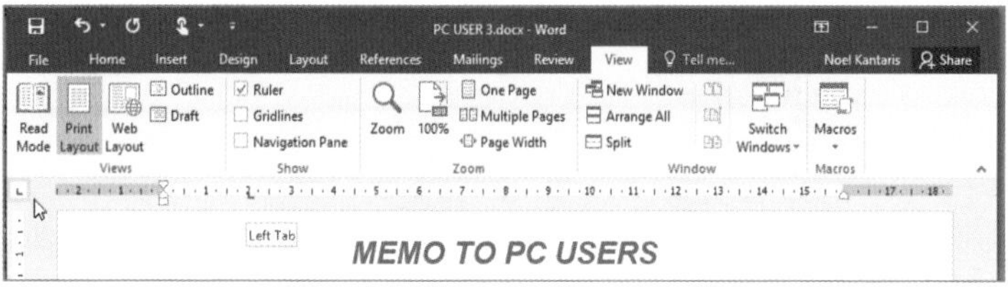

Fig. 4.1 The Ruler and Tab Setting.

To set tabs, tap or click on the tab type button (which cycles through the available types) until the type you want is showing and then click on the ruler. To remove a tab, just drag it off the ruler.

The tab stop types available have the following functions:

Button	***Name***	***Effect***
	Left	Left-aligns text after the tab stop.
	Centre	Centres text on tab stop.
	Right	Right-aligns text at the tab stop.
	Decimal	Aligns decimal point with tab stop.
	Bar	Inserts a vertical line at the tab stop.

The tab type button actually cycles through two more types, first line indent and hanging indent. These give you a quick way of adding these indents to the ruler.

To place tabs exactly, use the **Layout** tab, tap or click the **Paragraph** box launcher to display the **Paragraph** dialogue box (see Fig. 3.11, page 49). Follow this by taping or clicking the **Tabs** button at the bottom of the displayed dialogue box in Fig. 3.11 to open the **Tabs** box shown here in Fig. 4.2. Next type the distance from the left margin for the tab under the **Tab stop position** and tap or click **Set** followed by **OK**. To clear the ruler of tabs press the **Clear All** button. To remove one tab, select it in the list and click the **Clear** button. Tab stops apply either to the paragraph containing the cursor, or to any selected paragraphs.

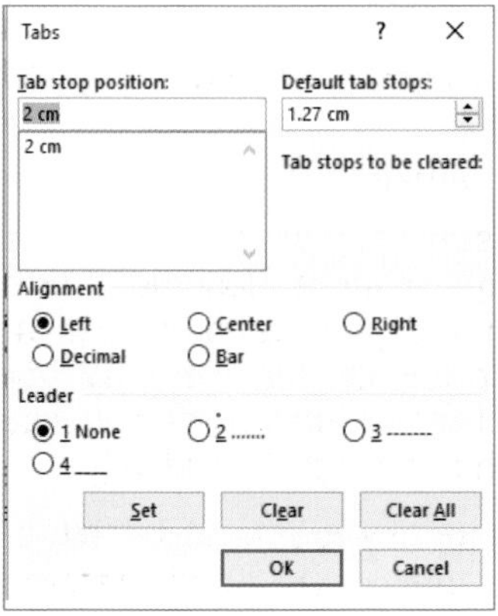

Fig. 4.2 The Tabs Box.

If you want tabular text to be separated by characters instead of by spaces, select one of the four available characters from the **Leader** box in the **Tabs** dialogue box. The options are none (the default), dotted, dashed and underline. The Contents pages of this book are set with right tabs and dotted leader characters.

When you are finished tap or click the **OK** button to make your changes active. Now using the **Tab** key on either keyboard, displays the selected leader characters. If you don't like what you see, press the **Clear All** button in the **Tabs** dialogue box which takes you back to the default **Tab** settings.

Note: All paragraph formatting, such as tab stops, is placed at the end of a paragraph. To carry the formatting to the next line or paragraph, press **Enter**. To cancel formatting, press the down arrow key instead.

Formatting with Styles

In Chapter 2, I discussed how you can format your work using **Styles**, but I confined myself to using the default styles only. In this section I will give an overview of how to create, modify, use and manage styles. Word's **Style** controls, shown in Fig. 4.3, are in the **Home**, **Styles** group.

Fig. 4.3 The Home Styles Group.

A **Style** is a set of formatting instructions which you save so that you can use it repeatedly within a document or in different documents. A collection of **Styles** can be placed in a **Template** which could be appropriate for, say, all your memos so it can be used to preserve uniformity and save time by not having to format each paragraph individually.

Further, should you decide to change a style, all the paragraphs associated with that style can reformat automatically. To provide a pattern for shaping a final document, use a **Template**. By default all documents which have not been assigned a template, use the **Normal.dotm** global template.

Paragraph Styles

Styles contain paragraph and character formats and a name can be attached to these formatting instructions. From then on, applying the style name is the same as formatting that paragraph with the same instructions. With **Word** you can create your styles by example.

Creating a New Paragraph Style

Previously, I spent some time manually creating some hanging indents in the last few paragraphs of the **PC USER 3** document. Open that document and display the **Styles** dialogue box by tapping or clicking the **Styles** dialogue box launcher on the **Home**, **Styles** group.

Next, place the insertion pointer in one of the previously created hanging indent paragraphs, situated at the bottom of the document, and click the **New Style** button pointed to at the bottom of the **Styles** box in Fig. 4.4 below.

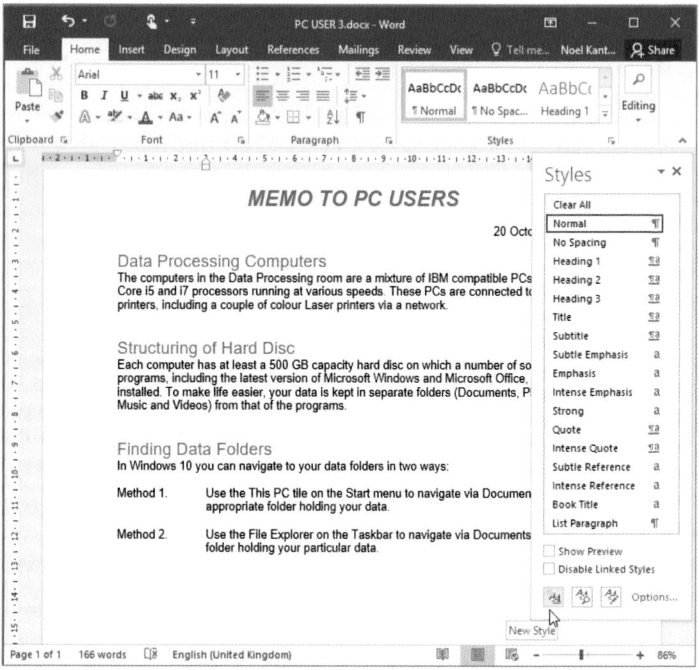

Fig. 4.4 Creating a New Style.

This opens a dialogue box, the top half of which is shown in Fig. 4.5, in which you type the new style name you want to create in the **Name** text box, say, ‘Hanging Indent’, then click **OK** to confirm your changes.

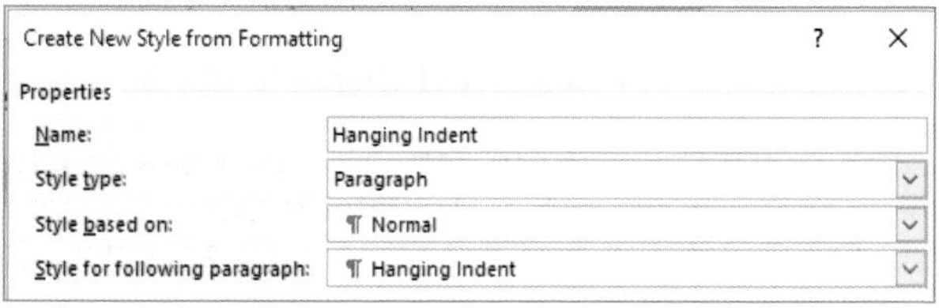

Fig. 4.5 Creating a New Style from Formatting.

Finally, change the style of the other paragraphs to the new 'Hanging Indent', by selecting the new style either from the list in the refreshed **Styles** dialogue box similar to Fig. 4.4 or from the **Styles** gallery as shown in Fig. 4.6.

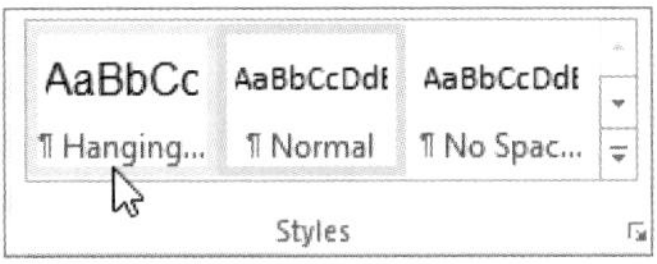

Fig. 4.6 New Quick Style.

Save the result as **PC USER 4**. If you want some help on **Styles**, type 'Help with styles' in the **Tell me what you want to do** box in the **Ribbon**, and select the **Get Help on "help with styles"** option.

Inserting Page Numbers

To insert page numbers in a document, use the **Insert**, **Header & Footer**, **Page Number** command button, and tap or click, say **Bottom of Page**, then select **Plain Number 2** which places the number in the middle of the page. This places the number as shown in Fig. 4.7 and displays a **Header & Footer Design Options** box, also shown in Fig. 4.7.

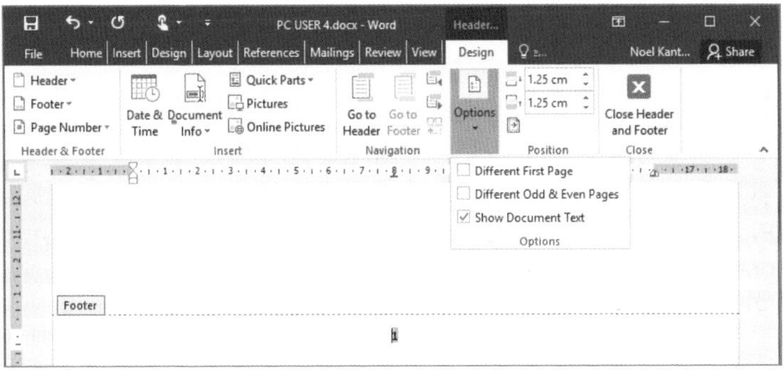

Fig. 4.7 Placement of Page Numbers.

From the displayed **Options** list, you can select **Different First Page** number or one of the other options. I leave this to you to experiment and find out what each selection does to your document. When you finish, tap or click the **Close Header and Footer** button.

Document Templates

A document template provides the overall pattern of your final document. It can contain:

Styles to control your paragraphs and formats.

A Theme to control document colours and fonts.

Page set-up options.

Boilerplate text, which is text that remains the same in every document.

AutoText, which is standard text and graphics that you could insert in a document by typing the name of the AutoText entry.

Macros, which are programs that can change the menus and key assignments to comply with the type of document you are creating.

Customised shortcuts, toolbars and menus.

If you don't assign a template to a document, then the default **Normal.dotm** template is used by **Word**. To create a new document template, you either modify an existing one, create one from scratch, or create one based on the formatting of an existing document.

Creating a Document Template

To illustrate the last point above, I will create a simple document template, which I'll call **PC User Memo**, based on the formatting of the **PC USER 4** document. But first, make sure you have defined the 'Hanging Indent' style as explained earlier.

To create a template based on an existing document do the following:

Open the existing document, if not already opened.

Tap or click the **File** command button, and select the **Save As** command which displays the **File Save** dialogue box, shown in Fig. 4.8 on the next page.

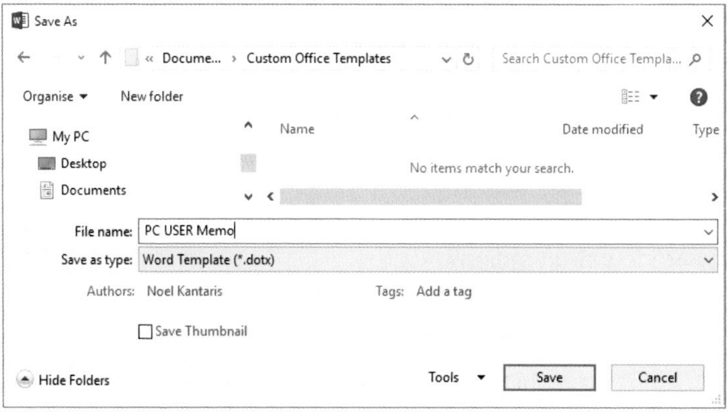

Fig. 4.8 Saving a Document as a Template.

In the **File name** box, type the name of the new template (**PC USER Memo** in our example). In the **Save as type** box, select **Word Template** and press the **Save** button.

To edit a template, tap or click the **Open** button in **File**, then select **Browse** which, in my case, automatically opened the box in Fig. 4.9 – if necessary, navigate to where you saved it. You can then choose the template and tap or click the **Open** button.

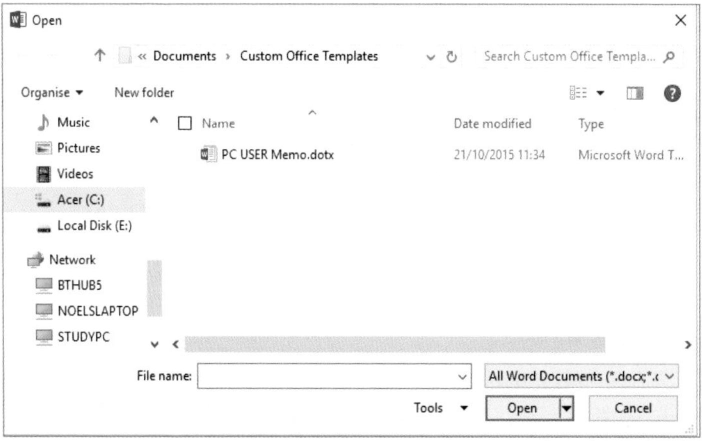

Fig. 4.9 Opening a Template.

Add the text and graphics you want to appear in all new documents that you base on this template, and ***delete*** any items (including text) you do not want.

In this example, I deleted everything in the document except the heading and date, then inserted the picture using **Insert**, **Pictures** to create the screen below.

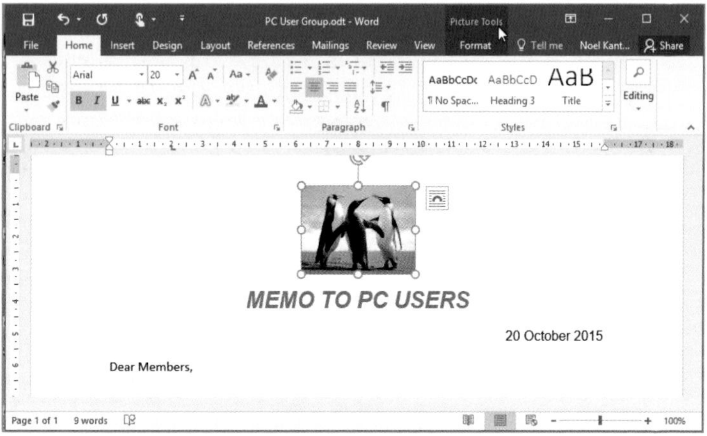

Fig. 4.10 Artwork and Text in the New Template.

Note that when a picture is inserted in **Word**, a new tab appears on the **Ribbon**, called **Picture Tools, Format**, as shown in Fig. 4.10, which allows you to manipulate the picture without the need for any additional programs. However, this new tab only displays when the inserted picture is selected. Do spend a bit of time here to examine these additional tools. Finally, tap or click the **File**, **Save As** command to save the changes using the template name **PC User Group**.

To use the new template, open it, type the rest of your memo, then use the **File**, **Save As** command, but this time choose 'Word Document' as the **Save as type** and give it the name **PC User 5**.

Don't forget that **Word** has a series of built-in templates to suit 'every occasion'. To see these, tap or click the **File**, **New** command button which displays all the available **Word** templates with a preview of what they will look like when selected.

Comments and Tracked Changes

Another of **Word**'s powerful features is the facility to add comments and to track changes made to a document. These actions are all carried out from the **Review** tab on the **Ribbon** as shown in Fig. 4.11.

Use **Comments** to annotate a document. These display in the margin. A tracked change is a mark that shows where a deletion, insertion or other editing change have been made.

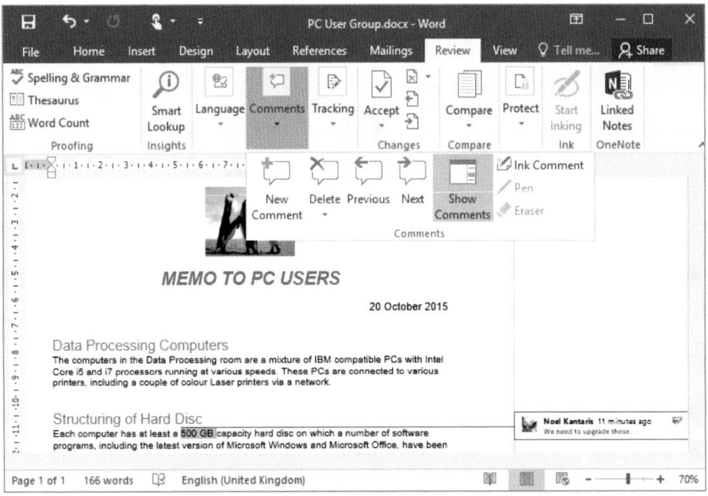

Fig. 4.11 A Comment in a Document.

To hide a comment, tap or click **Review**, **Show Comments** command which collapses the comment to a bubble button. Tap or click this bubble to display the comment again. For more options use the **Review**, **Tracking**, **Show Markup** command button, and select what you want to display on the screen, such as **Insertions and Deletions**, **Formatting** or even comments from **Specific People**. To add a comment, place the pointer in the correct location, tap or click the **New Comment** button, and type the comment into the 'balloon' that opens. You can print a document with mark-ups to keep a record of any changes made.

Sharing & Exporting Word Documents

With **Word** you can share documents in several different ways. Having opened a document, use the **File**, **Share** option to open the screen shown in Fig. 4.12 below.

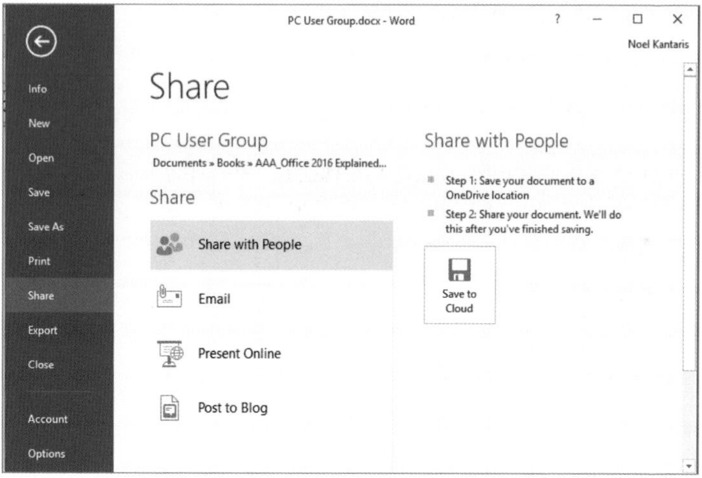

Fig. 4.12 Sharing a Document with People.

You can select one of the displayed options:

If you choose to send your document to the cloud (to **OneDrive**), then you are given the opportunity to **Invite people** to share it and automatically share any changes made to the document. This also happens if you tap or click the **Share** tab on the **Ribbon**.

If you choose **Email** the document will be sent to people you choose as an **Attachment**.

If you choose **Present Online**, the document will be presented to selected people as a link, who then can view it in their Web browser.

If you choose the **Post to Blog** option, it allows you to create a new blog post using the current document.

The **File**, **Export** option allows you to create a **PDF/XPS Document** format that you can publish or send to friends in a form that cannot be changed while the **Change File Type** option (also within **File Export**) can be used to change the current format to a **Word 97-2003** format, **OpenDocument** text, **Template**, **Plain Text** or **Rich Text**. These facilities are very useful and easy to implement.

Printing Documents

To print a document, open it in **Word**, then use the **File**, **Print** command which displays the screen below.

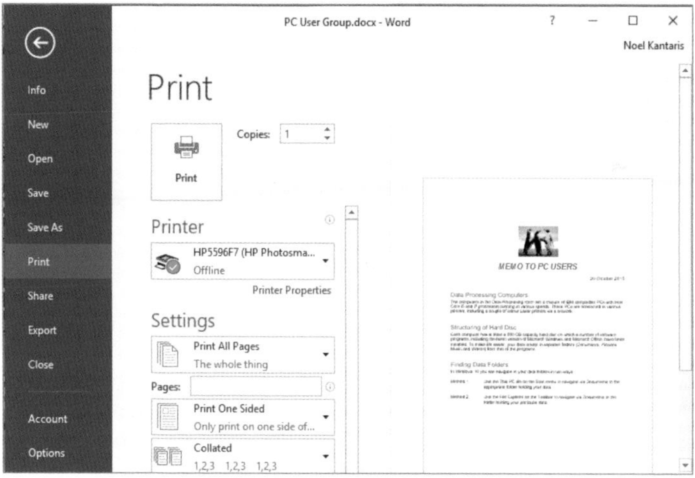

Fig. 4.13 The Print Screen.

You can print a document in various ways, as follows:

Tap or click the **Print** button to print the document using the default printer and current settings. You can also specify the number of copies to be printed in the **Print**, **Copies** box.

The **Settings** in the **Print** screen of Fig. 4.13, allow you to select which pages to print, whether one sided or not, collated or not, in **Portrait** or **Landscape**, etc.

On the **Settings** option, you can also select the paper size, change margins and choose the number of pages per sheet. You might have to scroll down to see some of these facilities.

In the **Printer** box you can select which printer to use, as shown for one of my computers in Fig. 4.14 below.

One thing to remember is that, whenever you change printers, the appearance of your document may change, as **Word** uses the fonts available with the newly selected printer. This can affect the line lengths, which in turn will affect both the tabulation and pagination of your document.

Throughout the process of selecting printers, etc., the document is displayed in the **Preview** pane to the right of the **Print** screen, so you can see what you'll get before printing to paper.

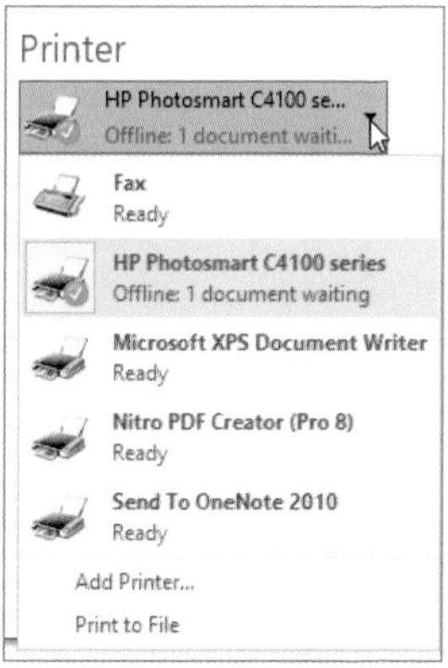

Fig. 4.14 The Printer Selection Screen.

Using Mail Merge

There are times when you may want to send the same basic letter or e-mail to several different people, or companies. The easiest way to do this is with a **Mail Merge** operation from **Word**. For this to work, the basic content of all the letters or e-mail messages must be the same, the differences being specific to each recipient, such as name, address, etc. You can also use **Mail Merge** for the following:

Envelopes The return address is the same on all the envelopes, but the destination address is unique on each one.

Labels Each label shows a person's unique name and address.

Two files are prepared; a 'Data' file with the names and addresses of recipients, and a 'Form' file, containing the text and format of the letter. The two files are then merged together to produce a third file containing an individual letter to each party listed in the original data file.

Before creating a list of names and addresses for a mail merge, you need to select the **Office** application that is most suited to the task. For example:

For a long list which is frequently updated and you are required to sort and search, you should use either the **Outlook**'s **Contacts** list of names and addresses, **Excel** or **Access**.

For a small to medium size data list in which you do not expect to make too many changes, it is easiest to create a list in **Word**.

To illustrate the merge procedure, I will use the **PC User 5** document and a table I shall create in **Word**. First open the memo (or your own letter), then place two empty lines at the very top of it by tapping or pressing **Enter** twice. Next, select these two empty lines and **Format** them the same as the text in the memo, then tap or click the **Mailings** tab, **Start Mail Merge** and select **Step-by-step Mail Merge Wizard** from the drop-down list of options, as shown in Fig. 4.15.

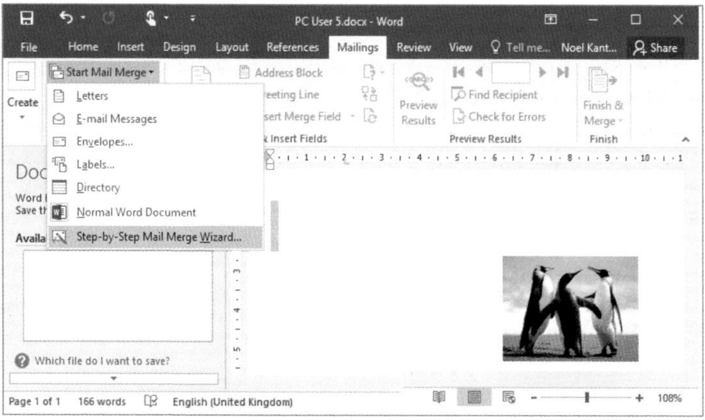

Fig. 4.15 Starting a Mail Merge.

This opens the **Mail Merge Task** pane in which you select the document type to be used: **Letters** (the default), **E-mail messages**, **Envelopes**, **Labels**, etc., as shown in Fig. 4.16. Next, choose **Select Recipients** (the second command in the **Start Mail Merge** group), also shown in Fig. 4.16 which allows you to: **Type a New List**, **Use an Existing List**, or **Choose from Outlook Contacts**.

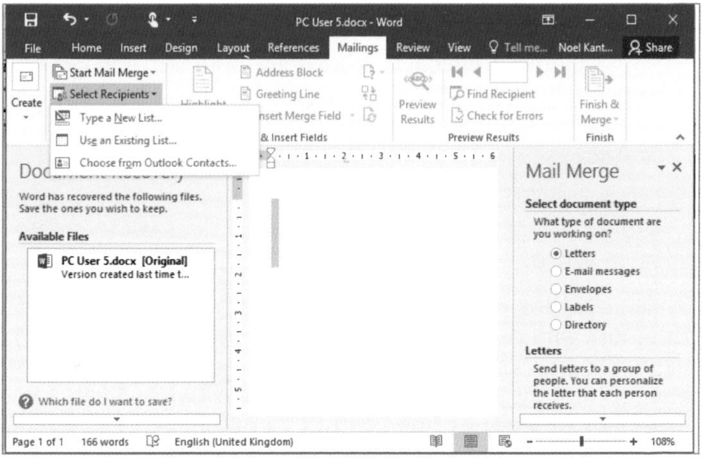

Fig. 4.16 Selecting Recipients and the Mail Merge Task Pane.

Creating an Address List in Word

On selecting **Type a New List**, the **New Address List** dialogue box opens as shown in Fig. 4.17.

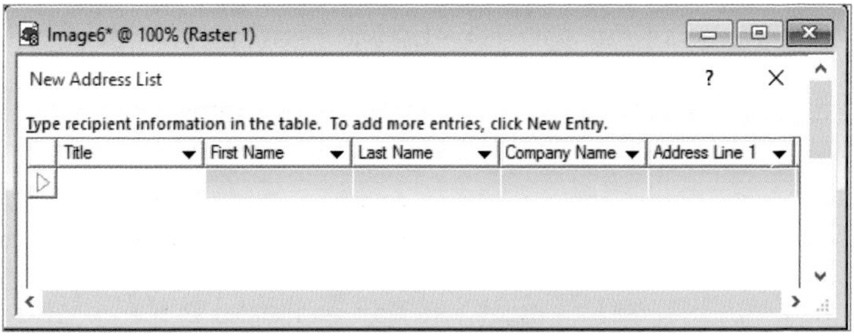

Fig. 4.17 The New Address List Dialogue Box.

Word provides commonly used field names for your address list. As you start filling in the first entry, additional buttons are displayed at the bottom of the **New Address List** box, as shown in Fig. 4.18.

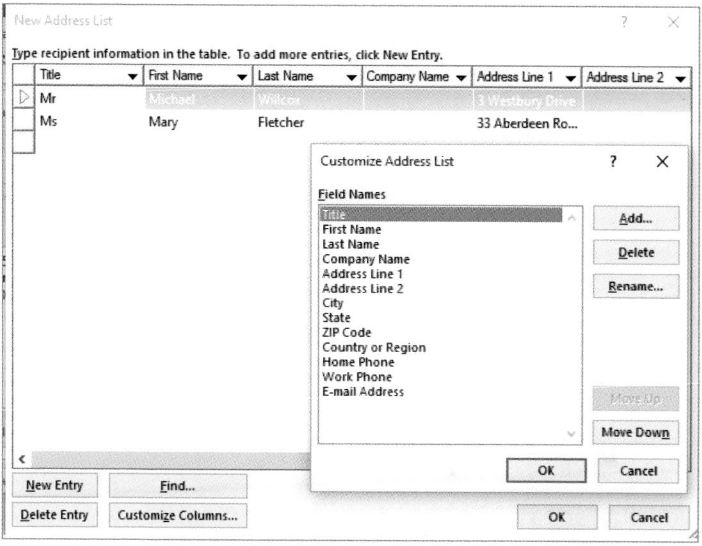

Fig. 4.18 Customising the New Address List Columns.

The various fields in the list can be changed by using the **Customize Columns** button which opens the **Customize Address List** box, also shown in Fig. 4.18. Filed names can be deleted, renamed, moved and new ones added.

Once the columns are customised and entries added to the list, you can sort them by tapping or clicking on the down-arrowhead of the field you want to use as your sort criteria. Having completed your list, tap or click the **OK** button to display the **Save Address List** window. Name your data list, say **Customers** – **Word** adds the extension **.mdb**.

Next, place the insertion pointer where the name and address should be on the letter and select **Mailings**, **Insert Merge Field** and choose the appropriate fields from the drop-down menu, with **Title**, **First Name** and **Last Name** on one line, with a space in between, tapping **Enter** to change lines.

In Fig. 4.19, you'll see the fields as they should appear at the top of your letter – you might have to select them all and format them in Arial, 11 point.

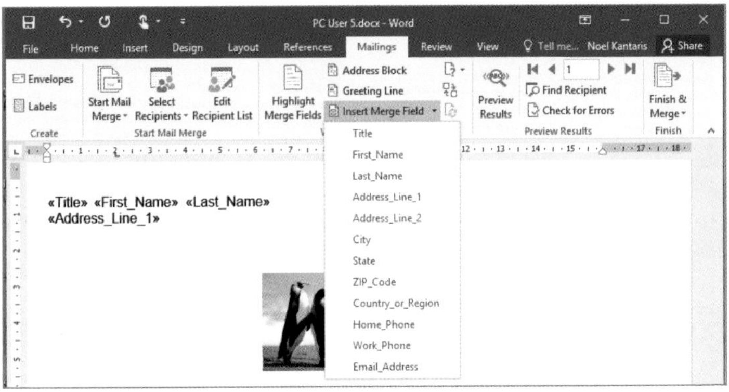

Fig. 4.19 Placing Address Fields on a Letter.

To see a preview of the merged results, tap or click the **Mailings**, **Preview Results** button to display Fig. 4.20.

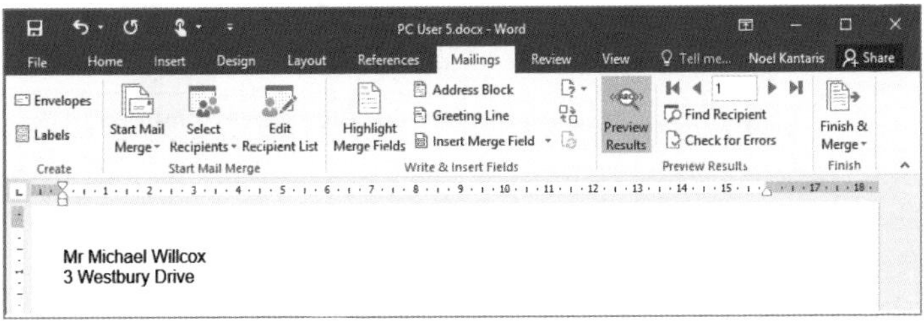

Fig. 4.20 The Name and Address Preview.

Finally, tap or click the **Mailings**, **Finish & Merge** command and select to either edit, print, or send the letter using e-mail. Try it, it is an easy, but a very powerful feature.

***

Word has many more features, far too many to discuss in the space allocated to this book. What I have tried to do so far, is give you enough information so that you can have the confidence to forge ahead and explore the rest of **Word**'s capabilities by yourself. Try investigating tables, frames and drawing amongst other topics. I leave it to you.

5

Microsoft Outlook 2016

Microsoft's **Outlook** is a powerful electronic communication and personal information manager. You can use most of the skills gained in editing and formatting **Word** documents equally well with **Outlook**.

Starting Outlook 2016

To start Microsoft **Outlook**, either tap or click its icon on the **Taskbar**, shown here on the left, which opens a screen similar to that in Fig. 5.1.

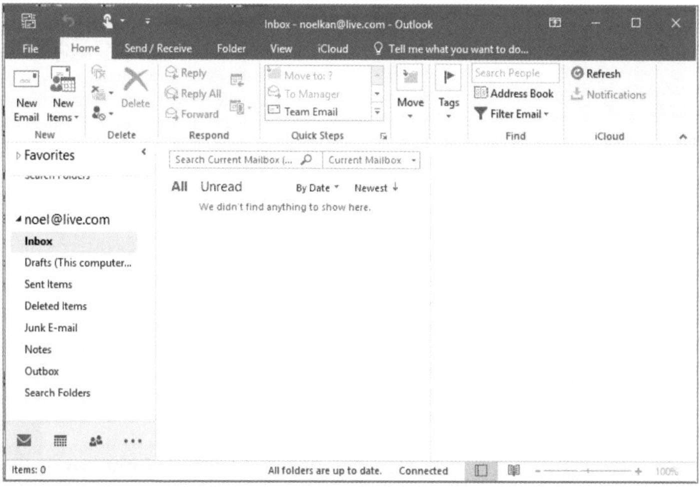

Fig. 5.1 Outlook 2016's Opening Screen.

If you are wondering where the **Outlook** templates are, don't worry as **Outlook** doesn't have any, but you can format e-mail messages in the same way as **Word** documents.

The Outlook Screen

As you can see, **Outlook** also supports the **Ribbon**. What you see may not be the same as shown in Fig. 5.2, because it depends on the settings you have activated.

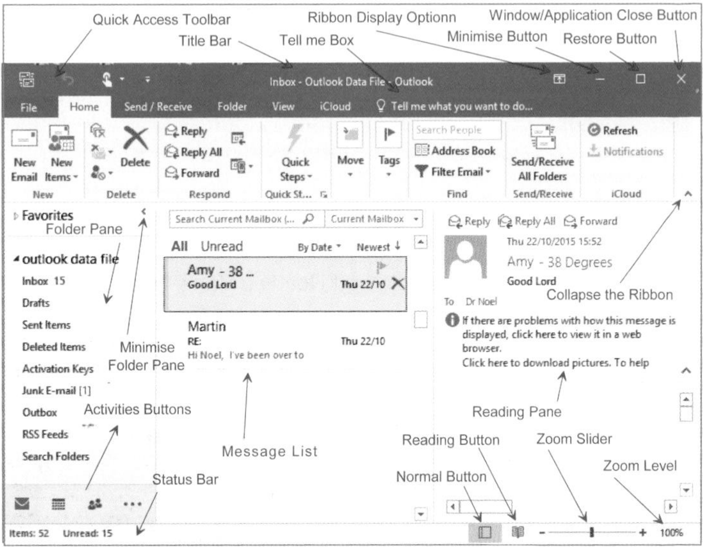

Fig. 5.2 Outlook 2016's Three Different Panes.

Below the **Ribbon** the window is split into three areas at present – which will change the moment you tap or click one of the other activities, such as **Calendar**, **Contacts**, **Tasks**, **Notes**, etc., which display as icons at the bottom left of the screen. To see all the available activities, tap or click the **More** button, the one with the 3 dots. The windows of the various activities of **Outlook** will be different, but for the time being I'll concentrate on **Mail**.

With the **Mail** activity selected, tapping or clicking the **Inbox** folder displays the screen in Fig. 5.2 above. The **Reading** area on the right of the screen is where you read your e-mail messages, but at present is rather small. To substantially increase it, tap or click the **Minimise the Folder Pane** ‹ button. What now displays is shown in Fig. 5.3 on the next page.

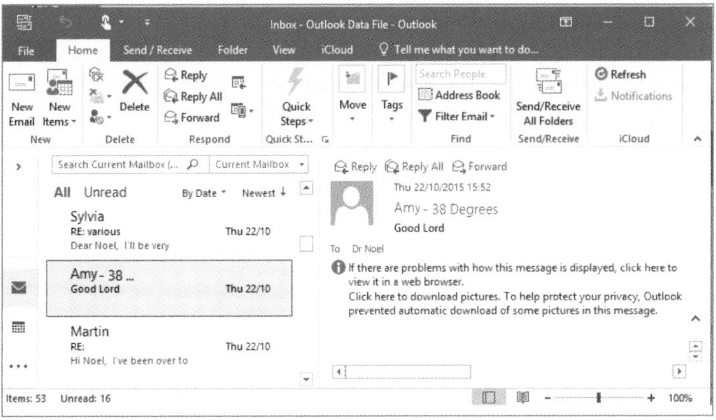

Fig. 5.3 The Enlarged Reading Pane Area.

Note that the **Minimise the Folder** button has now been replaced by a **Maximise the Folder** › button. To return to the former state (Fig. 5.2 on the previous page) use this button, followed by the **Expand the Folder Pane** button to pin it in place. Having maximised the **Folder** pane, now tap or click the **Reading** button at the bottom of Fig. 5.3, to quickly collapse the **Folder** pane, then tap or click the **Normal** button to return the **Outlook** window to its former state.

The Folder Pane

In **Outlook**, the **Folder** pane makes it easier for you to navigate to different **Outlook** folders. You can re-size it or display it in a minimised form to use less screen space.

The contents of the **Folder** pane change depending on what view (such as **Mail** or **Calendar**) you are using. Each view offers access to **Outlook** information relevant to that view.

The view buttons at the lower part of the **Folder** pane correspond to **Outlook**'s different views, or activity areas, such as **Calendar**, **Tasks** or **Contacts**. Depending on the view that you choose, you see a different set of panes, folders, and information, as shown in Fig. 5.6 on the next page for **Calendar**.

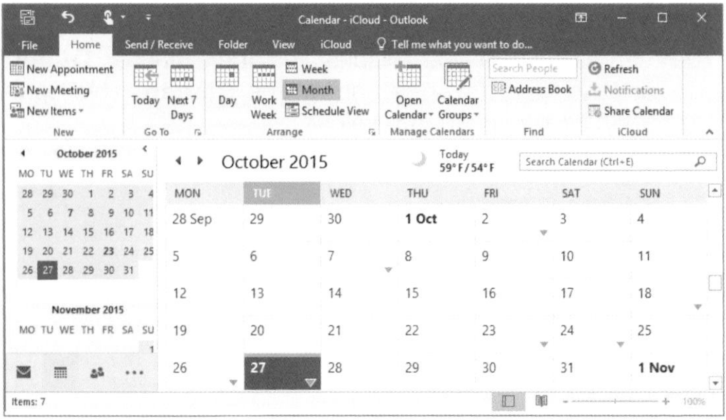

Fig. 5.4 Folder Pane Configuration for Calendar.

To re-size the **Folder** pane, point to its right border and when the pointer becomes a double-headed arrow ↔, drag it to the left or right. The buttons in the **Activities** pane (below the **Folder** pane), opens the following **Outlook** views when they are tapped or clicked:

Mail	The Mail activity where you read and send e-mail messages and feeds.
Calendar	The Calendar and Scheduling activity in which you can create and manage appointments, meetings and events.
People	The activity that accesses details of your contacts or connection to a social network.
Tasks	Used to manage tasks and small projects.
Notes	Used to make and manage 'stick on' type notes.
Folders	Displays your Mail, Calendar, Contacts, etc., folders in the Folders Pane from where you can switch to other activities.
Shortcuts	Gives quick access to your favourite folders or to Web pages, if you have created any.

The View Tab

You can configure the display of the various **Outlook** activities by using the **View** tab on the **Ribbon**. This opens the screen shown in Fig. 5.5 below.

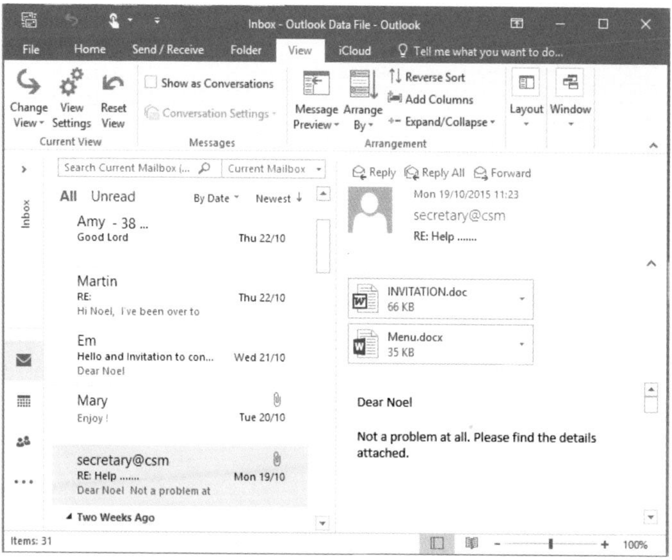

Fig. 5.5 Using the View Tab to Configure your Display.

It is worth spending some time here trying the various display views to see which suits you best.

Importing Data into Outlook

In my experience when **Office** 2016 is installed it does a good job of finding and including your previous e-mail settings, data and saved messages, especially if you previously used an older version of **Outlook**.

If you also hold personal or business information, such as contacts or tasks to perform, it is easy to import these into **Outlook** as well, by using the **File**, **Open & Export** command on the **Ribbon**, then selecting the **Import/Export** option as shown in Fig. 5.6 on the next page.

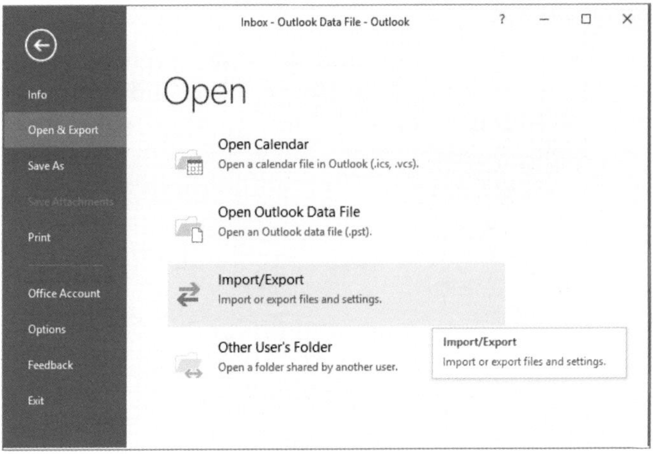

Fig. 5.6 Selecting the Import/Export Option from Open & Export.

This starts the **Import and Export** set of screens, the first one of which is shown in Fig. 5.7.

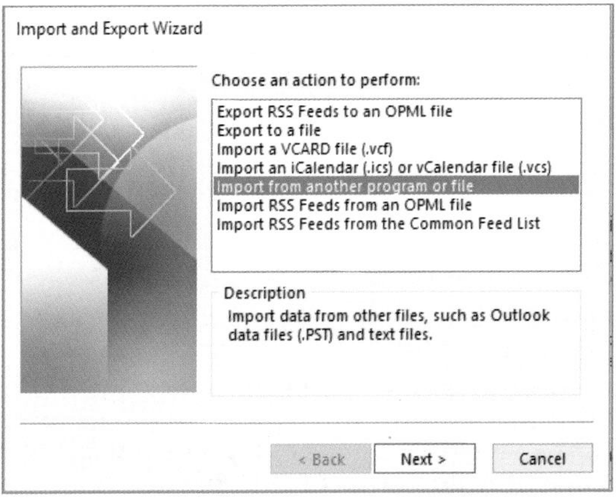

Fig. 5.7 The Import and Export Wizard.

Next, highlight the **Import from another program or file** entry and tap or click **Next**, which displays a list of possible organiser-type formats that it can handle as shown in Fig. 5.8 on the next page.

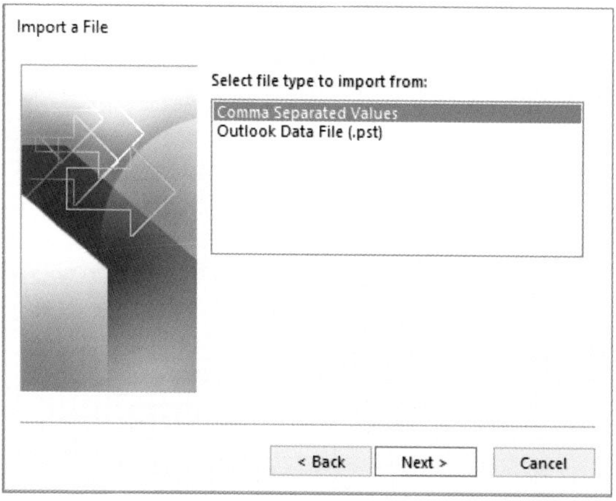

Fig. 5.8 Selecting the File Type to Import.

If the file type to import appears on the list above, all is well. Just select it and specify on the next screen where to find it.

However, if the file type does not appear in the list, then you will have to go back to your previously used organiser and export the data into **Comma Separated Values**, so that you can use this file type to import your data into **Outlook**.

Having selected the type of file you want to convert, tapping or clicking the **Next** button displays the following screen in which you are asked to locate the file to be converted. After that the conversion is automatic – just follow the on-screen instructions.

I found the data conversion to be faultless and was particularly impressed that the extensive information in my **Contacts** folder was converted fully and accurately.

Obviously I cannot show you the outcome of this process, as it contains private and sensitive information, but you may see some conversion entries as I examine the individual sections of **Outlook** in later pages.

E-mail with Microsoft Outlook

It is most likely that you will spend most of your time with **Outlook** dealing with e-mail messages. For this to work, you must be connected to the **Internet** or a local area network (LAN). A connection to the **Internet** these days uses mainly plugged-in or wireless **Broadband** using your telephone wires to the exchange. Some providers use a fibre-optic connection from their telephone exchange to the **Internet** which results in a very fast service. There are other methods of connection, of course, such as an **Ethernet** card connected to a LAN which itself is connected to the **Internet**.

To use a telephone-based connection you will need to subscribe to an **Internet Service Provider** (ISP) which is a company that allows you to connect to its **Internet** host. All ISPs offer an e-mail address and a mailbox facility to hold your incoming messages until you connect and download them to your computer. The whole procedure of connecting to your ISP, downloading e-mail messages, filtering unwanted junk e-mail, saving and managing e-mail messages and other information, such as addresses of Web sites, can be done very easily in **Outlook** and will be explored later.

The Folders Pane

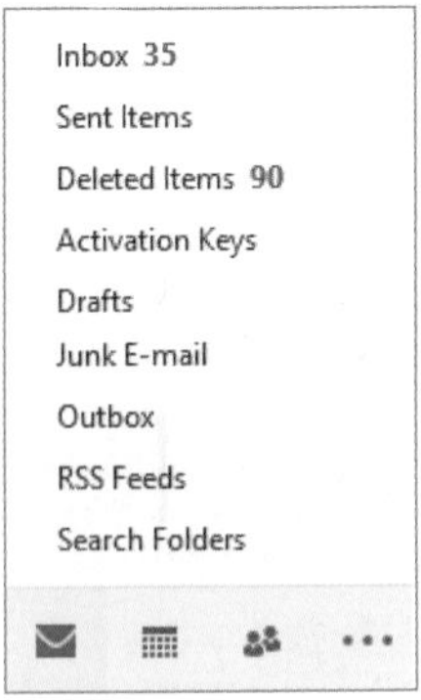

Fig. 5.9 Outlook Mail Folders.

Most of the default **Mail** folders in **Outlook**, shown here in Fig. 5.9, are self-explanatory.

Inbox – contains all your received e-mail messages (35 unread in this case).

Drafts – contains any messages under preparation that you intend to complete later.

Outbox – contains prepared e-mail messages which are waiting to be sent.

Other folders are used for housekeeping, such as:

Deleted Items – used to hold deleted items before you finally clear them from your system or reinstate them.

Sent Items – used to hold a copy of all e-mail messages you have sent.

Junk E-mail – can be made to hold filtered junk e-mail.

Search Folders – hold specified e-mail searches, so that you can use them again.

RSS Feeds – contains any live **Feeds** that you might have subscribed to. **RSS** stands for 'Really Simple Syndication'.

Here, I have also created a folder called **Activation Keys** to hold all the e-mail messages I've been sent by companies containing information relating to activation keys for purchased software. You may have something similar.

As you receive new e-mail messages, unless they are filtered out they are all placed in the **Inbox** which means that it gets bigger and bigger. Perhaps most of them you will delete, but you will want to save some for future reference. You might like to create folders to hold your stored messages, in some sort of order, like my **Activation Keys** folder. You might, for example, create folders to hold e-mail messages from specific members of your family, or messages dealing with a specific business, etc.

Creating a New Folder

You can add new folders, under a selected folder, by tapping or clicking the **Folder** tab on the **Ribbon**, then selecting the **New Folder** command, shown selected in Fig. 5.10, which opens the box shown in Fig. 5.11 on the next page.

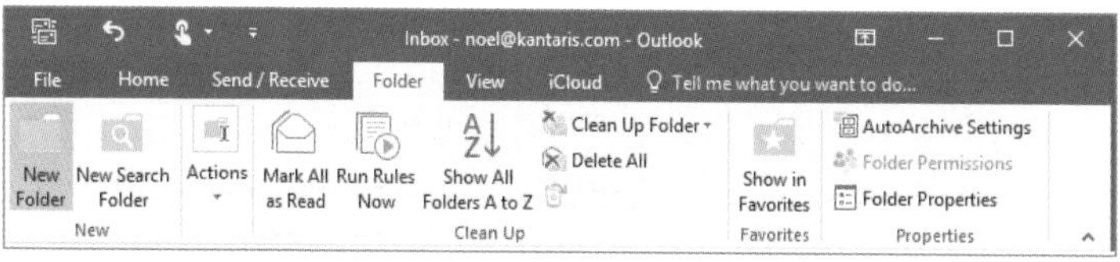

Fig. 5.10 Creating a New Mail Folder.

You enter the new folder **Name** and what the **Folder contains**. Here, as can be seen in Fig. 5.11, the **Inbox** folder is selected, therefore on pressing the **OK** button the new folder will become a sub-folder of that folder.

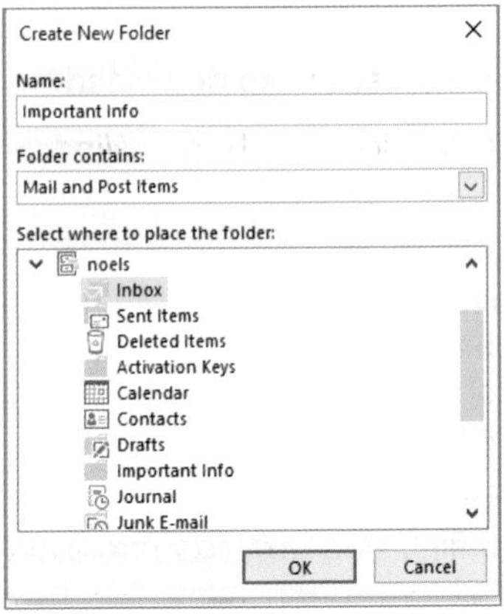

Fig. 5.11 The Create New Folder Dialogue Box.

Had you selected the containing folder (**noels** in my example) instead of the **Inbox** folder, the new folder would have appeared in the main listing, like the **Activation Keys** folder, also shown in Fig. 5.11.

You can move and copy messages from one folder into another by either touching and holding or right-clicking its header line in the **Messages** pane then selecting **Move** from the displayed menu. This opens a list of all the folders available to you for such an operation. All you have to do is choose one.

You can also move or copy messages by dragging them to another folder, but when copying with the mouse, you must also have the **Ctrl** key depressed during the operation. When a copy operation is taking place, the mouse pointer shows a '+', as shown here.

E-mail Accounts

Outlook supports several types of e-mail accounts:

Microsoft Exchange – An e-mail based communications server often used by networked businesses. Home users typically do not have an Exchange account so cannot use the features in **Outlook** that require Exchange.

POP3 – A common protocol that is used to retrieve e-mail messages from an Internet e-mail server.

IMAP – **I**nternet **M**essage **A**ccess **P**rotocol – Creates folders on a server to store and organise messages for retrieval by other computers. You can read message headers only and select which messages to download.

HTTP – Web-based e-mail service, such as Windows Live, Mail or Gmail.

For most accounts, **Outlook** automatically detects and configures the account by using just a name, an e-mail address and a password. **Exchange** account users usually don't have to type any information, because **Outlook** identifies the network credentials used to connect it.

The **Outlook**, e-mail accounts are included in profiles, which consist of accounts, data files and settings containing details about where your e-mail is stored. You can have several e-mail accounts in a single **Outlook** user profile and you could also add an **Exchange** account for your business e-mail and a **POP3** account for your personal e-mail.

Adding a New Account

To add a new e-mail account to your profile, click the FILE button, then click the **Account Settings** icon highlighted in Fig. 5.12, to display additional buttons, as shown below.

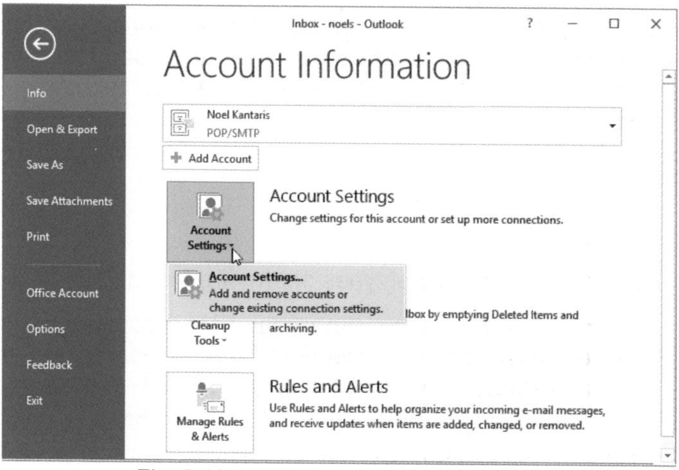

Fig. 5.12 The Account Settings Button.

To add or remove accounts or configure a connection to social networks, tap or click the **Accounts Settings** button to open the dialogue box shown in Fig. 5.13.

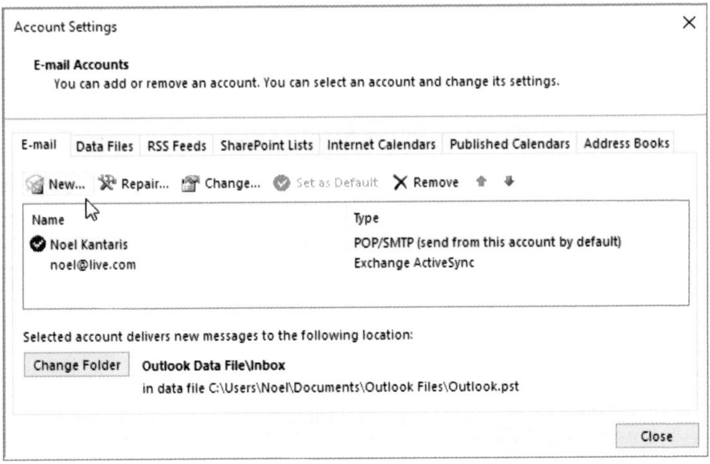

Fig. 5.13 Adding a New E-mail Account.

Next, click **New** to open the **Add Account** dialogue box shown in Fig. 5.14.

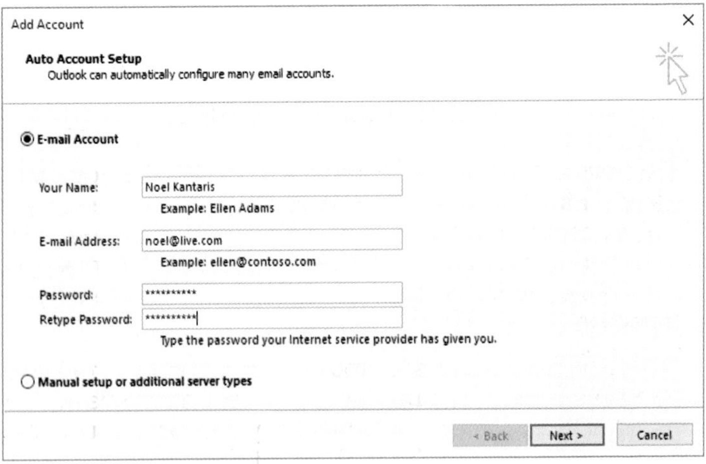

Fig. 5.14 The Add Account Auto Account Setup Box.

It is in Fig. 5.14 where you enter the information for your account. In the **Your Name** box, type your name as you want it to appear to other people. In the **E-mail Address** box, type the complete e-mail address as obtained from your mail administrator or ISP.

In the two **Password** boxes, type the password for your e-mail account followed by the **Next** button. Hopefully the rest is automatic and results in the following actions.

First, your e-mail server is contacted and **Outlook** is configured for your account, as shown in Fig. 5.15 below.

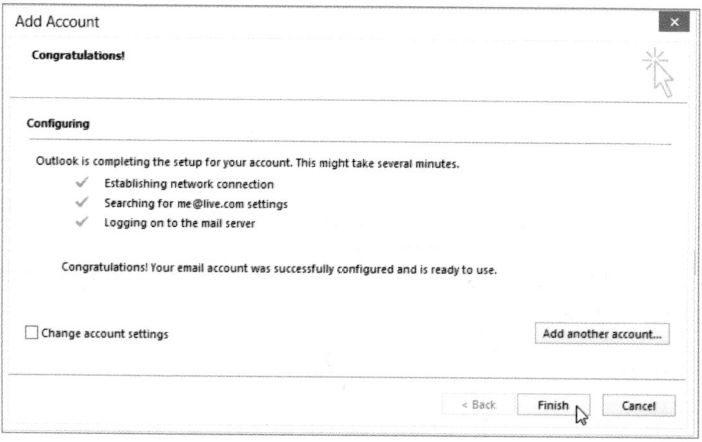

Fig. 5.15 Configuration Procedure.

After your account is configured successfully, and you tap or click the **Finish** button you should find a new message in **Outlook** confirming that all is as it should be. If an encrypted connection cannot be established to the e-mail server, you are prompted to tap or click **Next** to attempt an unencrypted connection.

This new semi-automatic procedure is a great improvement and makes setting up e-mail accounts very easy indeed. You only need three pieces of information: your name, your e-mail address and password. **Outlook** does the rest.

You are now in a position to send and receive e-mail messages. Tapping or clicking the **Send/Receive All Folders** command button in the **Send / Receive** tab of the **Ribbon**, shown here in Fig. 5.16, downloads instantly any messages you might have waiting for you in your e-mail accounts.

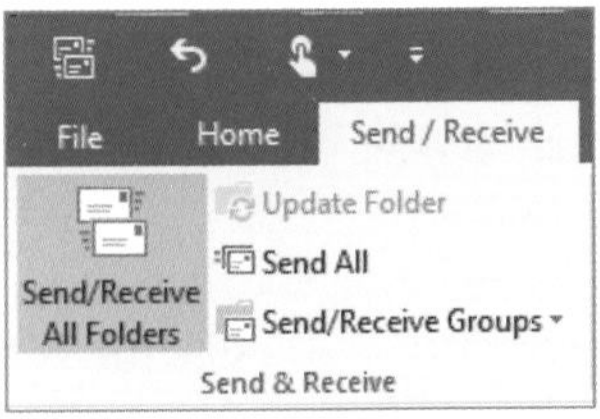

Fig. 5.16 The Send/Receive All Folders Button.

Creating and Sending E-mail Messages

The best way to test out new e-mail features is to send a test message to your own e-mail address. This saves wasting somebody else's time, and the message can be very quickly checked to see the results. So, tap or click the **New E-mail** button on the **Home** tab of the **Ribbon** to open a new **Message** window shown in Fig. 5.17.

Note the address in the **To...** box is shown underlined. This was automatically done by **Outlook** after I typed in the text string and moved to the **Subject:** box, because it is recognised as an e-mail address by **Outlook**. Later on I'll discuss how to choose an address from **Contacts**.

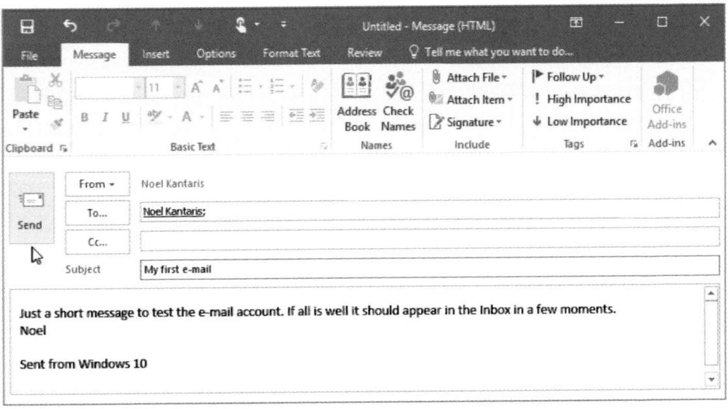

Fig. 5.17 A Test E-mail in Outlook 2016's Message Window.

Each e-mail should have a short subject, which is what will appear on the **Messages List** when the message is received. The **Cc** box is where you include the address of additional persons that you would like to receive a copy of the same

message. To send the message, simply press the **Send** button which closes the **Message** window. If you are connected to the **Internet**, the message will be sent immediately. If not it will be placed in the **Outbox**, waiting for you to go online.

In a few moments, the message appears in the **Inbox**, as in Fig. 5.18 below. You can tap or click the **Send/Receive All Folders** command button on the **Send / Receive** tab to force **Outlook** to check the mailbox.

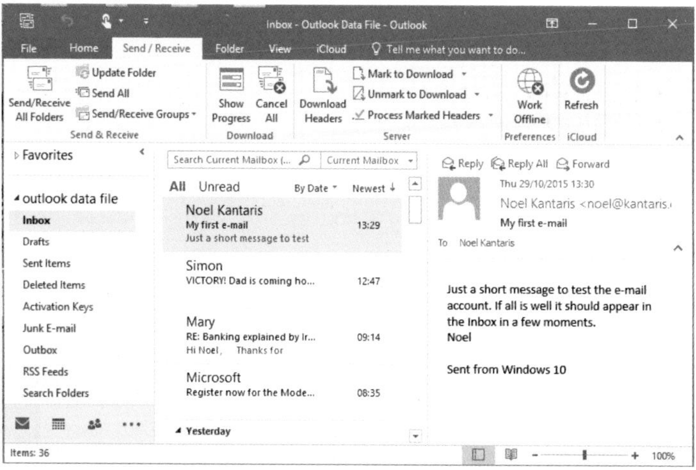

Fig. 5.18 The Test Message Received in our Inbox.

As you can see, the contents of a selected message in the **Messages List** appear in **Outlook**'s **Reading** pane. Here the **Reading** pane appears to the right of the **Messages List**. Double-tapping or double-clicking an e-mail title, opens the message in its own **Message** window which is less cluttered and easier to read. Try it to see for yourself.

Outlook's Message Formats

Outlook 2016 supports four types of message formats:

HTML This message format can produce highly formatted messages with different fonts, colours, bullet lists and graphics.

Plain Text A format supported by all e-mail programs, but does not support text formatting or display graphics in the body of the message, but pictures can be included as attachments.

RTF A Rich Text Format which supports text formatting.

MHT A Web page archive file format which is an MHTML document that saves the Web page content and incorporated external resources, such as images, Flash animation, etc., into an HTML document.

When you reply to a message in **Outlook** it automatically uses the same format as the original message. So if someone sends you a message in **Plain Text**, your reply to that message is automatically sent in the same format as the original message.

So, try to avoid excessive text enhancement as there are still some people out there who use e-mail programs that are only capable of receiving plain text and, therefore, not everyone will appreciate the artwork you spent ages creating!

Outlook automatically converts **RTF** formatted messages to **HTML** by default when you send them to an **Internet** recipient, so that the message formatting is maintained and attachments are received.

Formatting Text

There are several ways to format the text of your message. After selecting the text you want to format you can use the various command buttons on the **Message** tab, in the **Basic Text** group, as shown in Fig. 5.19 on the next page.

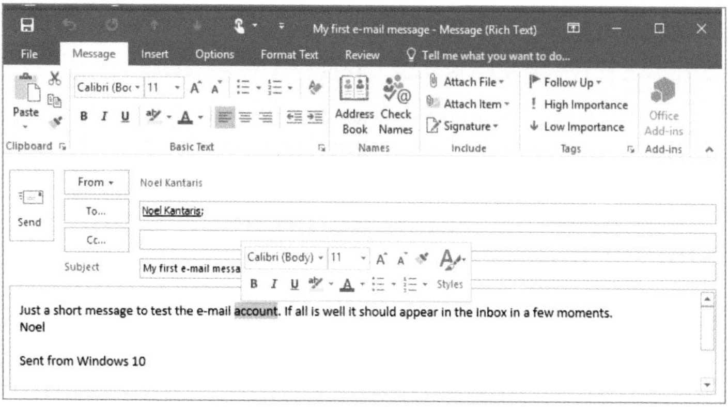

Fig. 5.19 The Message Tab Command Buttons.

Also, you can format text either by using the **Mini** toolbar, (see Fig. 5.19), which displays when you double-tap or double-click on a word, or when you use the drop-down list of options that appears when you right-click the selected word. This also opens the **Mini** toolbar as shown in Fig. 5.20.

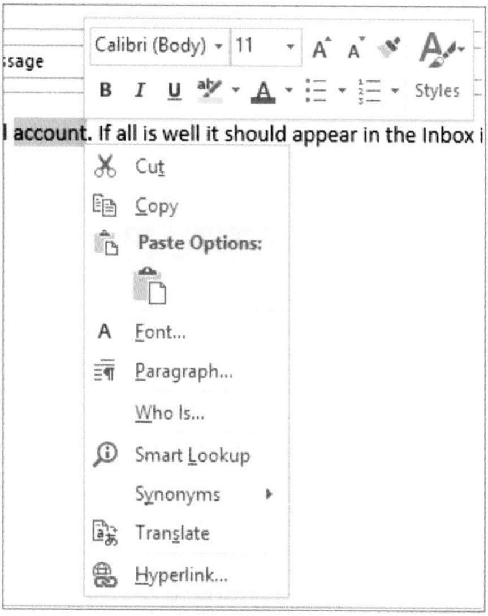

Fig. 5.20 The Mini Toolbar and Right-click Options.

If, however you touch and hold a word on a touch-sensitive screen, a similar **Mini** toolbar is displayed, but slightly different to the one shown in Fig. 5.20. The **Mini** toolbar now has a downward pointing arrowhead (Fig. 5.21) which, when touched, displays a slightly different sets of drop-down formatting options to those in Fig. 5.20.

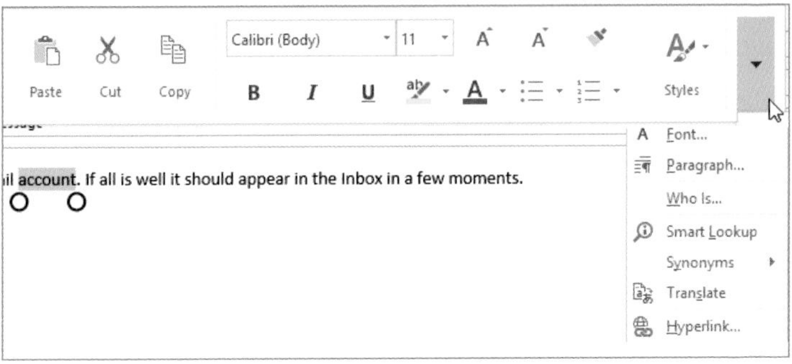

Fig. 5.21 The Mini Toolbar and Touch and Hold Options.

The difference has to do with the relative size of finger versus mouse pointer, but in both cases you can change the font, increase or decrease the size by one increment, use the **Format Painter**, select the font style (bold, italic or underline). You can also, change paragraph styles, check the spelling of text, find a synonym and translate a word or a phrase from English into another language and insert a hyperlink.

Adding Graphics to an E-mail

Using the **Insert** tab, in the **Illustrations** group, shown in Fig. 5.22, you can add **Pictures** from a file, **SmartArt Graphic**, or ready made **Shapes** to visually communicate information and **Charts** to illustrate and compare data. In the **Tables** group you can add a **Table**.

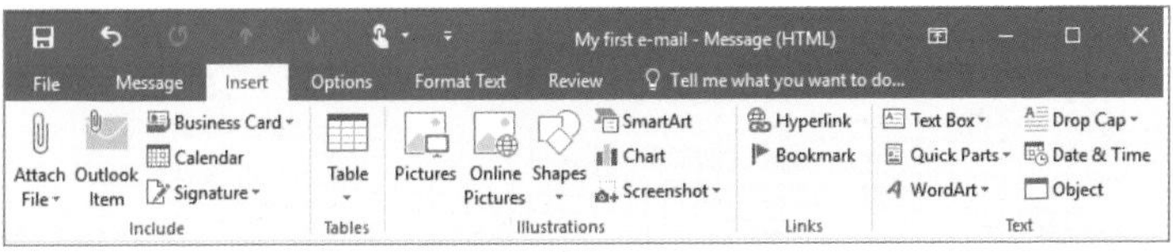

Fig. 5.22 The Insert Tab.

However, although including graphics in a message can have startling visual results, it also increases the file size of your e-mail message, so it might take longer to send and to receive. I leave it to you to experiment with these features.

There are three more tabs that you need to consider when composing an e-mail message. These are: (a) the **Options** tab (see Fig. 5.23), (b) the **Format Text** tab (see Fig. 5.24), and (c) the **Review** tab (see Fig. 5.25).

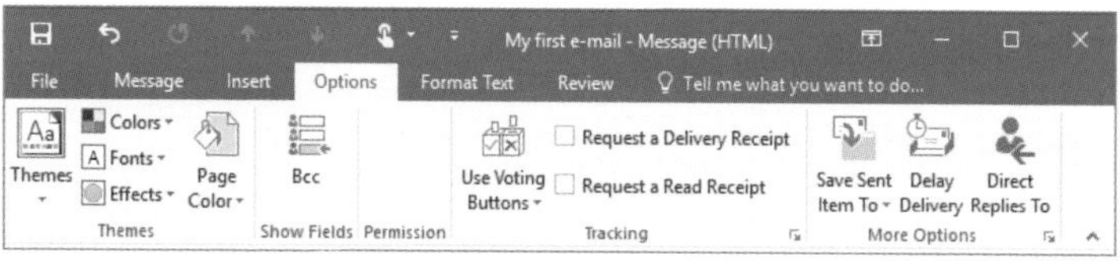

Fig. 5.23 The Options Tab.

You use the **Options** tab to select different **Themes**, **Show Fields** such as showing or hiding the **Bcc** field which allows you to send a message to someone secretly without the knowledge of the other recipients of your e-mail. The **From** options (see Fig. 5.19 on page 87) allows you to send an e-mail from another person's account by simply typing their name in the field.

Under **Tracking** you can request either a **Delivery Receipt** and/or a **Read Receipt** which assures you that the recipient has received and/or read your e-mail.

The **Format Text** tab shown below is similar to the **Message** tab discussed earlier (see Fig. 5.19, page 87). You use this tab to specify the **Format** of your e-mail; **HTML**, **Plain Text** or **Rich Text**. You can also change the **Font**, the **Paragraph** layout, change **Styles** and **Find and Replace** text to be found under the **Editing** group of commands.

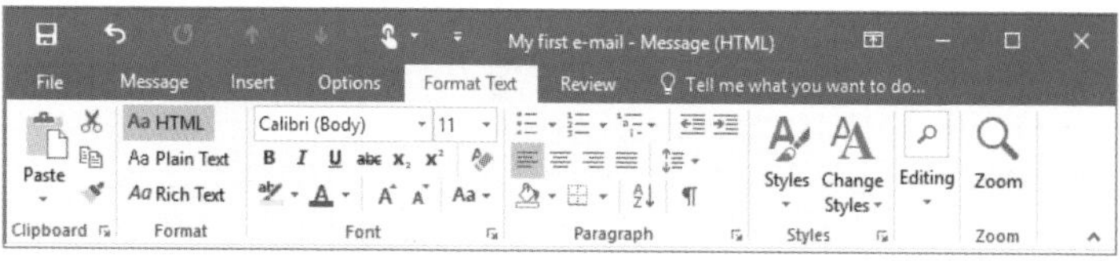

Fig. 5.24 The Format Text Tab.

Finally, the **Review** tab (Fig. 5.25) allows you to check your **Spelling & Grammar**, use the **Thesaurus** and **Word Count** in the **Proofing** group of commands, while in the **Language** group you can either translate text from one language to another or choose the proofing language. A very useful command is **Start Inking** which allows you to add freehand pen and highlighter strokes.

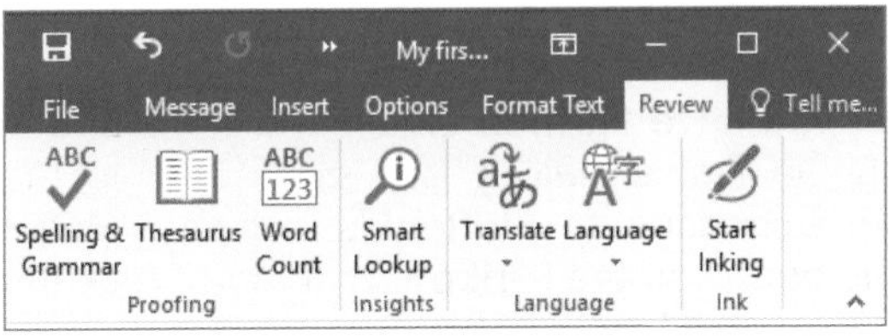

Fig. 5.25 The Review Tab.

It is worth spending some time here to examine the available facilities. Again, I leave it to you to do so.

* * *

In the next chapter, amongst other topics, I shall discuss how to respond to e-mail messages, create e-mail signatures, deal with junk mail, search folders, and how to send photos as e-mail attachments.

* * *

6

Other E-mail Features

Selecting Options Settings

Now that you have finished experimenting with sending and receiving the first e-mail, it is a good idea to make some permanent changes to **Outlook**'s settings. Use the FILE command button on the **Ribbon**, and tap or click the **Options** command pointed to in Fig. 6.1 below.

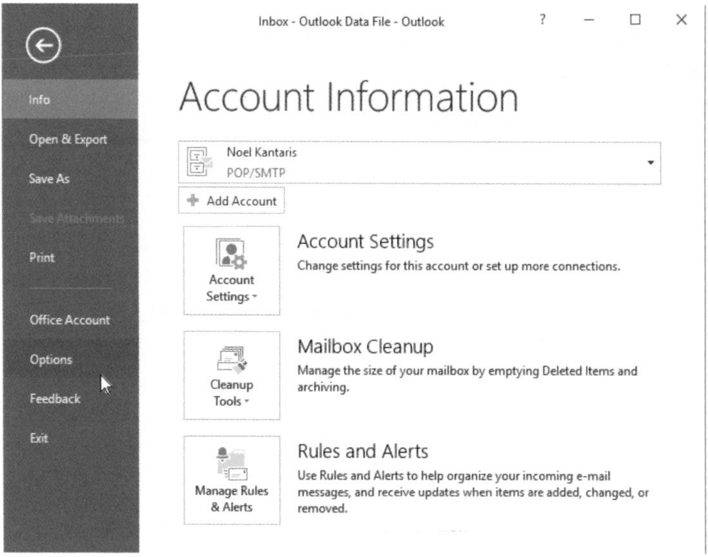

Fig. 6.1 The File Backstage View.

This opens the **Outlook Options** dialogue box and selecting **Mail** on the left pane, displays the screen shown in Fig. 6.2 on the next page.

I suggest you check and if necessary, make the following selections:

- Make sure that the **Always check spelling before sending** option is ticked, so that every message you write is checked before it is sent.
- Press the Spelling and Autocorrect... button and check or change the default options for spelling and auto-correcting.
- Scroll down to **Replies and forwards**. In the **When replying to a message** and **When forwarding a message** list boxes you can select to include or exclude the original message with your reply.

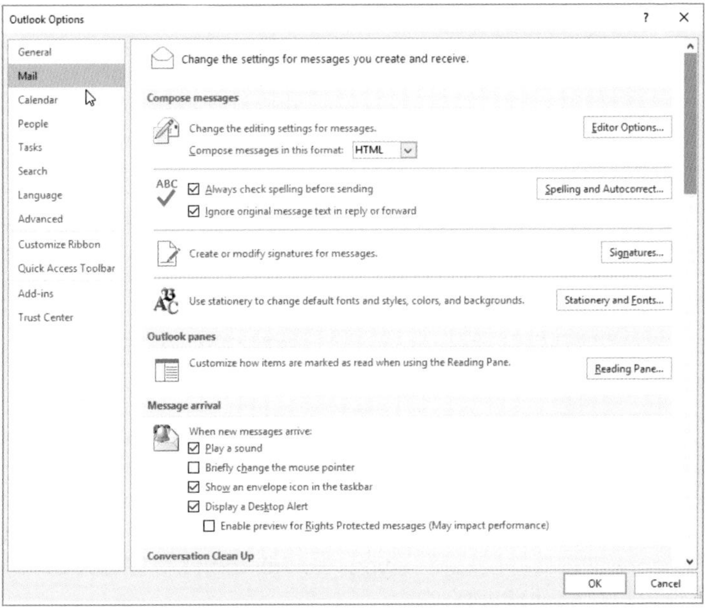

Fig. 6.2 The Outlook Options Box.

To implement any changes made in this dialogue box, tap or click the **OK** button. Obviously there are a lot more selections you could make, but I leave these to you. Very soon, after you have been using **Outlook** for a while, you will know yourself what options and preferences to choose.

Spell Checking E-mail Messages

Just because e-mail messages are a quick way of getting in touch with friends and family, there is no reason why they should be full of spelling mistakes, as **Outlook** is linked to the spell checker that comes with **Office**. Misspelled words that cannot be corrected automatically by **Outlook**, will be underlined in red, as shown in Fig. 6.3 below.

Do try it out by preparing a message in the **New Message** window, but with obvious spelling mistakes, as shown below.

Fig. 6.3 Correcting Spelling Mistakes.

Touching and holding or right-clicking a flagged 'error' opens a drop-down menu. You can accept a suggestion, **Ignore All** occurrences, or add your original word to the dictionary for future use. This works very well. However, make sure that the spelling of an added word is correct, otherwise you will end up with a dictionary full of misspelled words!

Using the Thesaurus

If you are not sure of the meaning of a word, or you want to use an alternative word in your e-mail, then the **Thesaurus** is an indispensable tool.

Simply place the cursor on the word you want to look up and tap or click the **Review**, **Proofing**, **Thesaurus** button, shown in Fig. 6.4 on the next page. This opens the **Thesaurus Task** pane, and as long as the word is recognised, synonyms are listed, as shown in Fig. 6.4 on the next page.

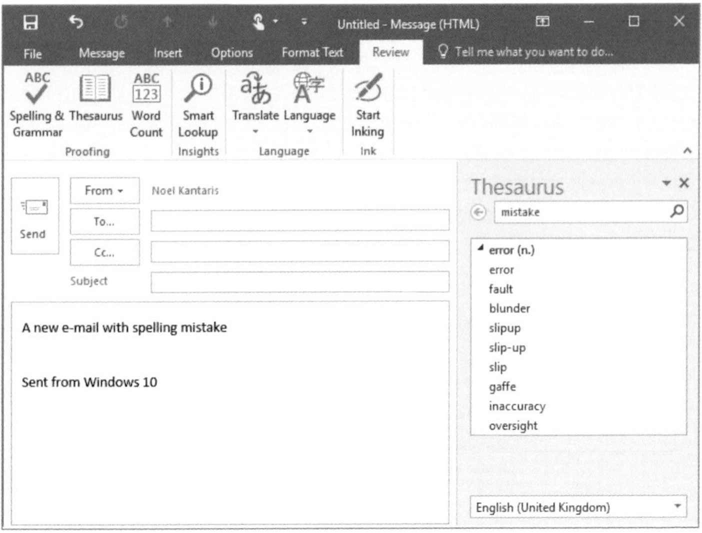

Fig. 6.4 Using the Thesaurus.

You can use the **Thesaurus** like a simple dictionary by typing any word into the **Search** box and then tapping or clicking the **Search** button. Again, if the word is recognised, lists of its meaning variations and synonyms will be displayed.

For a quick way to get a list of alternatives to a word in your e-mail, please refer to Chapter 5 (Fig. 5.20, page 87 when using the mouse), or (Fig. 5.21, page 88 when using a touch-sensitive screen). In both cases, choose the **Synonyms** option from the respective drop-down menu.

Incoming E-mail Messages

In Chapter 5 (see Fig. 5.3, page 73), I discussed how you can get a quick overview of an incoming e-mail message by selecting its header in the **Messages List** and looking at its contents in the **Reading** pane. However, it is easier to work with your messages in the **Message** window, shown in Fig. 6.5 on the next page. This is opened by double-tapping or double-clicking the message header in the **Messages List**.

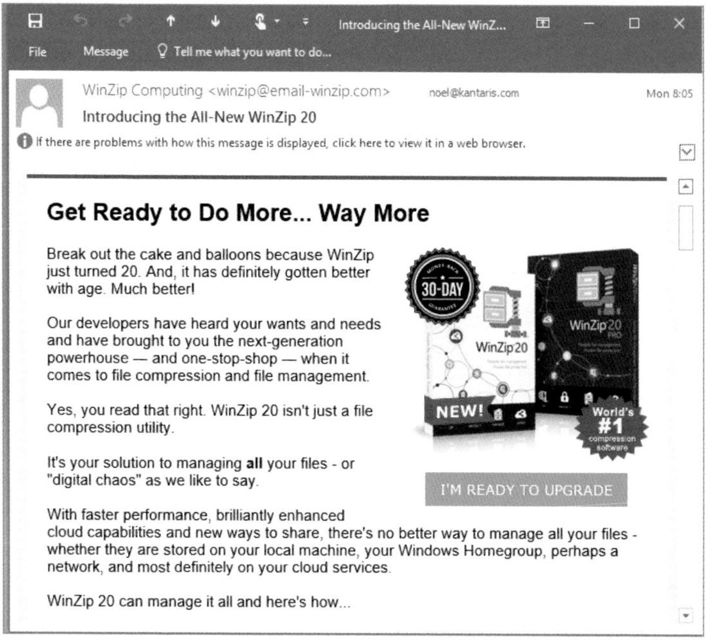

Fig. 6.5 Viewing a Message in its Own Window.

As you can see, in this view I have minimised **Outlook**'s **Ribbon**. Also, by default, **Outlook** deactivates links to pictures in received e-mail messages until you have checked and given your permission to display them. This is because some 'spammers' (people who send masses of unsolicited e-mail messages) use such pictures to prove to themselves that an e-mail address is alive.

Responding to a Message

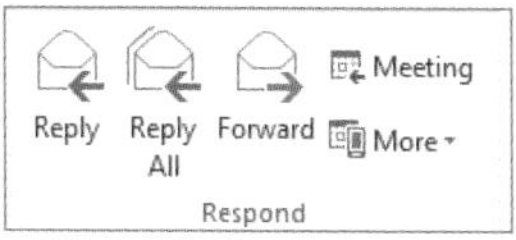

Fig. 6.6 Responding.

Some messages will require some sort of answer or response action, which you carry out from the **Respond** group on the **Ribbon**.

To reply to the original sender, tap or click **Reply**. To reply to the sender and everyone else who received the message, tap or click **Reply to All**.

A new already addressed **Message** window is opened, for you to type your reply. By default, the original message text is included at the end of the message body.

To forward a message to somebody else, tap or click **Forward** and enter their name in the **To** box. You can also add recipient names to the **Cc** and **Bcc** boxes, to send copies and 'blind copies'. You use **Bcc** if you don't want anyone else to know that the recipient was sent a copy.

E-mail Filing Actions

Even if an e-mail message doesn't require a direct response, it may need some sort of filing action, such as deleting it using the **Delete Ribbon** group, shown in Fig. 6.7 or saving, printing, etc., which is carried out from the **File** button menu shown in Fig. 6.8.

Fig. 6.7

Deleted items are held in the **Deleted Items** folder, in case you want to resurrect them. To empty this folder, touch and hold or right-click it in the **Folders** pane and select the **Empty Folder** option from the drop-down menu in Fig. 6.9.

Fig. 6.8 The File Menu.

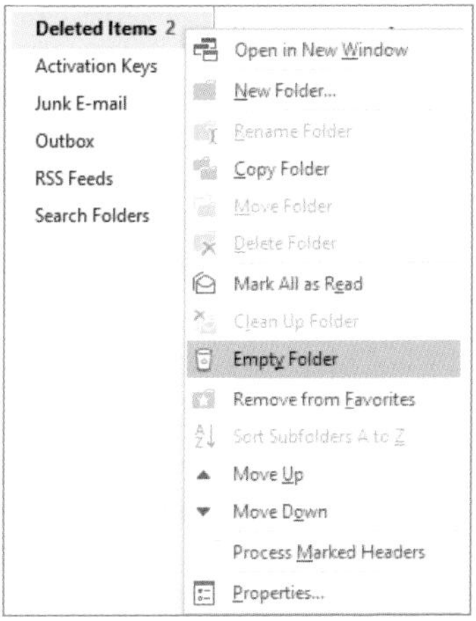

Fig. 6.9 The Empty Folder Option.

Flagging Messages

When a message needs a future action, either touch and hold or right-click the greyed flag against its header on the **Message List**, or select the **Follow Up** button (Fig. 6.10) which displays when you tap or click the **Home**, **Tags** button. Both actions display the drop-down menu which allows you to attach a 'flag' to the message header.

Fig. 6.10 The Tags Group.

Messages that you flag for follow-up also show in the **To-Do Bar**, in the **Task List**, and on your **Calendar**. Also, you can set reminders for them so that you actually remember to do the follow-up.

Assigning Categories to Messages

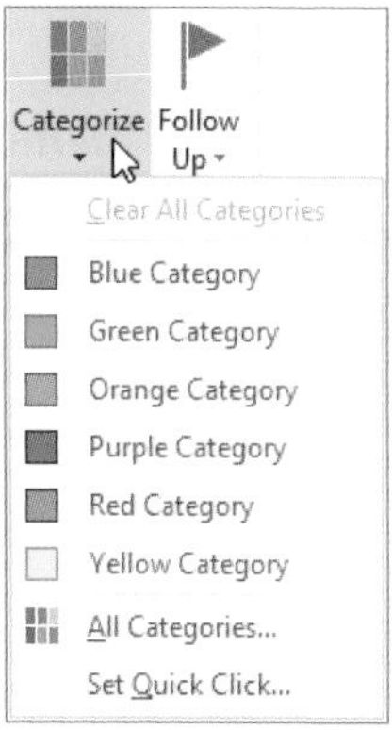

Fig. 6.11 The Coloured Categories Menu.

You might also want to attach coloured categories to your messages to make them more visible and easier to sort. At first, **Outlook** categories do not have proper names, only **Red** or **Orange Category**, etc., as shown in Fig. 6.11. When you first use one of these, **Outlook** prompts you to rename it. You could create names such as **Holiday**, **Birthdays**, etc.

Once you have assigned a category to a message, you can quickly scan your **Inbox** and find the message just by looking for its coloured tag.

Other Follow Up Actions

Using the mouse – You can drag messages from the **Messages List** to the appropriate button on the **Navigation** pane which is situated under the **Folder** pane. What the result is depends on which button in the **Navigation** pane you use.

To set up a meeting, drag the message to the **Calendar** button on the **Navigation** pane. A new appointment opens for you to fill in the rest of the details, such as the date, time and location of the meeting. All you need to do then is invite the person to the meeting, and tap or click **Send**.

When you drag a message to the **Contacts** button on the **Navigation Pane**, a new **Contact** form opens and the e-mail address in the message is automatically added to it. If you like, you can then fill in the rest of the details, such as an address and phone numbers.

Finally, if you drag a message to the **Tasks** button, a new **Task** is formed. With all these actions, dragging creates a new item, but leaves the message still in your **Inbox**. You need to delete it yourself if you don't need it any more.

Using a touch-sensitive screen – To achieve any of the above tasks on a touch-sensitive screen, touch and hold on a message until a small square appears around your finder on the screen. Letting go displays a menu of options, one of which is **Move**. Tapping this option opens a secondary menu as shown in Fig. 6.12 and tapping the **Other Folder** entry displays a third list of options which includes **Calendar**, **Contacts** and **Tasks**, as shown below.

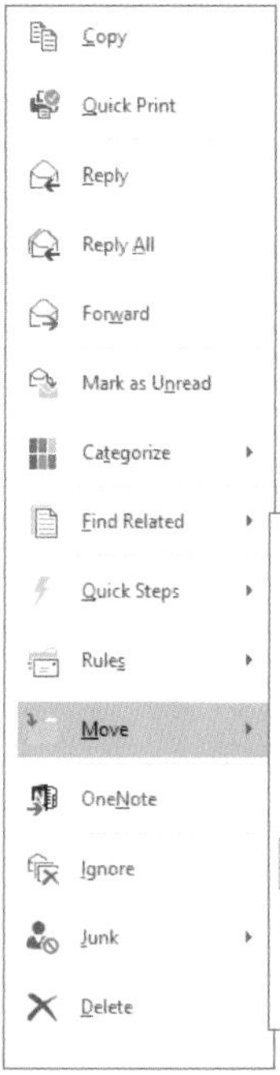

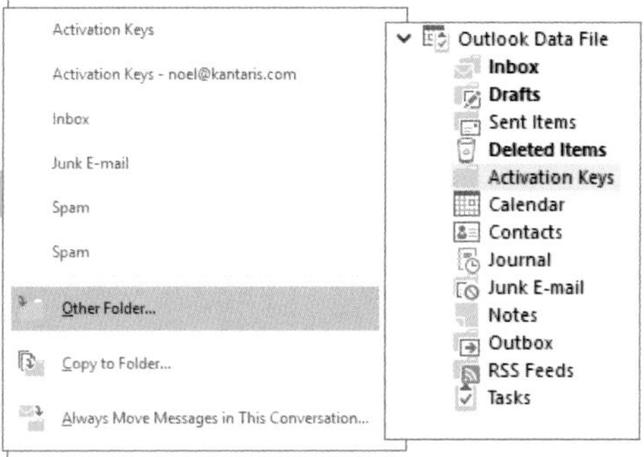

Fig. 6.12 Moving a Message.

Desktop Alerts

By default **Outlook**, if running, flashes a desktop message briefly whenever a new message is placed in the **Inbox**, as shown in Fig. 6.13. The alert displays the name of the sender, the subject and the first two lines of the message.

Fig. 6.13 Desktop Alert of an Incoming E-mail.

Similar messages display when a meeting or a task request is received.

Desktop Alerts appear whatever you are doing on your PC, but provided **Outlook** is minimised on the **Task** bar. As long as you move quickly, you can either open the message in its own window so that you can read it or delete it. If you need to keep a **Desktop Alert** visible so that you can see who sent it, place a finger or the mouse pointer on the **Desktop Alert** before it fades away.

To turn off alerts, select the **File**, **Options**, **Mail** and remove the check mark pointed to in Fig. 6.14.

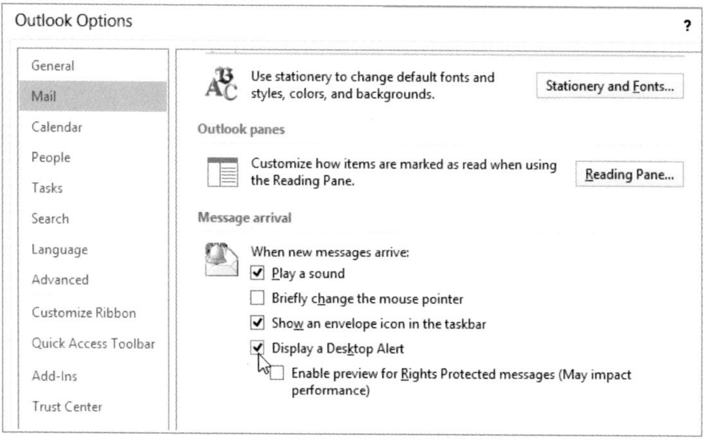

Fig. 6.14 The Display a Desktop Alert Option.

Creating E-mail Signatures

It is often useful to supply your name, address, phone number and perhaps your Fax number at the bottom of your outgoing e-mails. It is up to you how much information you want to provide. **Outlook** lets you do this with the **Signature** feature.

To create a signature, use **File**, **Options**, **Mail**, then under **Compose messages**, tap or click the Signatures... button to open the dialogue box shown in Fig. 6.15.

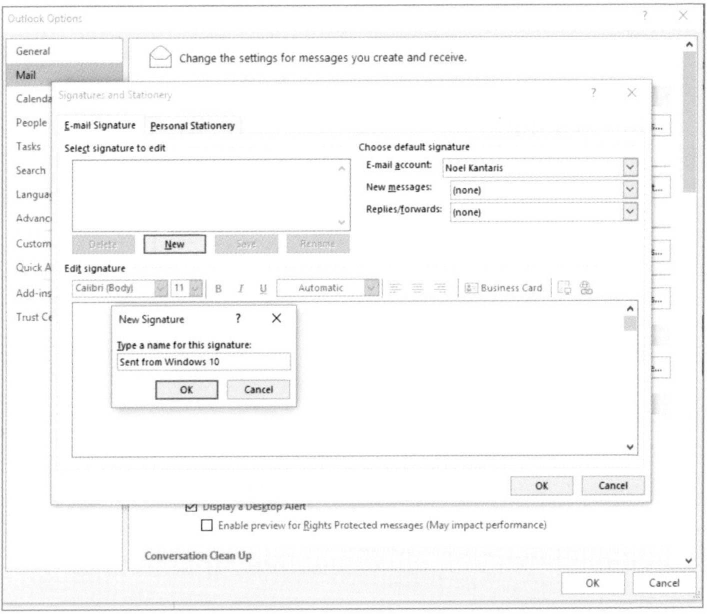

Fig. 6.15 The Signatures and Stationery Dialogue Box.

If necessary, tap or click the **E-mail Signature** tab and then tap or click the **New** button. Type 'a name for the signature', and then tap or click **OK**. Next, you type the text (such as your name) that you want to include in the signature and format it with the style and formatting buttons. You can format your signature even if you use plain text as your message format. However, the formatting will only be visible to your mail recipients who use HTML or RTF message formats.

You can add an **Electronic Business Card**, a **Picture** or a **Hyperlink** to your signature by tapping or clicking the appropriate buttons.

In the **Choose default signature** section, select the **E-mail account** which you always want to associate with the signature. If you only have one, this is automatic! In **New messages** and **Replies/forwards** boxes, select the signature you want to be automatically added to the end of each message. Select '(none)' if you don't want a signature used. After you finish creating the signature, tap or click **OK**.

You could create several signatures with different content to be used depending on whether your e-mail is casual, formal or professional, and switch between them as required.

You can add or change the signature on a new message by tapping or clicking the **Signature** button in the **Include** group on the **Ribbon** and selecting from the drop-down list, as shown here in Fig. 6.16.

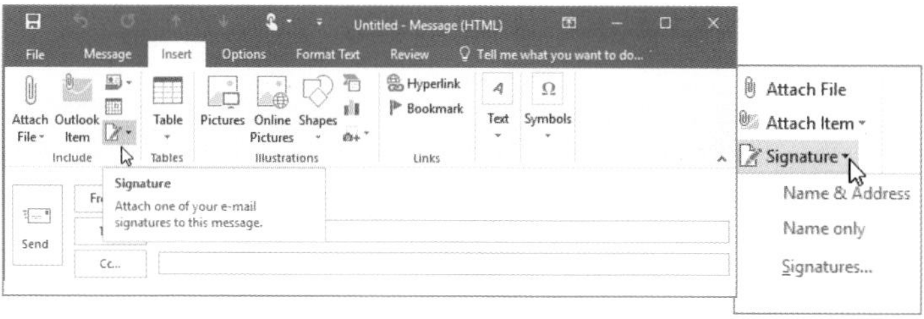

Fig. 6.16 Selecting a Signature.

Junk E-mail Filter

The **Junk E-mail** filter in **Outlook** is designed to catch junk messages or spam and send them to the **Junk E-mail** folder. It does this by examining each incoming message based on, when it was sent, its content and structure. The filter is turned on by default, with 'No automatic filtering' protection (see Fig. 6.18 on the next page). I suggest you change this to 'low' which is designed to catch the most obvious spam. You can make the filter more aggressive by changing the level of protection.

Messages sent to the **Junk E-mail** folder are converted to plain text and any links are disabled. You should check the messages in the **Junk E-mail** folder as you might lose important messages that have been incorrectly filtered out.

When the **Junk E-mail** folder is active the **Not Junk** option is added to the drop-down menu shown here in Fig. 6.17, so that you can retrieve such messages, if necessary.

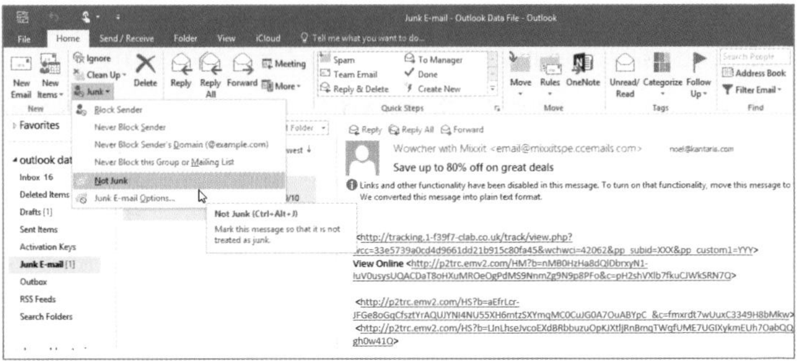

Fig. 6.17 The Junk E-mail Folder Options.

Selecting **Junk E-mail Options** from the above drop-down menu, displays the multi-tab **Junk E-mail Options** dialogue box shown in Fig. 6.18.

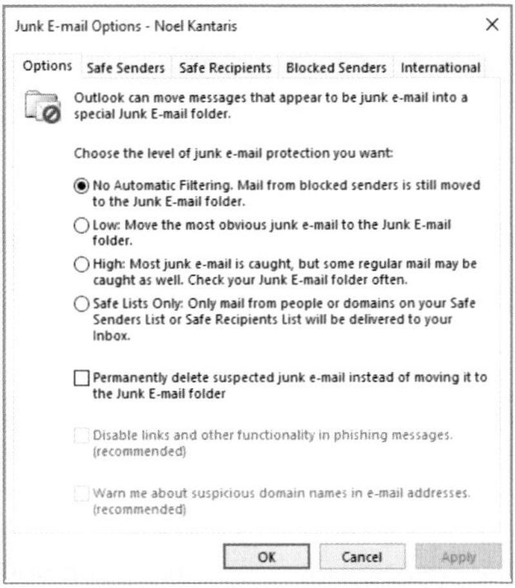

Fig. 6.18 The E-mail Options Dialogue Box.

As you can see, there is a lot to choose from here. In the **Options** tab you can choose the level of protection, disable links, etc. For the contents of the other tab screens, see the next page.

In short, you can use these tabs to specify the following:

Safe Senders List – E-mail addresses and domain names in the **Safe Senders List** are never treated as junk e-mail, regardless of the content of the message. By default, all of the e-mail addresses in your **Contacts** are included in this list. E-mail addresses of people not listed in your **Contacts** but with whom you correspond are included in this list if you select the **Automatically add people I e-mail to the Safe Senders List** check box in the **Safe Senders** tab. This check box is not selected by default.

You can configure **Outlook** so that it accepts messages only from people in your **Safe Senders List**. This configuration gives you complete control over which messages are delivered to your **Inbox**, but can exclude people who might be trying to contact you for the first time!

Safe Recipients List – If you belong to a mailing list or a distribution list, you can add the list sender to the **Safe Recipients List**, so that messages sent from these e-mail addresses or domain names are never treated as junk, regardless of the content of the message.

Blocked Senders List – You can easily block messages from particular senders by adding their e-mail addresses or domain names to the **Block Sender List**. To do this, select the offending message in the **Messages List** and use the **Junk**, **Block Sender** option.

Fig. 6.19 Blocking a Sender.

If you have existing lists of safe or blocked names and addresses, you can import them into **Outlook**.

International – To block unwanted e-mail messages that come from another country or region, you can add country/region codes to the **Blocked Top-Level Domains List**. To block unwanted e-mail messages in another language, add encodings to the **Blocked Encodings List**.

Deleting Junk Mail

To get rid of your junk mail, touch and hold or right-click the **Junk E-mail** folder and select the **Empty Folder** option as shown in Fig. 6.20.

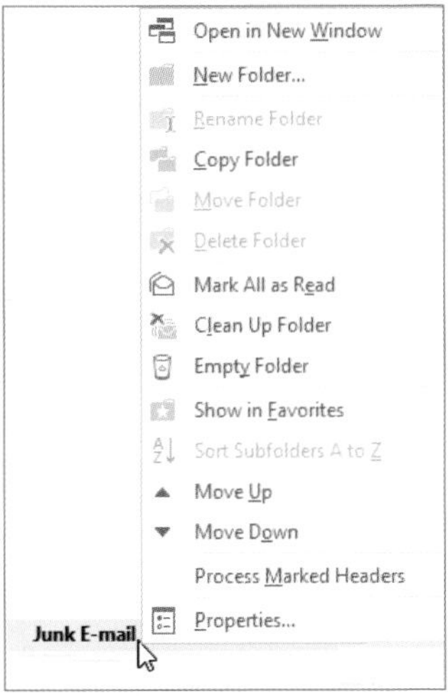

Fig. 6.20 The Context Menu Options.

To permanently delete individual messages from the **Junk E-mail** folder without emptying it, select the message, and then press the **Delete** key on your keyboard.

You can also carry out some of these options from the **Folder** tab of the **Ribbon**, as shown below in Fig. 6.21 when the **Junk E-mail** folder is selected. The commands within the **Clean Up** group of the **Folder** tab change depending on which folder is selected.

Fig. 6.21 The Folder Tab on the Ribbon.

Searching Folders

Selecting a folder and clicking the **New Search Folder** icon in Fig. 6.21 above, displays the dialogue box part of which is shown in Fig. 6.22. You can use this to create searches of your e-mail folders based on specific criteria, such as **Unread mail** or **Mail from people and Lists**.

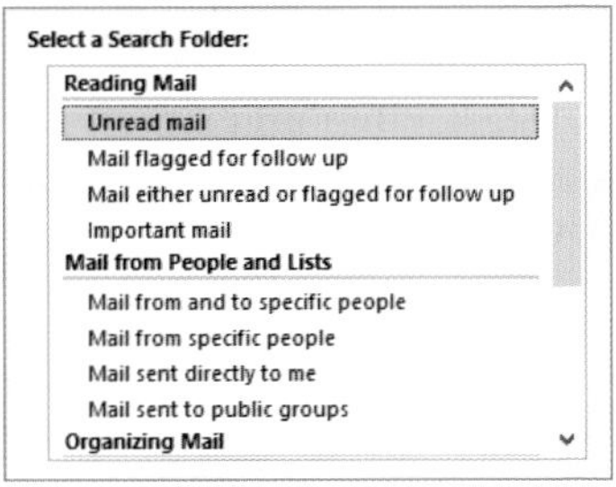

Fig. 6.22 Searching Folders.

Using E-mail Attachments

Attachments are files or **Outlook** items that can be sent as part of an e-mail message. **Files** can be drawings, documents, photos, or even sound and video files, and **Outlook** items can be messages, appointments, contacts, tasks, journal entries, notes, posted items and documents.

When you receive an e-mail in **Outlook** with an attachment it will have a paper clip icon in the **Message List** and the details of the attachment will appear in the attachment box below the **Subject** line, as shown in Fig. 6.23.

Fig. 6.23 The Attachment Box.

For security reasons, **Outlook** blocks potentially unsafe attachment files with name extensions such as **.bat**, **.exe**, **.vbs** and **.js**, as they could contain viruses. **Outlook** does not block **Microsoft Office** document files, but make sure your anti-virus program has scanned them before you open them.

Previewing an Attachment

To quickly see what an attachment contains without opening it, touch or click the down-arrowhead and select **Preview** to display it as shown in Fig. 6.24.

Fig. 6.24 Previewing an Attachment.

Sometimes you might get the warning message telling you that "You should only preview files from a trustworthy source". Obviously if you don't know the sender of the message, it is best not to preview or open the attachment.

At other times you might get a message telling you "This file cannot be previewed because there is no previewer installed for it". This message was displayed in my case even thought the e-mail came from a trusted source and the attachment was an **Excel** file!

To open an attachment you just double-tap or double-click it or touch and hold or right-click and select **Open** from the drop-down menu in Fig. 6.24. To return to the body of the e-mail, tap or click the **Back to Message** button at the top-left of the screen.

Saving Attachments

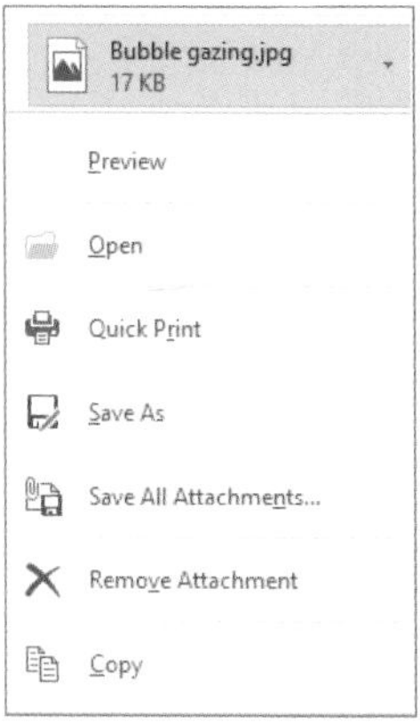

There are several ways to save attachments, the easiest is probably to touch and hold or right-click the attachment button and on the displayed menu (Fig. 6.25) select **Save As**. Choose a folder location, and then tap or click **Save**.

To save multiple attachments tap or click the **Save All Attachments** option on the menu.

Fig. 6.25 A Contextual Menu.

Adding Attachments to your E-mail

If you want to include an attachment to your e-mail, simply tap or click the **Message**, **Include**, **Attach File** (or **Attach Item**) button on the **Ribbon** (Fig. 6.26), then select the file to attach in the dialogue box that opens.

Fig. 6.26.

Printing E-mail Messages

It was originally thought by some that computers would lead to the paperless office. That has certainly not proved to be the case, as most people need to keep a paper copy for various reasons.

Outlook lets you print to paper either lists of details of all e-mail messages in a selected folder (details being: who sent the e-mail, its subject, when it was received and its size), or the actual contents of an e-mail.

To print a list of messages in a folder, select the folder, then use the **File**, **Print** command which displays the **Print** dialogue box and select **Table Style**, as shown in Fig. 6.27.

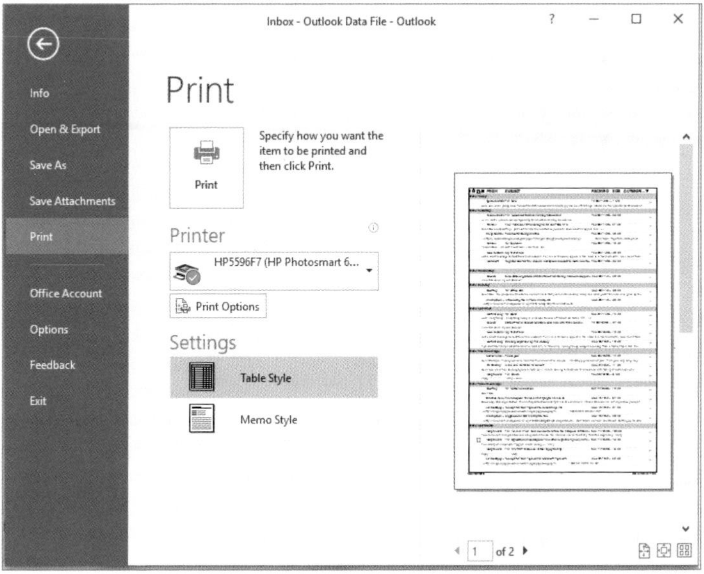

Fig. 6.27 Printing Table Style from Outlook.

The **Print** Options allow you to use the **Page Setup** option to select the size and font of both the column headings of your lists and their rows. You can also choose the paper size, and whether to add headers or footers to the tables. Selecting **Preview** will show you what the print output will look like.

Selecting the **Memo Style** (the default), sends the contents of the selected message to the printer and prints out the actual contents of the message. Make sure the correct printer, page range and number of copies you want are selected, then tap or click the **OK** button.

You can also start the printing procedure by tapping or clicking the **Print** button shown here. In this case the print job will be sent to the currently selected printer, using the current settings, so be careful when you use the **Print** button.

If the message has files attached to it and you want to print everything, then first tap or click the **Memo Style** button, followed by the **Print Options** button (the one below the **Printer** selection box in Fig. 6.27) to open the dialogue box in Fig. 6.28.

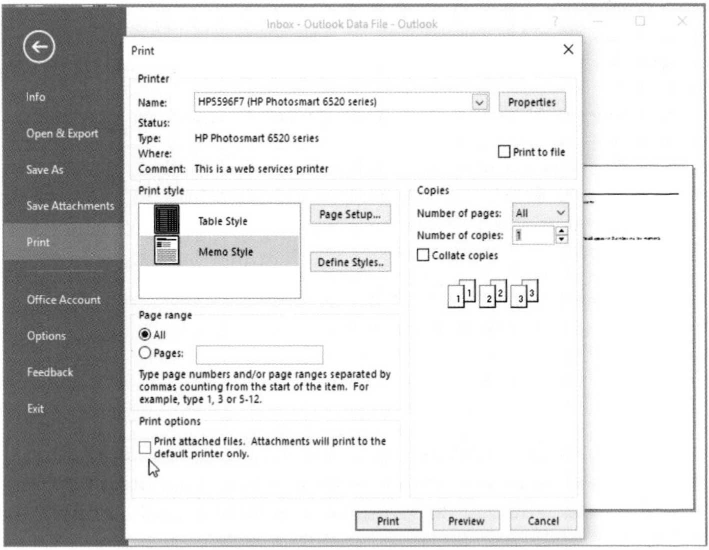

Fig. 6.28 Printing Attachments.

To print the attachments, tap or click the **Print attached files** box pointed to at the bottom of Fig. 6.28. However do note that attachments will print only to the default printer.

For example, if you have a colour printer set as the default, and you open a message with an attachment and choose to print the e-mail on a black and white printer, then the message will be sent to the black and white printer, but the attachment will go to the colour printer. So, if you have two such printers and you want to print the attachments in colour make sure you assign the colour printer as the default.

To do this with Windows 10, touch and hold or right-click the **Start** button, then select the **Control Panel** from the displayed menu, then choose **Devices and Printers** to open a screen part of which is shown in Fig. 6.29 below.

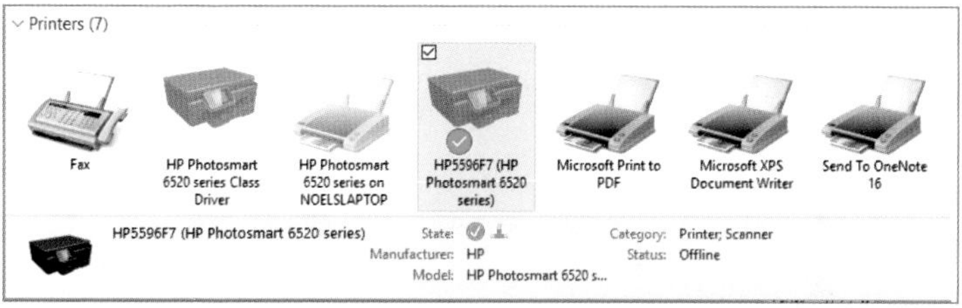

Fig. 6.29 The Windows Devices and Printers Folder.

Here, several printer drivers have been installed and the **HP Photosmart** 6520 colour printer is set as the default printer, indicated with a tick in its icon. To change this, touch and hold or right-click on another printer in the list, and select **Set as default printer** from the context menu.

Using RSS Feeds

With **Outlook**, you can read and manage your blogs and **RSS Feeds** from within the application, at the same time as handling your e-mail and calendar.

RSS stands for 'Really Simple Syndication'. They are also called 'Feeds' and are just Web pages, designed to be read by computers rather than people. **RSS** is a way for publishers of online news agencies and magazines to make news, blogs, and other content freely available to subscribers.

You find what you want, subscribe to it, and then every time the author updates the content or writes something new, it is delivered straight to **Outlook** on your desk. **Feeds** offer an easy way to keep up-to-date with what you are interested in.

The usual way to find a new **RSS Feed** is to look on your favourite Websites and, if they offer this feature, you will see the icon in colour, as shown in Fig. 6.30.

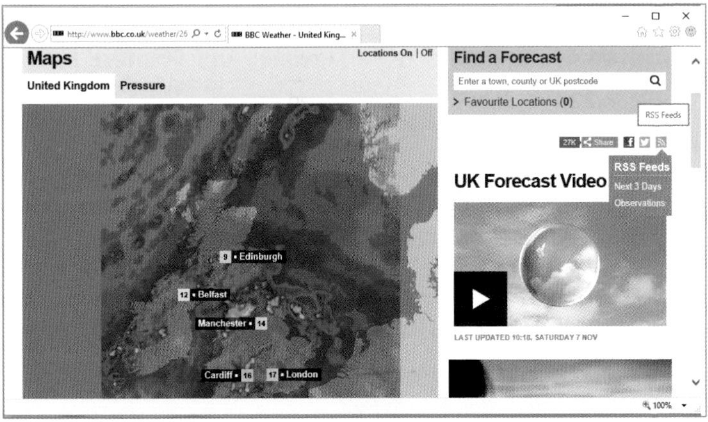

Fig. 6.30 An Example of a Website Supporting RSS Feed.

In this example you have two choices; **Next 3 Days** or **Observations**. Tapping or clicking the latter option, opens a **Feed** page. If you like it, look for the link that lets you 'subscribe', as shown in Fig. 6.31.

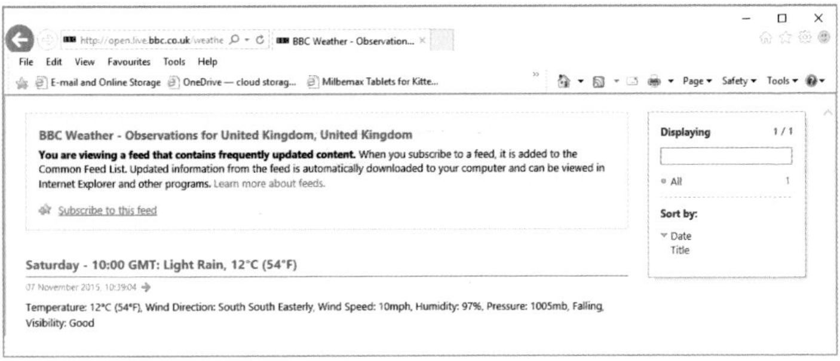

Fig. 6.31 Subscribing to a Feed Using Explorer.

Tapping or clicking the **Subscribe to this feed** link, opens the dialogue box, shown in Fig. 6.32. Selecting the **Subscribe** button completes the procedure. Now, you need to synchronise, as described next.

Fig. 6.32 The Subscribe to this Feed Dialogue Box.

Windows allows **Outlook** to share **RSS Feeds** via the **Common Feeds List in Windows**, which is a common location for **RSS Feeds**. However you need to synchronise **Outlook** with the **Common Feeds List**. To do this, select **File**, **Options**, **Advanced** in **Outlook**, and under **RSS Feeds** check the **Synchronize RSS Feeds to the Common Feed List (CFL) in Windows** option, as shown in Fig. 6.33.

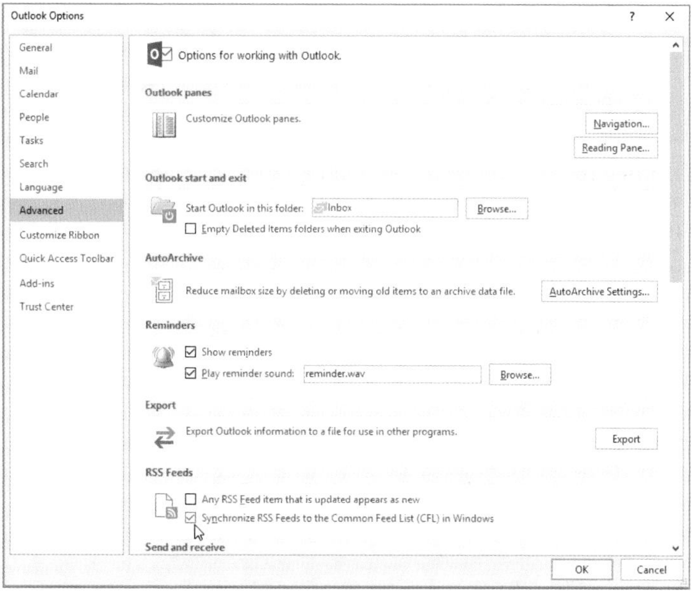

Fig. 6.33 Synchronising RSS Feeds.

Next time you start **Outlook**, expanding the **Folder** pane displays the **RSS Feeds** folder. Touch and hold or right-click this folder and select **Add a New RSS feed** option from the contextual menu to display a dialogue box in which you supply the URL of the **RSS Feed** you want to add to **Outlook**.

Selecting **Add**, displays a further dialogue box which warns against adding feeds from unknown sources, but if you want to continue, select the **Advanced** button so as to configure the new feed. This opens the **RSS Feed Options** dialogue box in which you choose whether to **Automatically download enclosures for this RSS Feed** or **Download the full article as an html attachment**.

Once a choice has been made (I chose the first option), the **RSS Feeds** folder gains a sub-folder containing (in my case) the **BBC Weather** feed I subscribed to, as shown in Fig. 6.34.

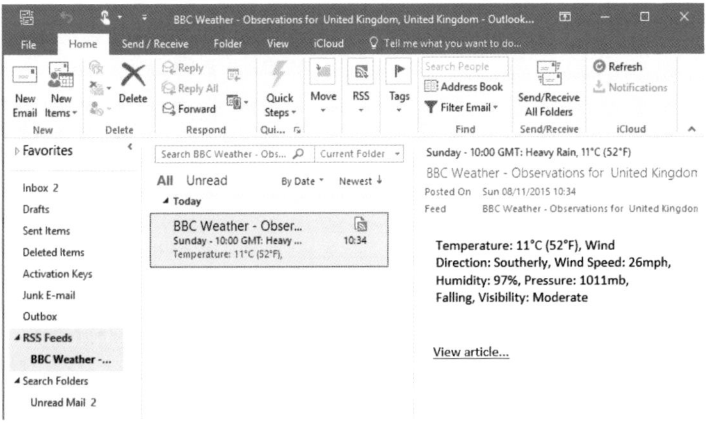

Fig. 6.34 Reading a Feed.

Outlook checks the **RSS** publisher's server for new and updated items regularly. To remove the **RSS Feeds** facility from **Outlook**, simply deselect the **Synchronize RSS Feeds to the Common Feed List (CFL) in Windows** check box. To remove an **RSS Feeds** sub-folder, touch and hold or right-click it and select **Delete Folder** from the displayed menu.

List of Contacts

In **Outlook** 'People' are the 'Contacts' you send the most messages to. The **Contacts** view displays your contacts in several ways, such as business cards or various list views. To change the way information is displayed, tap or click the **Change View** button and select one of the displayed formats, as in Fig. 6.35. What is shown here is an edited version of part of my **Business Cards** view.

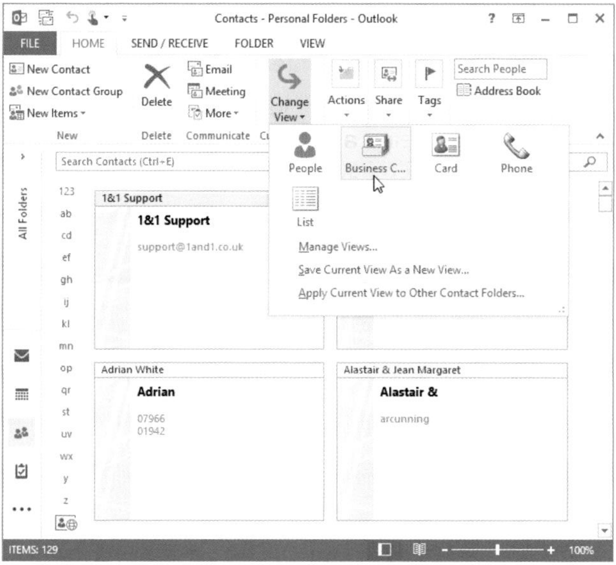

Fig. 6.35 Business Cards View.

To add a new contact, tap or click the **New Contact** button, or to edit an existing entry, double-tap or double-click on the contact name. Either action displays the **Contact** window, shown in Fig. 6.36 on the next page, in which you type relevant information. I usually only provide a few essential details, as shown, but you could include someone's whole history if you wanted to. You can even add a photograph for each of your contacts by double-tapping or double-clicking the photo button (Fig. 6.36) and browsing to the folder that holds it. Finally, tap or click the **Save and Close** button.

Fig. 6.36 Details of a Fictitious Contact.

Contact lists can be saved under different group names, so that you could have one list for your personal friends, and another for your business acquaintances.

The task of filling in such detailed information about an individual might be daunting at first, but if you persevere, you will find it very useful later. You can then use the controls in the **Communicate** group to instantly make contact in various ways. For example, you only have to tap or click on the **Web Page** button in the **More** command drop-down menu, to be automatically connected to a contact's Web page (provided you have included the information in their details). Tapping or clicking the **Call** button instead, opens the **AutoDialer** and connects to your contact by phone, as long as you are set up to do this!

Try tapping or clicking the **Map It** button. This opens a **bing Maps** Web page and locates the contact's address on it. This only works, though, provided you have entered the address in the **Address** box at the bottom of the **Contact** screen and included the **Postcode**. Try it with a real address, it works really well.

The Address Book

The **Name**, **Display Name** and **E-mail Address** of all your **Outlook Contacts** are added to the default **Address Book**. As e-mail addresses are often quite complicated and not at all easy to remember this can be a very useful feature. To open it you can tap or click the **Home**, **Find**, **Address Book** button on the **Outlook Ribbon**. Fig. 6.37 below shows part of mine.

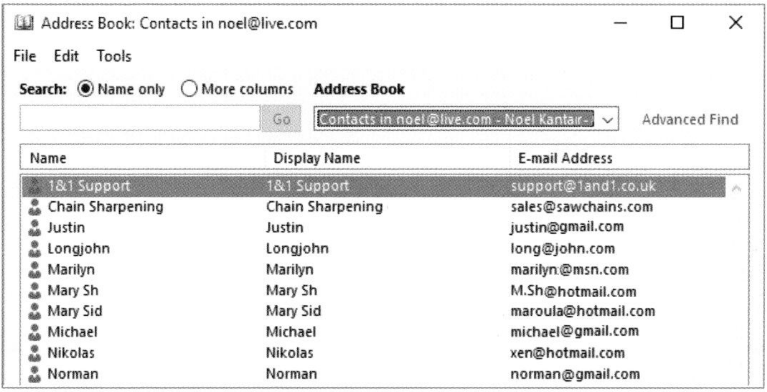

Fig. 6.37 Some Extracts from the Contacts Address Book.

Outlook allows you to access e-mail addresses from either the **Address Book** or from the **Contacts** list. If you are using a Microsoft **Exchange Server** e-mail account and its list contains the names and e-mail addresses of everyone in your organisation, then you could also use the **Global Address Book** for sending e-mail messages. The Microsoft **Exchange Server** administrator is the only person that can create and maintain this address book.

Once in the **Address Book**, you can edit an entry by double-tapping or double-clicking it to open the **Contact** window seen on the previous page in Fig. 6.36. If you want, you can manually add a new person's full details with the **File** menu option (at the top-left corner in Fig. 6.37), then the **New Entry** sub-menu command and select **New Contact** in the displayed **New Entry** dialogue box. Tapping or clicking the **OK** button, again opens the **Contact** window of Fig. 6.36. The **File**, **New Message** menu command starts a new message to the selected contact.

To send a new message to anyone listed in your **Address Book** or **Contacts** list, open a **New Message** window and tap or click on any of the **To:** or **Cc:** icons shown here on the left to open the window shown in Fig. 6.38.

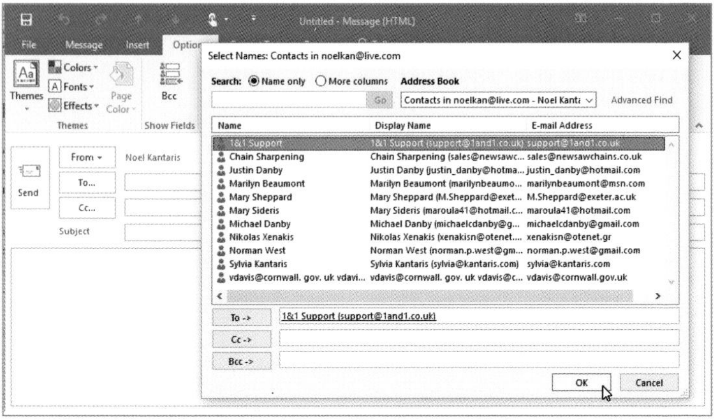

Fig. 6.38 Selecting a Contact to Use.

In the **Select Names** window, you can select a person's name and tap or click either the **To->** button to place it in the **To** field of your message, the **Cc->** button to place it in the **Cc** field, or the **Bcc->** button to place it in the **Bcc** field.

Note: Cc stands for carbon copy. If you add a name to this box, a copy of the message is sent to that recipient, and the recipient's name is visible to other recipients of the message.

Bcc stands for blind carbon copy. If you add a name to this box, a copy of the message is sent to that recipient, but the recipient's name is not visible to other recipients of the message.

7

Calendar, Tasks & Notes

Using the Calendar

The **Calendar** is the diary and scheduling view of **Outlook** in which you can create and manage appointments, meetings and events. Before starting to enter information in the **Calendar**, let us take a look at its opening screen which displays when you tap or click the **Calendar** button in the **Navigation** pane, pointed to in Fig. 7.1. Tapping or clicking a date on the **Date Navigator**, opens a **Day** view of **Calendar**. To display what is shown below, tap or click the **Month** button on the **Ribbon**, shown here highlighted (more about this on the next page).

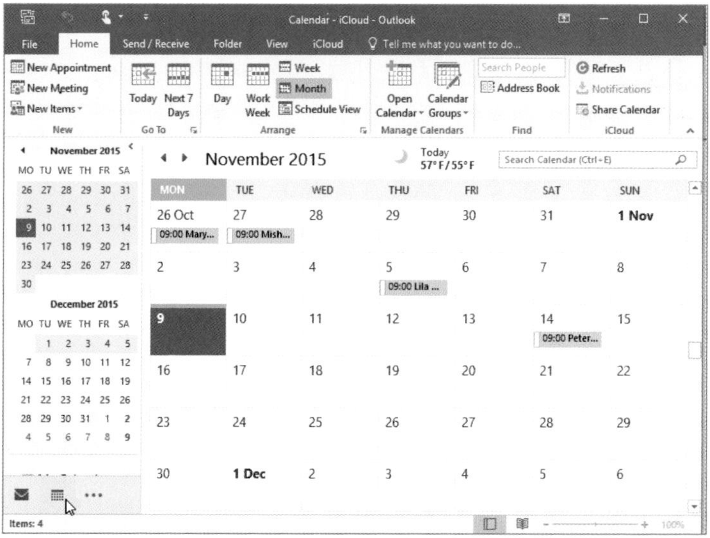

Fig. 7.1 The Outlook Calendar in Month View.

In Fig. 7.1, I have the **Navigation** pane open, which includes the **Date Navigator** and **My Calendars** just below it, but the latter is obscured – see below. You can close or minimise these to give more room for the **Calendar** itself.

Use the **Ribbon** buttons at the top of the **Calendar** window (in the **Arrange** group) to change your **Calendar** view, or the other buttons mentioned below to navigate through your **Calendar** and to show or hide other **Calendars** as follows:

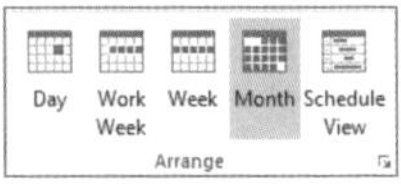

Click on **Day**, **Work Week**, **Week** or **Month** to quickly switch views.

You can use the **Date Navigator** at the top of the **Navigation** pane to open the **Calendar** on a specific day. The arrow button at the top moves only backward one month.

To move forwards or backwards through the **Calendar**, close the **Date Navigator** using the **Expand the Folder Pane** button to pin it in place, then select the **Back** or **Forward** buttons shown here.

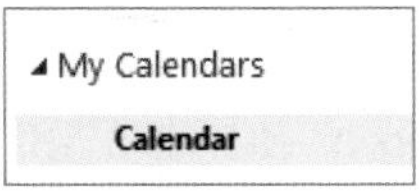

The **My Calendars** pane in the **Navigation** pane (the one mentioned above as being obscured) lets you see or hide additional **Calendars**, if you created or downloaded them, such as **Work**, **Shared** or **UK Holidays**.

The **Views** buttons on the **Status** bar shown in Fig. 7.2 also let you quickly change your view of the **Calendar**.

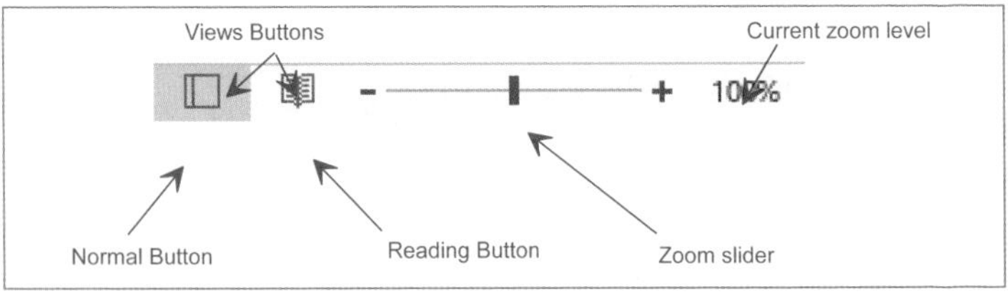

Fig. 7.2 The Views and Zoom Buttons on the Status Bar.

Some Definitions

Before you start scheduling an appointment, meeting or event, it is necessary to look at some **Calendar** definitions:

- An appointment does not involve other colleagues or resources, and can be recurring, that is it can be repeated on a regular basis, like birthdays.
- A meeting is an appointment that involves other people and possibly resources, and can also be recurring.
- An event is an activity that lasts one day or more, such as attendance at an exhibition or conference. An annual event occurs yearly on a specific date. Events and annual events do not occupy blocks of time in your **Calendar**; instead, they appear as a banner below the current day heading.
- A task is an activity that involves only you, and that doesn't need a scheduled time.

Entering Appointments

As an example let us create a recurring appointment to, say, meet 'Heads of Departments', that takes place on the second Friday every month starting at 10:00 a.m. on 13 November and lasts for 2 hours.

There are two ways of doing this: (a) tap or click the 13th November on the **Date Navigator**, move to 10:00 a.m., and double-tap or double-click the blue band, as shown in Fig. 7.3, or (b) navigate to the date in the **Calendar** and double-tap or double-click it. Either of these actions opens the new **Appointment** window, shown in Fig. 7.4 on the next page. Next, type 'Heads of Departments meeting' in the **Subject** box, 'My Office' in the **Location** box, set the **End time** to 12.00, and maybe enter some text in the main body with a little more detail.

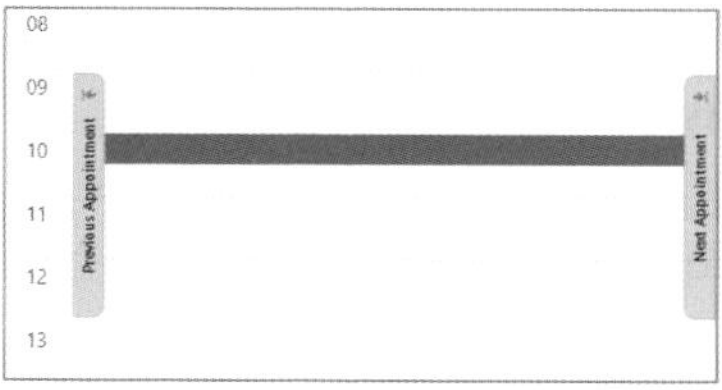

Fig. 7.3 Setting the Start Time.

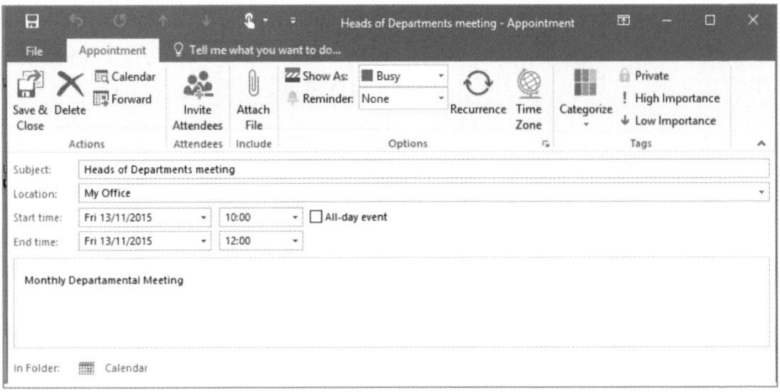

Fig. 7.4 Entering a New Appointment.

Next, tap or click the **Recurrence** button on the **Options** group of the **Ribbon**, as shown in Fig. 7.5, to open the **Appointment Recurrence** box shown in Fig. 7.6 below.

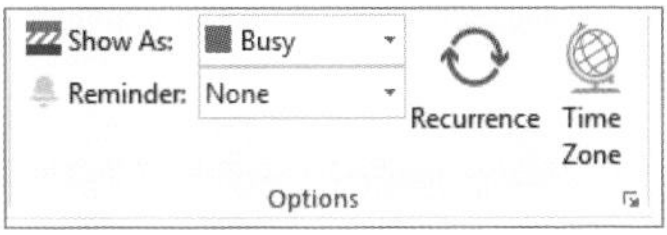

Fig. 7.5 Recurrence Button.

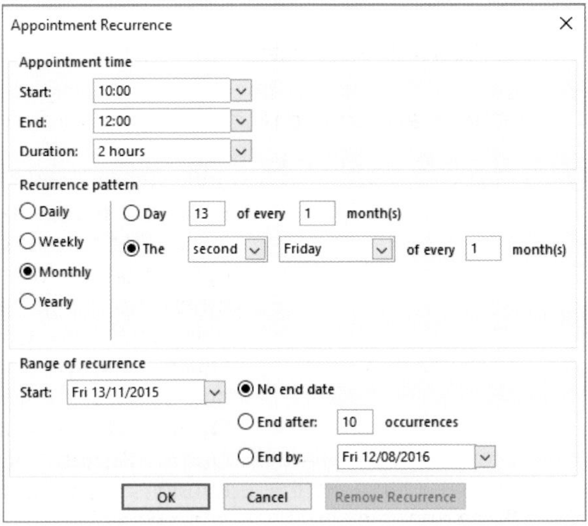

Fig. 7.6 The Appointment Recurrence Box.

In this dialogue box, select the **Monthly** radio button, under the **Recurrence pattern** and **The second Friday of every 1 month** radio button, then press **OK** followed by the **Save and Close** button on the **Ribbon**.

The **Calendar** entry, when you now point to the entry, displays the new appointment, including a more detailed explanation, as shown in Fig. 7.7.

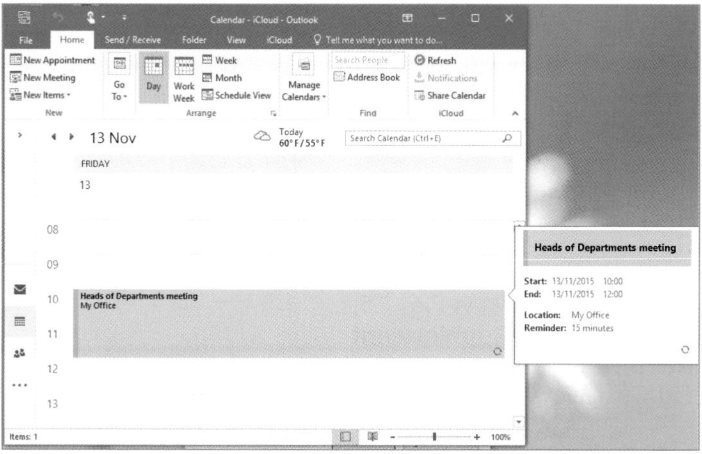

Fig. 7.7 The Appointment on Day View.

If you want to make any changes to the newly created appointment just touch and hold or right-click it to open the menu shown in Fig. 7.8. You can use the options on this drop-down menu to print, delete, categorise, etc. Choosing **Open**, displays two options, as shown here; **Open Occurrence** or **Open Series**, so that changes can be applied appropriately.

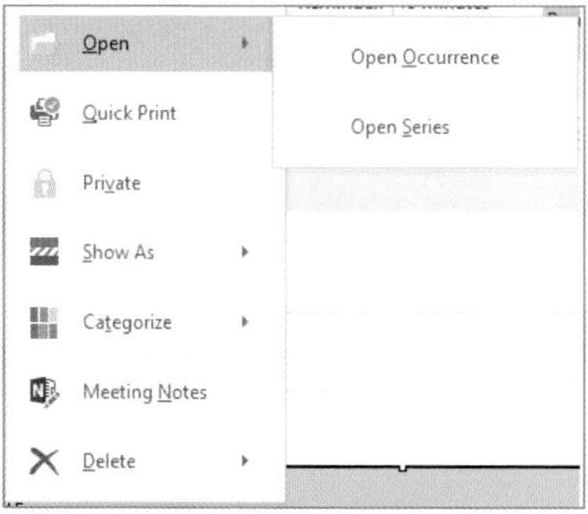

Fig. 7.8 The Appointment Context Menu.

By default you will get a reminder window opening on top of everything else on the screen 15 minutes before the appointment start time, once the appointment has been created and saved. If this is not long enough, you can set the reminder time to up to 2 weeks in advance in the **Options** group on the **Ribbon** (see Fig. 7.5, page 120).

What you select in the **Reminder** box depends on the type of entry. For example, for birthdays I usually select **3 days** to give me time to purchase a card and post it, while for meetings the choice will depend on where the meeting takes place and how long I need to get there.

Appointments also show on the **To-Do Bar** on the right of the screen when activated. I prefer to set up **Calendar** in the **Reading** view, which is also the default view of all other **Outlook** views (**Mail**, **Contacts**, **Tasks** and **Notes**). From all these views you can keep a check on your appointments.

In Fig. 7.9, you can see how to activate the **To-Do Bar**, as well as the other **View**, **Layout** options from the **Ribbon**

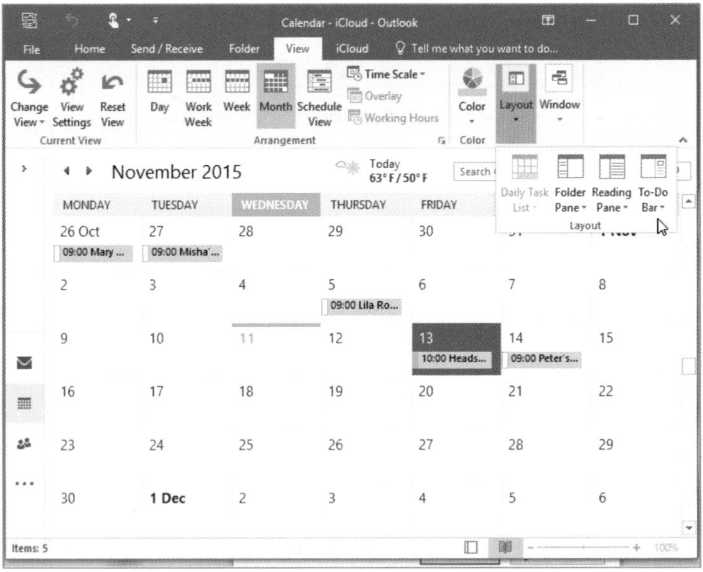

Fig. 7.9 The Layout Options on Monthly View.

Entering Events

An event is an activity that lasts all day long and is entered into the **Calendar** in the same way as an appointment. Conferences and holidays are events. Let us now assume that a conference is to take place on Monday the 11th of January for two days. To enter this tap or click the 11th January on the **Date Navigator** at the left pane of the **Normal** view and double-tap or double-click the displayed blue bar. It is important that you select **Normal** view otherwise the **Appointments** window will not be opened.

In the displayed **Appointment** window type 'Conference' in the **Subject** box and a location below it, then tap or click the **All day event** check box (pointed to in Fig. 7.10 below) and change the **End Date**. Starting and ending times are greyed out as the conference is an all day event - it is assumed that it starts early on the morning of the 11th and ends late on the afternoon of the 12th. The window now changes to an **Event** window, as shown below. Finally, select the **Save and Close** button to create the event, as shown in Fig. 7.11 on the next page when displayed in **Classic** view.

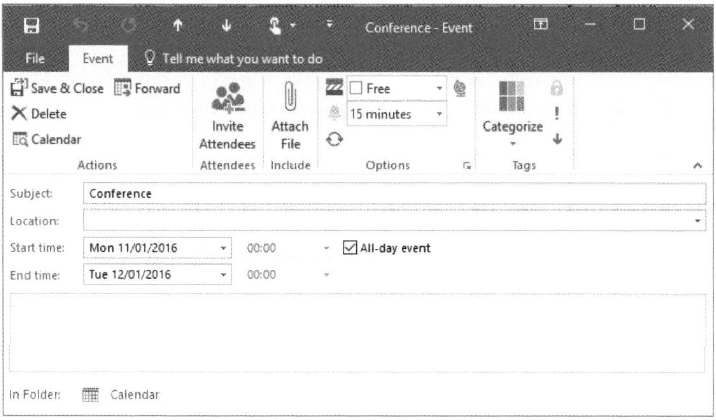

Fig. 7.10 Entering a New Event.

That's all there is to it; you should never miss your important dates again, but you must make time to enter them in **Calendar** in the first place. Do try it, you'll never regret it!

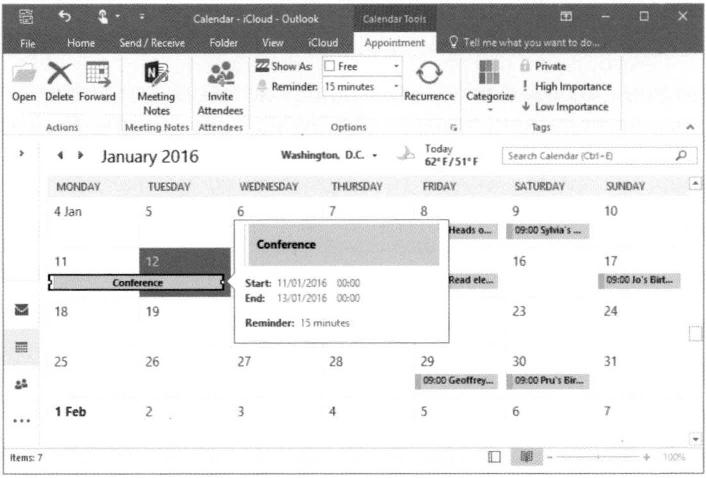

Fig. 7.11 The Calendar Monthly View.

Inviting Attendees and Taking Notes

When you tap or click an appointment or event, the **Ribbon** refreshes as showing above. Tapping or clicking the **Invite Attendees** button, displays Fig. 7.12 below.

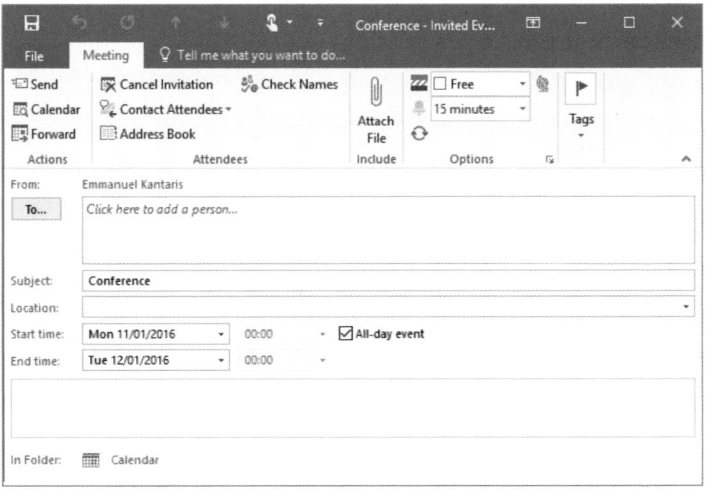

Fig. 7.12 Inviting People to an Event or a Meeting.

Tapping or clicking the **To...** button opens your **Address Book** so you can choose whom to invite.

You can even take notes during an event or meeting by tapping or clicking the **Meeting Notes** button on the **Ribbon** (see Fig. 7.11) to display the screen in Fig. 7.13.

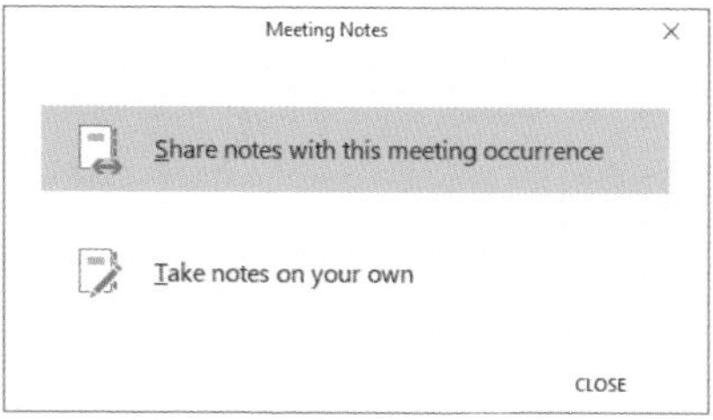

Choose one of these according to your needs.

Fig. 7.13 Taking Meeting Notes.

Printing Information

Information held in a diary can be printed on paper. Simply use the **File, Print** command to open the **Print** dialogue box shown in Fig. 7.14 below.

You can select a different installed **Printer** than the default and you can choose an appropriate option from the **Settings** list. You can also use the **Print Options** button and tap or click **Page Setup** to see the page **Format**, **Paper** size and **Header/Footer** options of the selected print style.

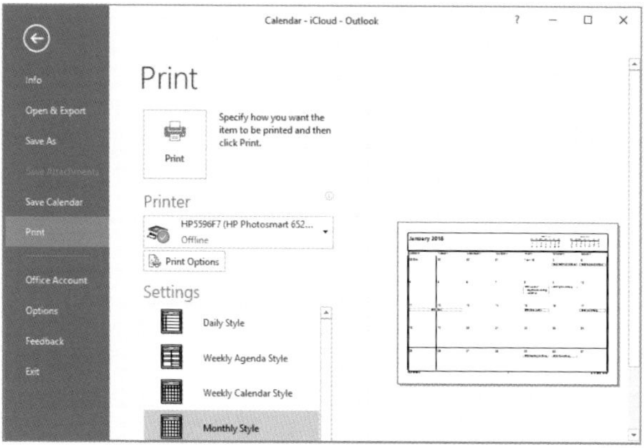

Fig. 7.14 The Calendar Print Dialogue Box.

Fig. 7.15 below, shows the **Page Setup** dialogue box with the **Header/Footer** tab selected. Note the five icon buttons pointed to below the **Footer** text boxes. These can be used to insert page numbers, total number of pages, date, time and user's name respectively, in both headers and footers. To do so, simply place the insertion cursor on one of the text boxes, then tap or click the appropriate button.

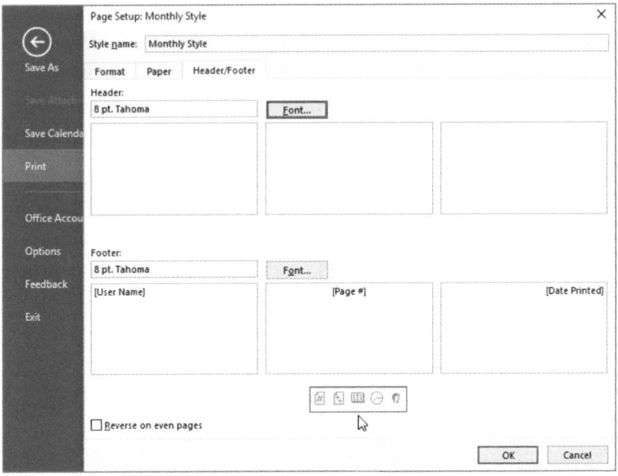

Fig. 7.15 Inserting a Footer in the Page Setup Dialogue Box.

In the footer set-up in Fig. 7.15 above, you can insert the user's name in the left panel of the footer, the page number in the middle panel, and the date printed in the right panel. If you decide to show such information on your printout, it is entirely up to you where you choose to insert it. You can also change the font type and font size of the information appearing on a header or footer.

If you want to change the font type and font size of the text appearing on the actual body of your printout, tap or click the **Format** tab of the dialogue box in Fig. 7.15 above, and make appropriate selections under the displayed **Fonts** section. Pressing the **OK** button on the **Page Setup** dialogue box returns you to the **Print** dialogue box. However, before committing anything to paper, tap or click the **Preview** button on the **Print** dialogue box and save a few trees!

Using Tasks

A 'task' is an item that you create in **Outlook** to track until it is completed. A 'to-do' item is an **Outlook** item, like a task, an e-mail message, or a contact, that has been flagged for follow-up. By default, all tasks are flagged for follow-up when they are created, even if they have no start date or due date. Therefore, whenever you create a task, or flag an e-mail message or a contact, a to-do item is created automatically. Both tasks and to-do items appear in **Tasks**, as shown below in the **To-Do Bar** and in the **Task List** in all the other **Outlook** activities (**Mail**, **Calendar**, **Contacts** and **Notes**).

To create a new **Task**, tap or click the **New Items** button on **Outlook**'s **Ribbon** and select **Task** from the drop-down menu, shown in Fig. 7. 16.

This opens the **Task**'s window for you to complete. I entered as subject 'Take Car for Service' and gave a date for it, as shown in Fig. 7.17.

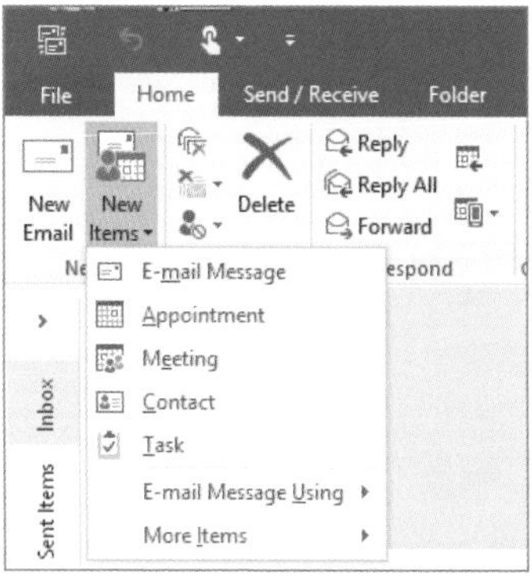

Fig. 7.16 New Items Options.

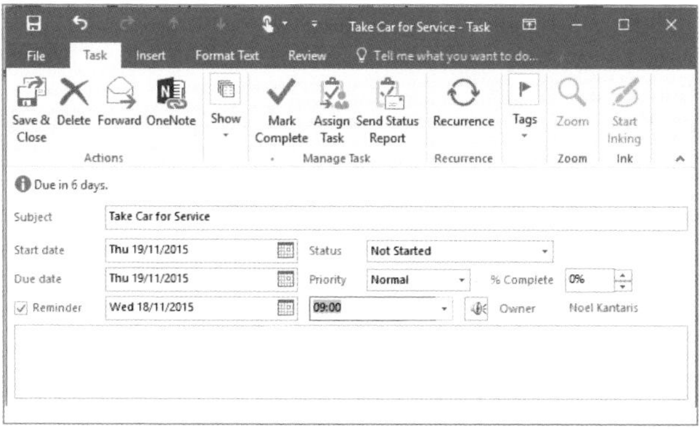

Fig. 7.17 Creating a New Task.

Having typed in all the required information, tap or click the **Save & Close** command button. To display your **Tasks**, use the **Tasks** button of the **Navigation** pane, pointed to in Fig. 7.18.

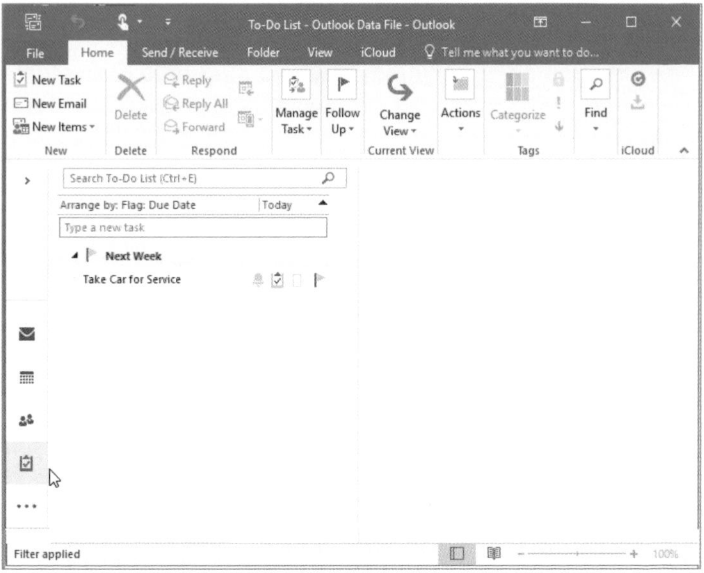

Fig. 7.18 A Simple To-Do Task List.

If you have the **To-Do Bar** open you can enter a task in its **Type a new task** text box from any view in **Outlook**. I tend to use the **To-Do Bar** most often to add and update tasks, and to mark them as completed.

To open the **To-Do Bar** tap of click the **View** tab on **Outlook**'s **Ribbon**, then in the **Layout** group, tap or click the **To-Do Bar** command and select the **Tasks** option from the drop-down menu, as shown in Fig. 7.19 on the next page. What is shown on the screen dump, is the result and the action required to get that result.

In addition, on the same screen in Fig. 7.19, I show what happens when the **Folder Pane** command is selected and the **Normal** option is chosen from the drop-down menu. What you choose to open on your screen depends on you.

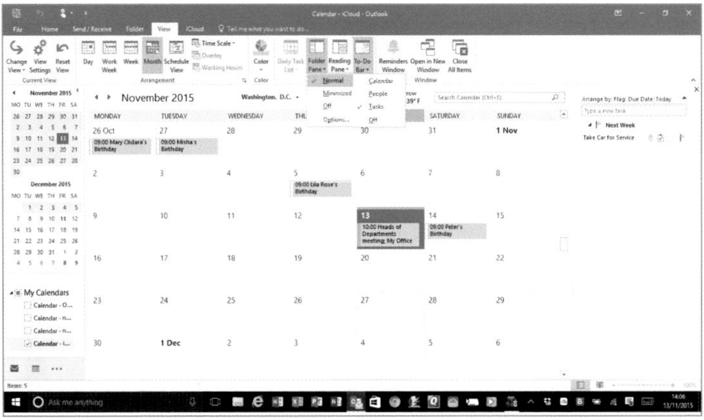

Fig. 7.19 Screen Displaying Folder Pane and Task Pane.

Delegating Tasks

Tasks can be assigned to other people within your organisation and can help you keep track of progress on work that they do for you. To assign a task, you first create it, then double-tap or double-click it to open it, then tap or click the **Forward** command on the **Ribbon** to display Fig. 7.20, ready to send it as a task request to someone.

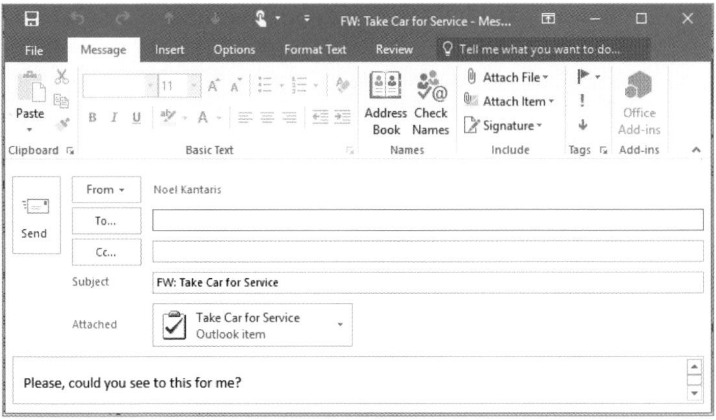

Fig. 7.20 Assigning a Task.

More To-Do Bar Details

It is worth looking at the **To-Do Bar** a bit closer. As we have seen, you can open it by using the **View**, **Layout**, **To-Do Bar** command, and selecting **Calendar** and/or **People** (Contacts) and/or **Tasks**, as shown in Fig. 7.21, where all are opened.

By default, the **To-Do Bar** is closed in all of **Outlook**'s activities, but you can activate it at any time. Once opened, the **To-Do Bar** will stay open until you click its '**x**' button (now called **Remove the peek**!) on each of the opened parts.

Fig. 7.21 Parts of the To-Do Bar.

The **To-Do Bar** consists of three parts, as shown in Fig. 7.21:

The **Task Input** panel where you can quickly add your tasks that need doing and below that the **Task** list, where your tasks and messages that have been flagged are shown.

The **Date Navigator**, which shows a small calendar display with the **Appointments** section below it (not shown here - for an explanation, see below) displays what you have planned for the next 7 days.

The **People Favorites** panel that allows you to access your favourite people which you must have categorised as such within your **Contacts**.

You can turn each part on or off by selecting or deselecting the option on the **To-Do** drop-down menu. You can even choose to turn everything off. Unfortunately, when you select the option **People**, the **Appointments** section below the small calendar is removed from the display. For me, today's tasks and appointments are by far preferable to displaying my favourite people!

Using Notes

If you are the type that sticks notes all over your desk to remind you of things, you will be happy to know that **Outlook** lets you create electronic 'sticky' notes. They remain on the **Desktop** until you close them or you close **Outlook**, but remain in **Notes** until you delete them.

When you start the **Notes** activity (tap or click the **...** more activities button and select **Notes**), as shown at the bottom left in Fig. 7.22. To create a new note, tap or click the **New Note** button on the **Ribbon**. The result for such a note is shown on both the **Notes** folder and the **Desktop**, as shown in Fig. 7.22.

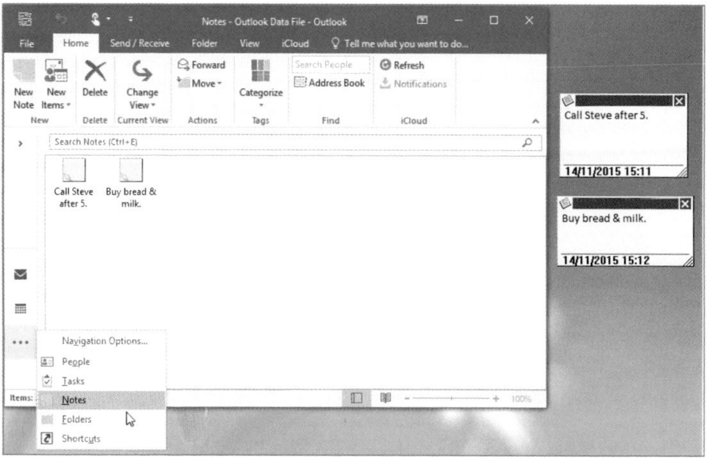

Fig. 7.22 The Notes Activity with Two Open Notes on the Desktop.

To create a new note from any other **Outlook** activity with a keyboard, use the **Ctrl+Shift+N** shortcut.

You can type whatever text you want in a note, and edit it at any time. Changes are saved automatically. You can also drag a note on the desktop.

To close the note displayed on the **Desktop** or in **Notes**, touch and hold or right-click it and select the **Delete** button on the **Ribbon**.

Backing Up Outlook Data

Unless you are using a Microsoft **Exchange** account or an HTTP account, such as Windows **Live Mail**, all of your **Outlook** data will be saved in the **Personal Folders** file (**Outlook.pst**). This file contains all of your **Outlook** folders, including the **Inbox**, **Calendar** and **Contacts**. By default you will have a single **.pst** file (usually called **Personal Folders** in your **Folder** pane).

To back up your **.pst** file, use the method discussed in Chapter 5, page 75, under **Importing Data into Outlook**. In particular, use the **File** button, then select the **Open & Export** entry on the screen and tap or click the **Import/Export** option. This opens the **Import and Export Wizard** dialogue box shown in Fig. 7.23 below.

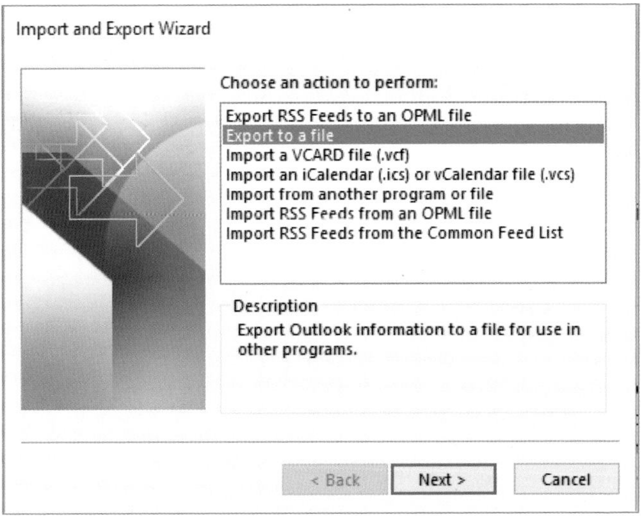

Fig. 7.23 The Import and Export Wizard.

Near the top of the screen select the **Export to a file** entry and press **Next**. In the displayed **Export to a File** dialogue box, select the **Outlook Data File (.pst)** entry, as shown in Fig. 7.24 on the next page, then press **Next**.

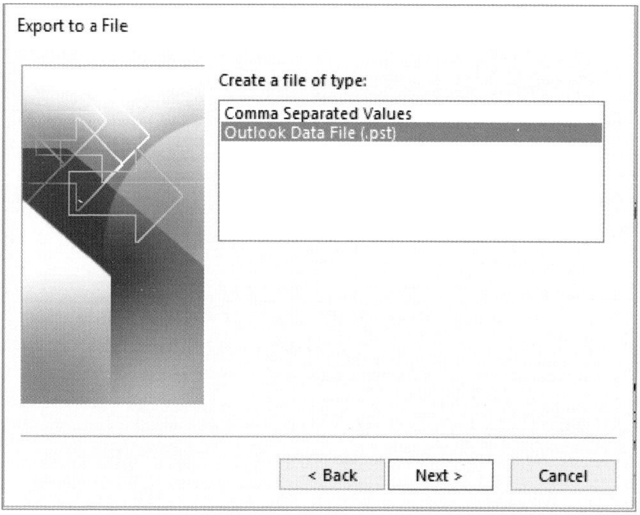

Fig. 7.24 The Export to a File Wizard Screen.

Now select the folder you want to back up, in this case the **Outlook Data File** folder shown in Fig. 7.25 and follow the screen instructions of the Wizard.

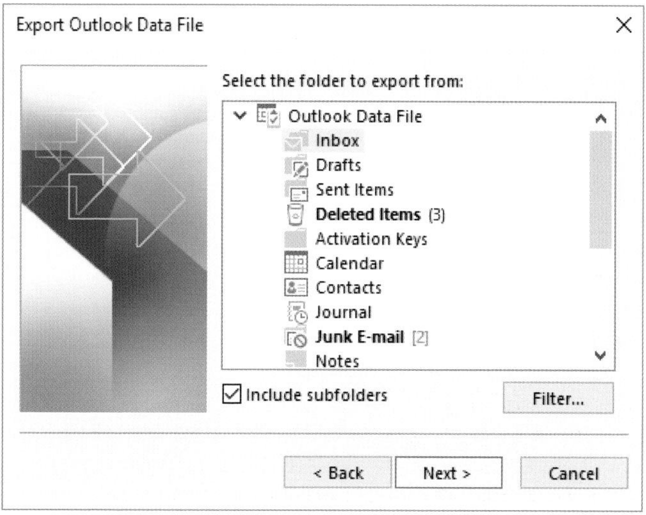

Fig. 7.25 The Outlook Data File Folder.

* * *

In the last three chapters, I have tried to cover sufficient information on **Outlook** 2016, so that you can get to grips with the program and get on with the job of sending and receiving e-mail messages effectively, this being one of the most used activities on the Internet. I also find that using the **Calendar** to record coming events and birthdays of all my friends and family members, an immense help.

Outlook has more features, too numerous to discuss in the space allocated here. What I have tried to do, is give you enough basic information so that you can have the confidence to explore the rest of **Outlook**'s capabilities by yourself. Above all, have fun!

* * *

8

Excel 2016 Spreadsheet Basics

Microsoft **Excel** 2016 is a powerful and versatile program which is used, not only in the business world, but also in science and engineering.

The program can emulate everything that can be done with a pencil, paper and a calculator. Thus, it is an 'electronic spreadsheet' or simply a 'spreadsheet', a name which is also used to describe it and other similar products. **Excel** is extremely flexible and can deal with the solution of complex problems which it can manage extremely fast. These can vary from budgeting and forecasting to the solution of complicated scientific and engineering problems.

The **Ribbon**, which groups tools by task and commands you most frequently use, has been updated and improved. As with all the other **Office** 2016 applications the FILE command button opens the **Backstage** full-screen interface for accessing all of the options relating to the application and the current **Workbook** document.

Excel 2016, just as its last three versions, supports worksheets with 1,048,576 rows by 16,384 columns and an unlimited number of types of formatting in the same workbook. It also provides a **Page Layout** view that lets you check how your sheet will look in printed format, a formula bar which automatically re-sizes to accommodate long, complex formulas and a powerful charting engine.

Starting Excel 2016

I have already discussed in Chapter 1 how to pin shortcuts on the **Taskbar** of all the applications that make up **Office** 2016. This makes it easier to access the individual Applications.

So, to start **Excel**, tap or click its icon on the **Taskbar**, shown here on the left, which opens a screen similar to that in Fig. 8.1.

Fig. 8.1 Excel 2016's Opening Screen.

Whether you have used a previous version of **Excel** or not, the first time you use the program, it might be a good idea to refer to the Help System as discussed at the end of Chapter 1 or 'Take a tour' as suggested above, before starting to experiment with anything else. Also note the number of templates available to you on the opening screen.

The Excel Screen

Tapping or clicking on the 'Blank workbook' on the opening screen, displays a window with a similar **Title** bar and **Ribbon** to those of **Word**, but with some differences.

As seen in Fig. 8.1, the opening screen includes a variety of templates for you to choose from, but it is worth looking at the **Blank Workbook** first which, when selected, displays the screen shown in Fig. 8.2 on the next page.

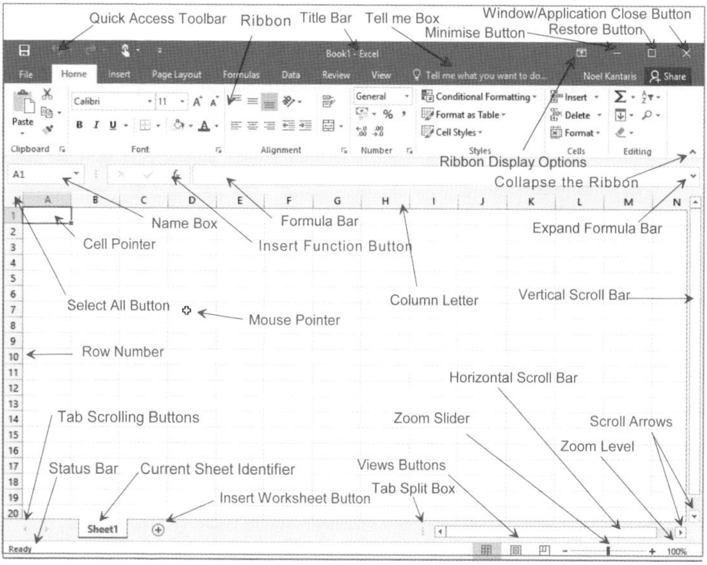

Fig. 8.2 The Excel Screen.

The layout, as shown in Fig. 8.2, is in a window, but if you click on the application **Restore** button, you can make **Excel** take up the full screen area available. Working in a smaller window can be useful when you are running several applications at the same time.

The **Excel** window, which in this case displays an empty and untitled book (**Book1**), has some areas which have identical functions to those of **Word** (see the beginning of Chapter 2), and other areas which have different functions. Below, I describe only the areas that are exclusive to **Excel**.

Area	***Function***
Name box	Identifies the selected cell (by name or by cell co-ordinates), chart item, or drawing object.
Formula Bar	Can display a number, a label, or the formula behind a result.
Expand Formula Bar	Use to expand the Formula Bar.

Insert Function	Use to open the Insert Function dialogue box.
Select All Button	Use to select the whole worksheet.
Cell pointer	Marks the current cell.
Column letter	The letter that identifies each column.
Row number	The number that identifies each row.
Tab Scrolling Buttons	Using these buttons, scrolls sheet tabs right or left, when there are more tabs than can be displayed at once.
Insert Worksheet	Use to insert another worksheet.
Tab split box	The split box which you drag left to see more of the scroll bar, or right to see more tabs.
Current sheet	Shows the current sheet amongst a number of sheets in a file. These are named Sheet1, Sheet2 and so on, by default, but can be changed to, say, North and South. To move to a particular sheet, click its tab.

The Ribbon

The **Ribbon** in **Excel** has seven tabs, each one with the most used controls grouped on it for the main program actions. For a general description of the **Ribbon**, see Chapter 1. Also on the **Ribbon** you'll find the FILE command button which allows you to **Open**, **Save**, **Save As**, **Print**, **Share**, etc., worksheets.

A quick look at the **Home** tab, displayed in Fig. 8.3 on the next page, shows that it contains groups for the more common worksheet activities. The **Clipboard Cut** and **Paste** commands, **Font**, **Alignment**, **Number Styles** and **Cells** groups for manipulating cells and their contents, **Editing** worksheets, etc.

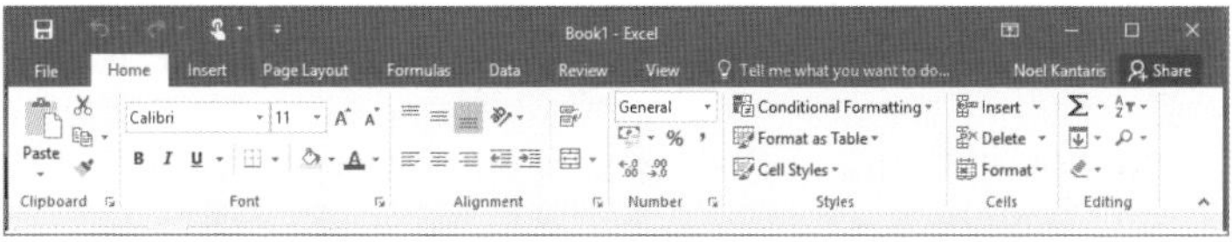

Fig. 8.3 The Home Tab of the Excel 2016 Ribbon.

Clicking a new tab opens a new series of groups, each with its relevant command buttons. The content of the other tabs allow you to do the following:

The **Insert** tab enables you to immediately insert Tables, Illustrations, Charts, Links and Text based features.

The **Page Layout** tab allows you to set your Themes, Page Setup, Scale to Fit, Sheet Options and to Arrange and group sheets.

The **Formulas** tab allows you to add and control formulas, consisting of a Function Library, Defined Names, Formula Auditing and sheet Calculation options.

The **Data** tab groups the actions used for handling and analysing your data. These include Get External Data from various sources, Connections for handling external links, Sort & Filter selected data, Data Tools and working with an Outline so that joined cells can be collapsed and expanded.

The **Review** tab groups controls for Proofing your worksheets and to initiate and track document review and approval processes. It lets you deal with Comments, and controls how Changes made to a worksheet will be handled.

The **View** tab allows you to set what you see on the screen. You can choose between Workbook Views, Show or Hide screen features, Zoom to different magnifications, control the viewing Window of workbooks by displaying them Side by Side, Synchronising scrolling, Freeze Panes and run and record Macros.

Workbook Navigation and Manipulation

When you first open **Excel**, it sets up a series of worksheets, in your computer's memory, many times larger than the small part shown on the screen. Individual cells are identified by column and row location (in that order), with present size extending to 16,384 columns and 1,048,576 rows. The columns are labelled from A to Z, followed by AA to AZ, BA to BZ, and so on, to XFD, while the rows are numbered from 1 to 1048576.

The point where a row and column intersect is called a cell, and the reference points of a cell are known as the cell address. The active cell (A1 at first) is boxed.

With the large size of **Excel**'s worksheets, finding your way around them is very important. There are four main ways of moving around a worksheet:

Using the **Go To** box.

Scrolling with your finger on a touch-sensitive screen or using the mouse.

Using the scroll bars.

Using key combinations with either the on-screen or physical keyboards.

The Go To Box

Pressing the **Ctrl+G** key combination on either keyboard, displays the **Go To** box shown here in Fig. 8.4.

Fig. 8.4 The Go To Box.

In the **Go To** box a list of named ranges in the active worksheet (to be discussed shortly, but not shown here) is normaly displayed, or one of the last four references from which you chose the **Go To** command.

In the **Reference** text box you type the cell reference or a named range you want to move to.

Mouse Scrolling and Scroll Bars

If you have a mouse with a wheel, you will be able to move easily around **Excel**'s enormous worksheets, as follows:

With a mouse – to scroll up or down: Rotate the wheel forward or back.

To pan through a worksheet: Hold down the wheel button, and drag the pointer away from the origin mark in any direction that you want to scroll.

To zoom in or out: Hold down **Ctrl** while you rotate the mouse wheel forward or back. The percentage of the zoomed worksheet is displayed on the **Status** bar.

With a finger or a mouse – to scroll one row up or down: Tap or click the ▲ or ▼ scroll arrowheads on the vertical scroll bar, while to scroll one column left or right: Tap or click the ◄ or ► scroll arrowheads on the horizontal scroll bar.

To scroll one window up or down: Tap or click above or below the scroll box on the vertical scroll bar, while to scroll one window left or right: Tap or click to the left or right of the scroll box on the horizontal scroll bar.

Key Combinations

To scroll to the start and end range of a worksheet: Press **Ctrl+→**, **Ctrl+←** with either keyboard to scroll to the start and end of each range in a column before stopping at the end of the worksheet or **Ctrl+↓**, **Ctrl+↑** with the physical keyboard to scroll to the start and end of each range in a row before stopping at the end of the worksheet.

To scroll one window up or down: Press **PgUp** or **PgDn** on the physical keyboard, while to scroll one window left or right: Press **Ctrl** then ← or **Ctrl** then → on either keyboards.

The area within which you can move the active cell is referred to as the working area of the worksheet, while the letters and numbers in the border at the top and left of the working area give the 'co-ordinates' of the cells.

The location of the active cell is constantly monitored by the 'Selection indicator' in the **Name Box**. As the active cell is moved, this indicator displays its address, as shown in Fig. 8.5 below.

The contents of a cell are displayed above the column letters within the **Formula Bar**. If you type text in the active cell, it appears in both the **Formula Bar** and the cell itself.

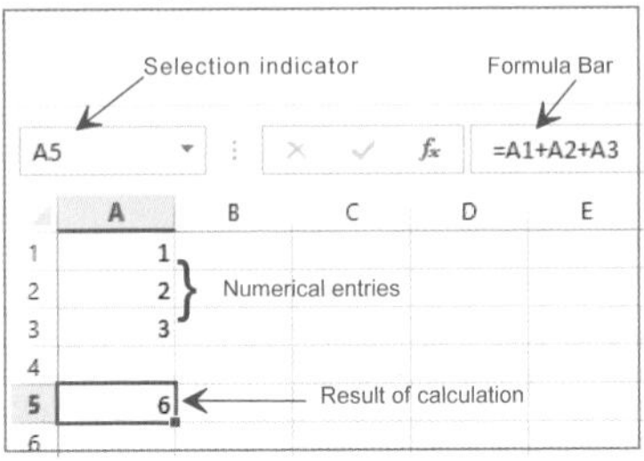

Fig. 8.5 The Selection Indicator and Formula Bar.

Typing a formula which is preceded by the equals sign (=) to, say, add the contents of three cells, causes the actual formula to appear in the **Formula Bar**, while the result of the calculation appears in the active cell when **Enter** is pressed.

Moving Between Sheets

You can scroll between worksheets by clicking one of the 'Tab scrolling buttons' situated to the left of Sheet1, as shown in Fig. 8.6. The inner arrows scroll sheets one at a time in the direction of the arrow, while the outer arrows scroll to the end, or beginning, of the group of available worksheets. A worksheet is then made current by clicking its tab.

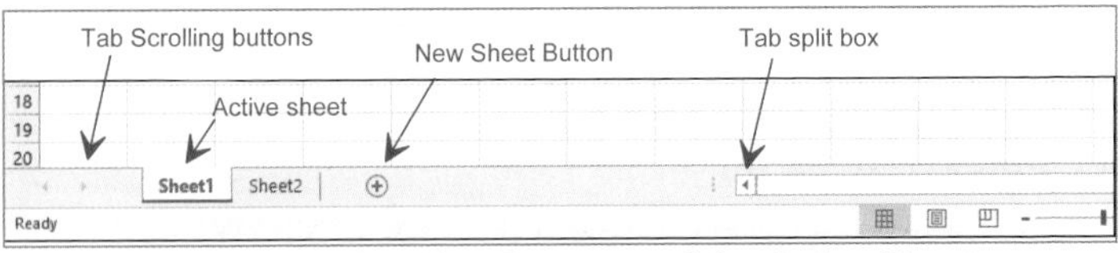

Fig. 8.6 Tab Scrolling Buttons and the Active Sheet.

To display more sheet tabs at a time, drag the **Tab Split** box to the right, or to the left to display less sheet tabs. To rename sheets, double-tap or double-click on their tab, then type the new name to replace the highlighted name.

To insert a sheet, tap or click the **New sheet** button and drag the new tab to where you want it in the stack (see Fig. 8.8).

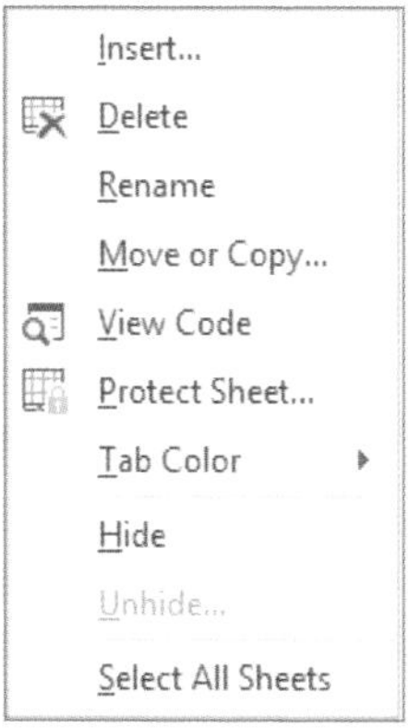

To delete a sheet, touch and hold or right-click on its tab and select **Delete** from the context menu shown in Fig. 8.7. As you can see, you can also **Insert**, **Rename** and **Move or Copy** sheets this way.

Fig. 8.7 The Touch and Hold or Right-click Context Menu.

Rearranging Sheet Order

To rearrange the order in which sheets are being held in a workbook, drag the particular sheet (point to it and with the left mouse button depressed move the mouse pointer) in the required direction, as shown in Fig. 8.8.

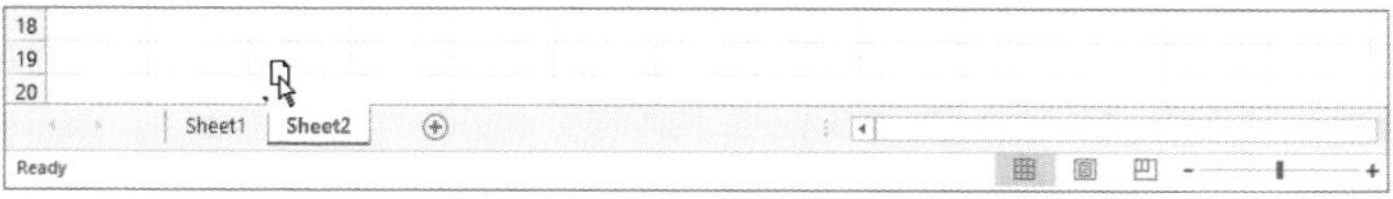

Fig. 8.8 Moving an Active Sheet.

While you are dragging the tab of the sheet you want to move, the mouse pointer changes to an arrow pointing to an image of a sheet. The small solid arrowhead to the left of the mouse pointer indicates the place where the sheet you are moving will be placed.

The above capability is not available to tablet users. On a touch-sensitive screen, first touch and hold the sheet you want to move, then on the displayed menu, shown in Fig. 8.7 above, select the **Move or Copy** option which displays a dialogue box in which you can choose where to move the selected sheet.

Grouping Worksheets

You can select several sheets to group them together so that data entry, editing or formatting can be made easier and more consistent.

To select adjacent sheets, click the first sheet tab, hold down the **Shift** key and then click the last sheet tab in the group. To select non-adjacent sheets, click the first sheet tab, hold down the **Ctrl** key and then click the other sheet tabs you want to group together.

Selecting sheets in the above manner causes the word '[Group]' to appear in the **Title** bar of the active window, and the tabs of the selected sheets to be shown in white. To cancel the selection, touch and hold or right-click a group tab and select **Ungroup Sheets**, or click the tab of any sheet which is not part of the selected group.

Selecting a Range of Cells

To select a range of cells, say, A3:C3, point to cell A3 and either (i) press the left mouse button and, while holding it pressed, drag the mouse to the right or (ii) double-tap the first cell and drag your finger to the right to display Fig. 8.9. The small circles only appear when you drag with your finger.

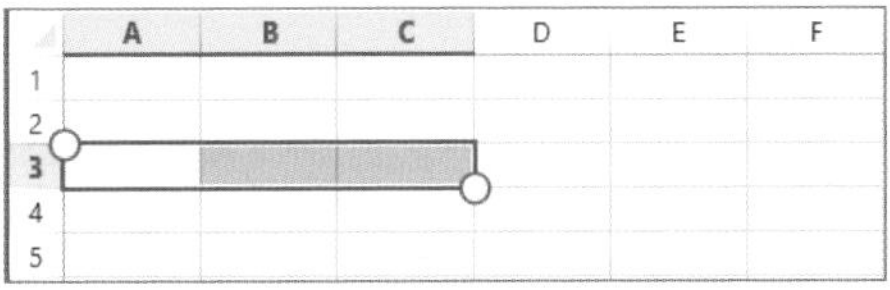

Fig. 8.9 Selecting a Range of Cells.

To select a range from the keyboard, first make active the first cell in the range, then hold down the **Shift** key and use the right arrow key (→) to highlight the required range.

Context Menus

Excel, like all the **Office** 2016 programs, lets you touch and hold or right-click on almost anything on the screen to open a 'context' menu of actions you can take.

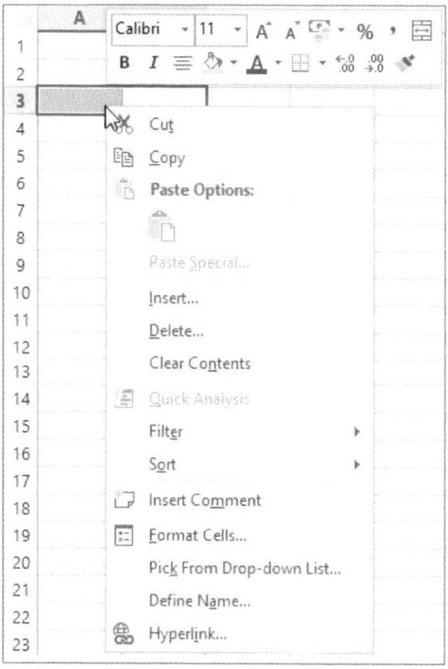

Fig. 8.10 shows the menu options available when you tap and hold or right-click a selected range of cells. It contains the most common commands you may want to carry out. Shown above this is the **Mini Toolbar**, an **Office** feature, which contains mostly formatting controls that you can instantly carry out.

Fig. 8.10 Context Menu and a Mini Toolbar.

Entering Information

We will now investigate how information can be entered into a worksheet. But first, make sure you are in **Sheet1**, then return to the **Home** (A1) position and type the words:

```
Project Analysis
```

As you type, the characters appear in both the **Formula Bar** and the active cell. If you make a mistake, press the **Backspace** key to erase the previous letter or the **Esc** key to start again. When you have finished, press **Enter** to move to the cell below or the **Tab** key to move to the next cell to the right.

Note that what you have just typed in has been entered in cell A1, even though the whole of the word 'Analysis' appears to be in cell B1. If you use the right arrow key to move the active cell to B1 you will see that the cell is indeed empty. Typing any letter at the beginning of an entry into a cell results in a 'text' entry being formed automatically, otherwise known as a 'label'.

If the length of the text is longer than the width of a cell, it will continue into the next cell to the right of the current active cell, provided that cell is empty, otherwise the displayed information will be truncated.

To edit information already in a cell, either double-tap the cell in question, or double-click it. The cursor keys on both keyboards can be used to move the cursor and/or edit information as required. You can also 'undo' the last 16 actions carried out since the program was last in the **Ready** mode, using the **Undo** button on the **Quick Access** toolbar or the **Ctrl+Z** keyboard shortcut.

Before you proceed, delete any information that might be in **Sheet1** of your workbook by selecting it (double-tap or double-click), then pressing **Del** or **Backspace**. Next, move the active cell to B3 and type:

```
Jan
```

Pressing the right arrow key (→) will automatically enter the typed information into the cell and also move the active cell one cell to the right, in this case to C3. The same thing can be achieved by tapping cell C3 on a touch-sensitive screen. Next, type in cell C3:

```
Feb
```

and press **Enter** or tap the next cell down.

The look of a worksheet can be enhanced somewhat by using different types of borders around specific cells. To do this, first select the range of cells, then tap or click the down arrow of the **Home**, **Font**, **Borders** button which opens an extensive list of border types, as shown in Fig. 8.11. In this example, I have selected the cell range A3:C3, then chose the **Top and Double Bottom Border** option.

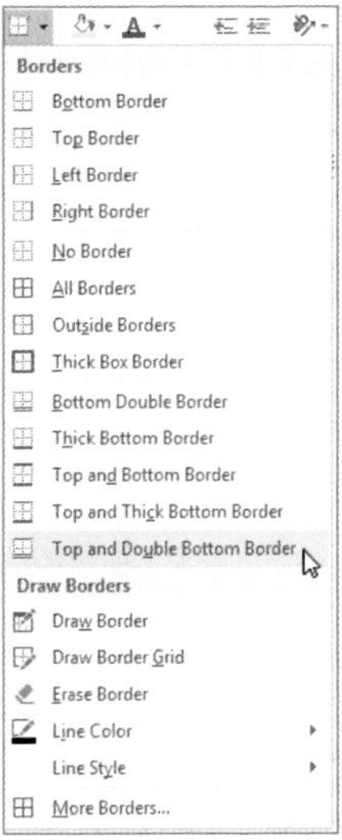

Fig. 8.11 The Borders Button.

Next, move to cell A4 and type the label **Income**, then enter the numbers **14000** and **15000** in cells B4 and C4, respectively, as shown below. Do note that by default, the labels **Jan** and **Feb** are left-justified, while the numbers are right justified, as shown in Fig. 8.12.

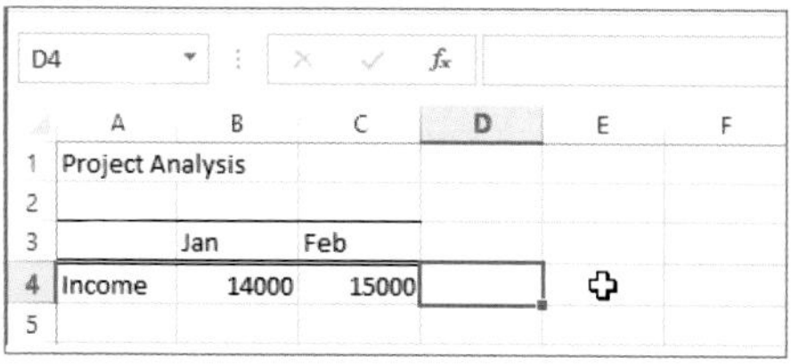

Fig. 8.12 Default Justification of Labels and Numbers.

Changing Text Alignment and Fonts

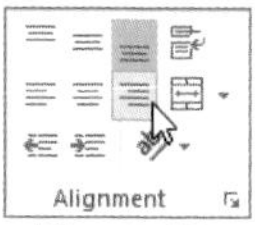

Fig. 8.13.

To somewhat improve this worksheet's looks, right-justify the text **Jan** and **Feb** within their respective cells. To do this, move the active cell to B3 and select the range B3 to C3, then select the **Home**, **Alignment**, **Align Text Right** command button, pointed to in Fig. 8.13.

For more control you can use the **Format Cells** dialogue box (Fig. 8.14). To open it, click the **Alignment Dialogue Box Launcher** and in its **Alignment** tab sheet select **Right (Indent)** in the **Horizontal** drop-down list.

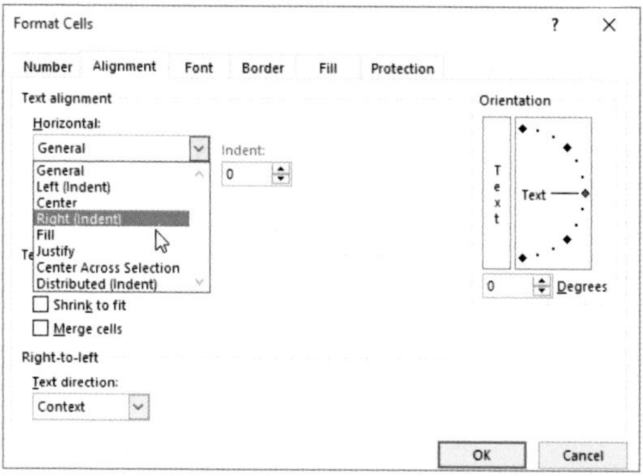

Fig. 8.14 Formatting Cells using the Alignment Tab Sheet.

No matter which method you choose, the text entries should now appear right-justified within their cells. The second method provides greater flexibility in displaying text, both in terms of position and orientation.

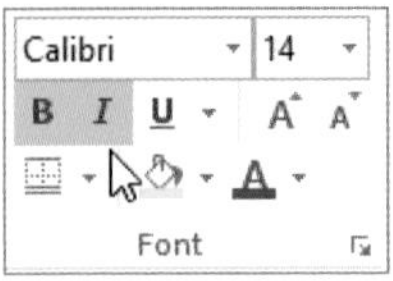

Fig. 8.15 The Font Group.

To improve the look of this work, select cell A1, then tap or click on the down arrowhead against **Font Size** button on the **Ribbon**, and choose point size 14 from the displayed list, then tap or click both the **Bold** and **Italic** buttons, shown in Fig. 8.15.

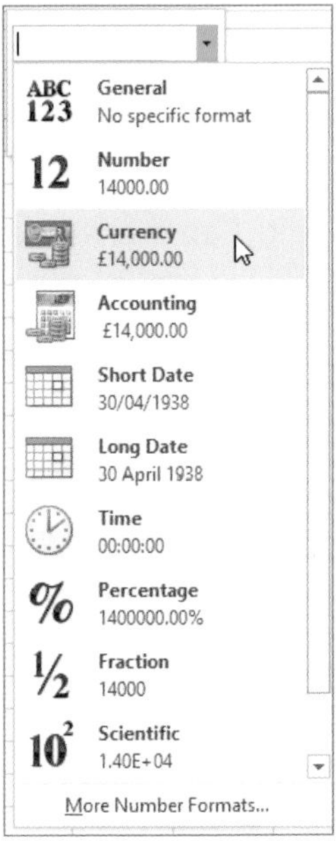

Fig. 8.16 Setting Currency Format.

Finally, since the numbers in cells B4 to C4 represent money, it would be better if these were prefixed with the £ sign. To do this, select the cell range B4:C4, and tap or click the **Home**, **Number** and select **Currency** from the drop-down list shown here in Fig. 8.16.

The numbers within the chosen range will now be displayed in currency form, and the width of the cells will automatically adjust to accommodate them, if they are too long which is the case in this example.

To see the actual new width of, say, column C, place the mouse pointer to the right of the column letter on the dividing line. When the mouse pointer changes to the shape shown in Fig. 8.17 on the next page, press the left mouse button without moving the mouse. The cell width will then display within a pop-up text box as 81 pixels, increased from the default column width of 64 pixels. To widen a column, drag the pointer to the right, until the required width is reached.

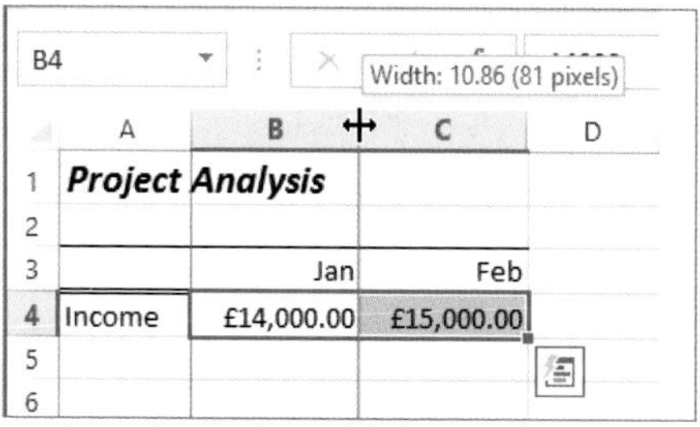

Fig. 8.17 Finding the Width of a Cell.

Filling in a Worksheet

I will use the few entries I've created so far (if you haven't got them, don't worry as you could just as easily start afresh, but refer to formatting made to those entries), to create the worksheet shown in Fig. 8.18 below.

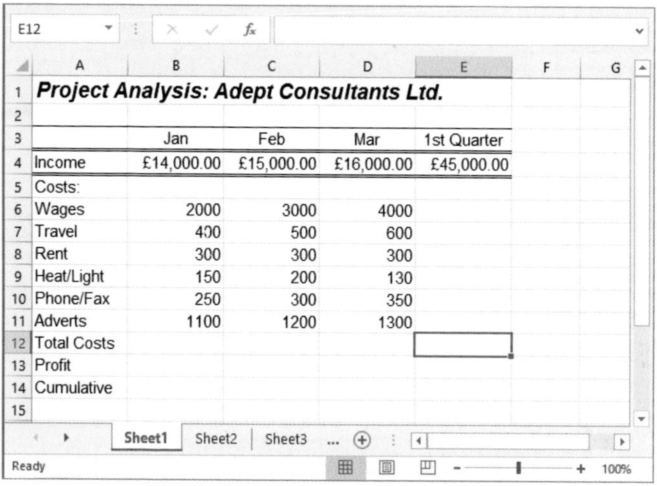

Fig. 8.18 Entering Data in a Worksheet.

The lines, like the double line at the bottom of the A3 to E3 and A4 to E4 ranges, were entered by first selecting each range, then right-clicking it and using the **Borders** button on the **Mini Toolbar** that hovers over the selection (see page 145). Alternatively, you could use the **Home**, **Font**, **Borders** button on the **Ribbon** and select an appropriate border.

Formatting Entries

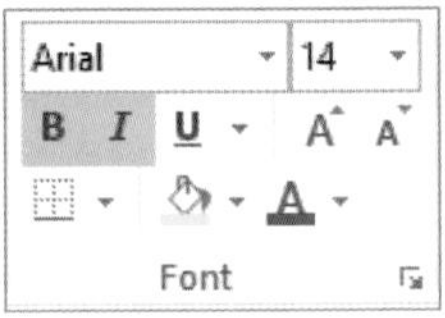

Fig. 8.19 Home, Font Group.

The information in cell A1 (Project Analysis: Adept Consultants Ltd.) was entered left-justified and formatted from the **Home**, **Font** group by selecting Arial from the drop-down **Font** list, and 14 from the drop-down **Font Size** list, and then clicking in succession the **Bold** and **Italic** buttons, as shown above.

The text in the cell block B3:E3 was formatted by first selecting the range and then clicking the **Home**, **Alignment**, **Center** command button, shown here, to display the text in the range centre-justified.

The numbers within the cell block B4:E4 were formatted by first selecting the range, then clicking the **Home**, **Number** and selecting **Currency** from the drop-down list.

All the text appearing in column A (apart from that in cell A1) was just typed in (left-justified), and formatted in Arial 11 font size. The width of all the columns A to E was adjusted to 12 characters; a quick way of doing this is to select one row of these columns, then click the **Home**, **Cells**, **Format** button, select **Column Width** from the displayed menu, partially shown in Fig. 8.20, type 12 in the displayed box in Fig. 8.21, and click **OK**.

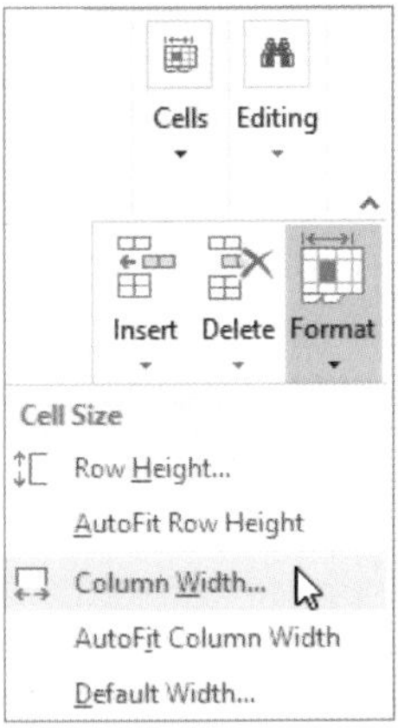

Fig. 8.20 Home, Cells Group.

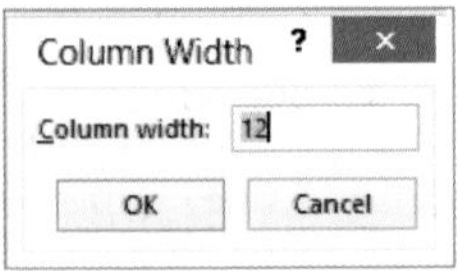

Fig. 8.21 Column Width Box.

Filling a Range by Example

To fill a range by example can be achieved by either using a mouse or a finger on a multi-touch screen. With a mouse you can fill ranges in both horizontal and vertical directions, while with a finger on a multi-touch screen you can only fill a range vertically.

With a mouse: Select the first cell of a range, point at the bottom right corner of the cell and when the mouse pointer changes to a small cross, as in Fig. 8.22, drag the mouse in the required direction. On releasing the mouse the range fills automatically. As I started with the abbreviation 'Jan', the next cell to the right will automatically fill with the text 'Feb'.

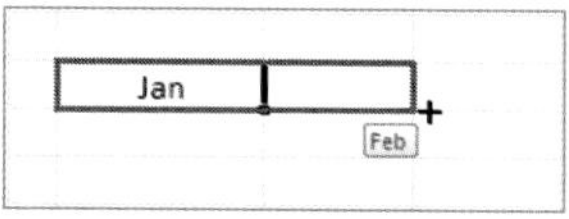

Fig. 8.22 Dragging a Range with a Mouse.

On a touch-sensitive screen: Touch and hold the first cell of a vertical range until the editing options appear above it as shown in Fig. 8.23. Next tap the **AutoFill** option which displays an auto-fill down-arrowhead against the cell, as shown here to the left. Drag the arrowhead downwards for a few cells, then release it. The range fills automatically, as shown here to the right.

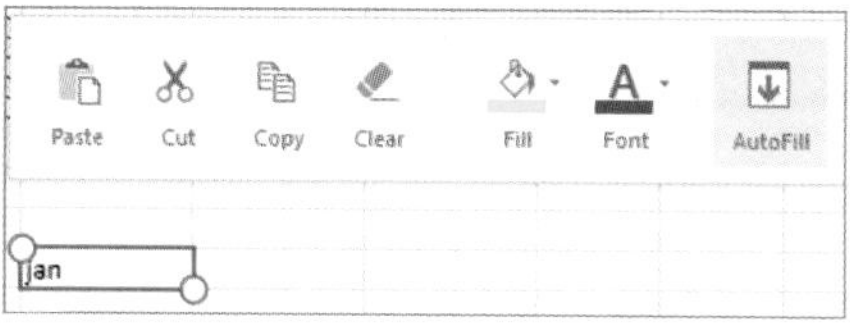

Fig. 8.23 Dragging a Range with a Finger.

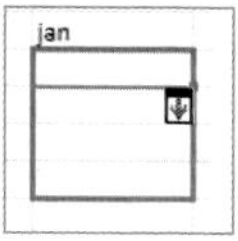

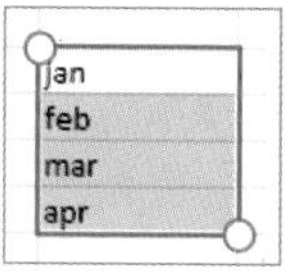

Entering Text, Numbers and Formulas

Excel allows you to format both text (labels) and numbers in any way you choose. For example, you can have numbers centre-justified in their cells.

When text, a number, a formula or an **Excel** function is entered into a cell, or reference is made to the contents of a cell by the cell address, then the content of the **Status** bar changes from **Ready** to **Enter**.

This status can be changed back to **Ready** by completing an entry and pressing **Enter**. To find the 1st quarter total income from consultancy, activate cell E4, type

=b4+c4+d4

and press **Enter**. The total first quarter income is added (£45,000) and placed in cell E4.

Saving a Workbook

To save your work before leaving the program, tap or click the **Save** button on the **Quick Access** toolbar. If this is the first time you use this facility, you will be asked to provide a filename and a location. Another way is to tap or click the command button and select the **Save As** command from the displayed **Backstage** screen, which gives you more control on the saving operation, as shown in Fig. 8.24 below.

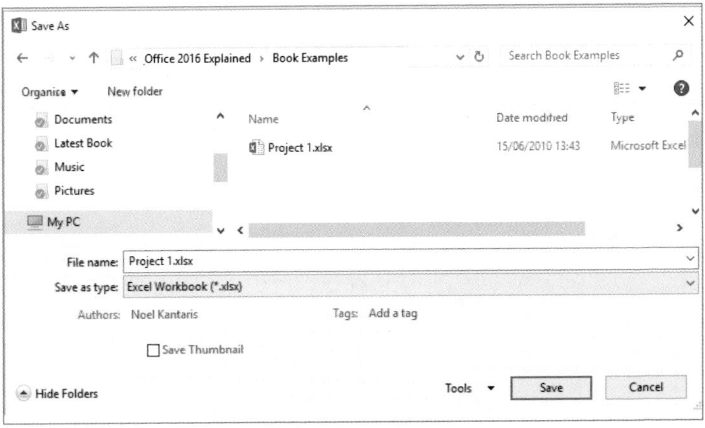

Fig. 8.24 Saving a Workbook.

Above I show the action (giving the workbook the filename **Project 1**), and the result of that action. If you tap or click the down-arrowhead against the **Save as type** box, you'll see the full list of available saving options. Try it.

9

Excel Functions & Page Setup

Opening an Excel File

To open a previously saved file in **Excel**, select it from the **Recent** list, shown in Fig. 9.1 or click the **Open Other Workbooks** (at the bottom of the list) which displays the **Open** screen, also shown on the composite in Fig. 9.1.

Next either find your work on **OneDrive** or use **This PC** option to navigate to the folder where you saved your work (in my case, **Documents**, **Books**, **Office 2016 Explained**, **Book Examples**). In your case this might be different.

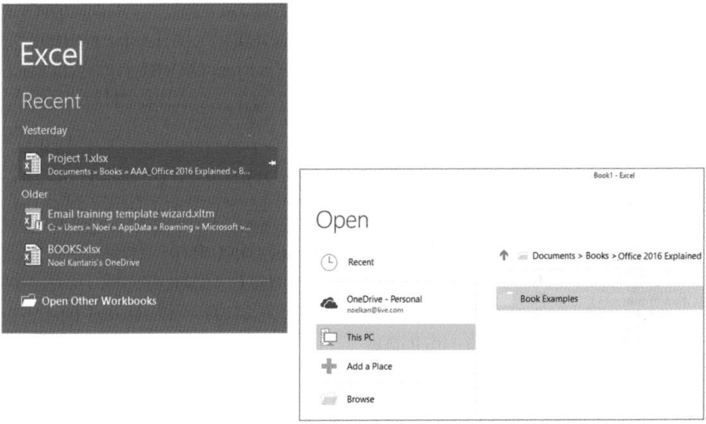

Fig. 9.1 Two Different Ways of Opening Excel Files.

In what follows, I will use the contents in **Project 1** to show you how to use functions and apply enhancements to it. So, before going any further, make sure that **Project 1** is opened in **Excel**.

Excel Functions

In the example **Project 1** (see Chapter 8), writing a formula that adds the contents of three columns is not too difficult or lengthy a task. But imagine having to add 20 columns! For this reason **Excel** has an inbuilt summation function which can be used to add any number of columns (or rows).

To illustrate how this and other functions can be used, activate cell E4 of **Project 1** and press **Del** to clear the cell of its formula, then tap or click the **Formulas**, **Insert Function** button on the **Ribbon** shown here to the left.

If the function you require appears on the displayed dialogue box under **Select a function**, choose it, otherwise use the **Search for a function** text box or select the appropriate class from the list under **Or select a category**.

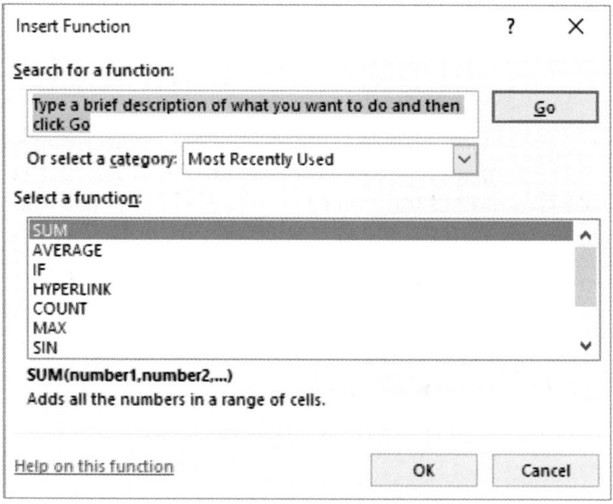

Fig. 9.2 Selecting a Function.

Choosing the **SUM** function and pressing **OK**, displays the screen in Fig. 9.3 shown on the next page. Note that the arguments in this case are given as B4:D4 in the **Number1** box and the actual result of the calculation is displayed lower down.

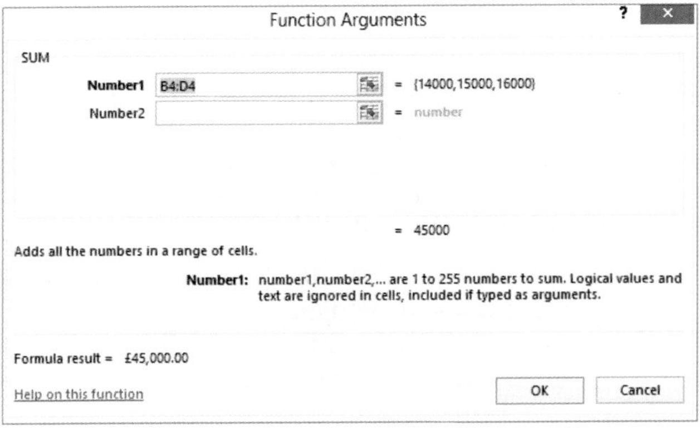

Fig. 9.3 The Function Arguments Dialogue Box.

Pressing the **OK** button, causes the function to be pasted into cell E4, but only the formula result is displayed in the cell. If you tap or click in the **Number2** box you can select another cell range to be summed. The overall result appears at the bottom of the box, as shown above.

The AutoSum Button

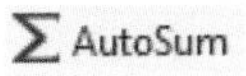

With addition, there is a better and quicker way of letting **Excel** work out the desired result. To illustrate this, select the cell range B6:E12, which contains the 'Costs' to be added up. To add these in both the horizontal and vertical directions, include in the selected range an empty column to the right of the numbers and an empty row below the numbers, as shown in Fig. 9.4.

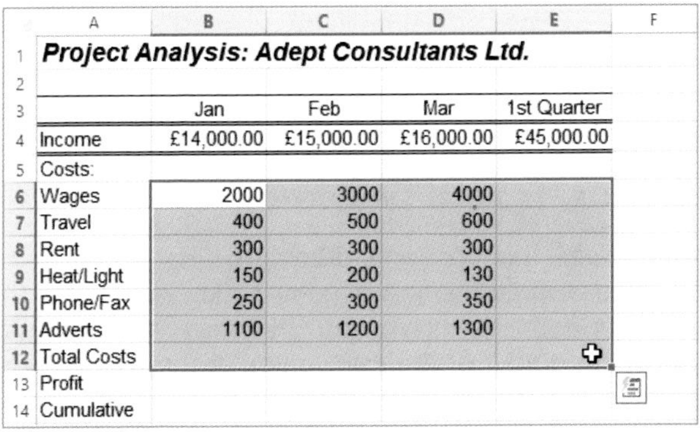

	A	B	C	D	E	F
1	***Project Analysis: Adept Consultants Ltd.***					
2						
3		Jan	Feb	Mar	1st Quarter	
4	Income	£14,000.00	£15,000.00	£16,000.00	£45,000.00	
5	Costs:					
6	Wages	2000	3000	4000		
7	Travel	400	500	600		
8	Rent	300	300	300		
9	Heat/Light	150	200	130		
10	Phone/Fax	250	300	350		
11	Adverts	1100	1200	1300		
12	Total Costs					
13	Profit					
14	Cumulative					

Fig. 9.4 Selecting Cells.

Pressing the **Formulas**, **AutoSum** command button, shown on the previous page, inserts the result of the summations in the empty columns and rows, as shown in Fig. 9.5.

	A	B	C	D	E	F
1	***Project Analysis: Adept Consultants Ltd.***					
2						
3		Jan	Feb	Mar	1st Quarter	
4	Income	£14,000.00	£15,000.00	£16,000.00	£45,000.00	
5	Costs:					
6	Wages	2000	3000	4000	9000	
7	Travel	400	500	600	1500	
8	Rent	300	300	300	900	
9	Heat/Light	150	200	130	480	
10	Phone/Fax	250	300	350	900	
11	Adverts	1100	1200	1300	3600	
12	Total Costs	4200	5500	6680	16380	
13	Profit					
14	Cumulative					

Fig. 9.5 The Result of the AutoSum Action.

The selected range remains selected so that any other formatting can be applied by simply pressing the appropriate **Ribbon** buttons.

Next, tapping or clicking the down-arrowhead in the **Autosum** button, displays a list of alternative options, as shown in Fig. 9.6. From this list you can choose to calculate the **Average**, **Count Numbers** in the entries, find the **Max** or **Min** values in a row or column, or open the **Insert Function** dialogue box discussed earlier by selecting the **More Functions** option.

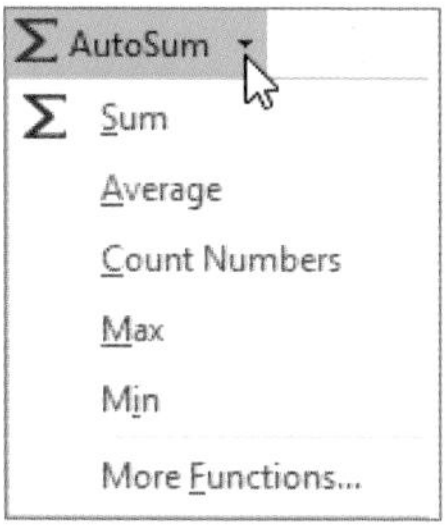

Fig. 9.6 AutoSum Menu.

Now complete the insertion of formulas in the rest of the worksheet, noting that 'Profit', in B13, is the difference between 'Income' and 'Total Cost', calculated by the formula **=b4-b12**. To complete the entry, this formula should be copied using the 'fill by example' method discussed in Chapter 8, page 151, into the three cells to its right.

The 'Cumulative' entry in cell B14 should be a simple reference to cell B13, that is **=b13**, while in cell C14 should be **=b14+c13**. Similarly, the latter formula is copied into cell D14 using the 'fill by example' method.

Next, format the entire range B6:E14 by selecting the range and clicking the **Home**, **Number**, **Accounting** option, shown here. This option puts the £ sign at the extreme left of each cell.

If you make any mistakes and copy formats or information into cells you did not mean to, use the **Undo** button on the **Quick Access** toolbar. The data in your worksheet, up to this point, should look like that in Fig. 9.7.

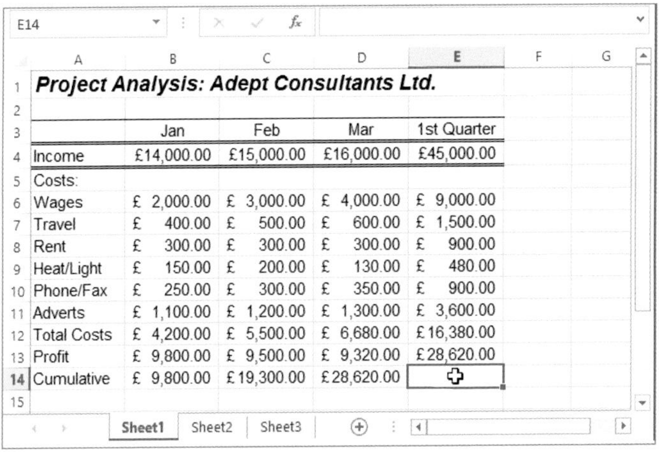

	A	B	C	D	E
1	*Project Analysis: Adept Consultants Ltd.*				
2					
3		Jan	Feb	Mar	1st Quarter
4	Income	£14,000.00	£15,000.00	£16,000.00	£45,000.00
5	Costs:				
6	Wages	£ 2,000.00	£ 3,000.00	£ 4,000.00	£ 9,000.00
7	Travel	£ 400.00	£ 500.00	£ 600.00	£ 1,500.00
8	Rent	£ 300.00	£ 300.00	£ 300.00	£ 900.00
9	Heat/Light	£ 150.00	£ 200.00	£ 130.00	£ 480.00
10	Phone/Fax	£ 250.00	£ 300.00	£ 350.00	£ 900.00
11	Adverts	£ 1,100.00	£ 1,200.00	£ 1,300.00	£ 3,600.00
12	Total Costs	£ 4,200.00	£ 5,500.00	£ 6,680.00	£ 16,380.00
13	Profit	£ 9,800.00	£ 9,500.00	£ 9,320.00	£ 28,620.00
14	Cumulative	£ 9,800.00	£ 19,300.00	£ 28,620.00	
15					

Fig. 9.7 The Completed 1st Quarter Worksheet.

Finally, use the **File**, **Save As** option to save the resultant worksheet as **Project 2** in the same folder as **Project 1**.

Formulas and Functions

As you have seen, **Formulas** in **Excel** are equations that perform calculations on values in your worksheet. A formula starts with an equal sign (=) and can contain any of the following:

Functions – Built-in **Excel** formulas that take a value or values, perform an operation and return a value or values. Use functions to simplify and shorten worksheet formulas.

References – Addresses of cells in the worksheet.

Operators – Signs or symbols that specify the type of calculation to perform in an expression. Operators can be mathematical, comparison, logical or reference.

Constants – Values that are not calculated and, therefore, do not change.

Excel Functions

Excel's functions are built-in formulas that perform specialised calculations. Their general format is:

NAME(arg1, arg2, ...)

where **NAME** is the function name, and **arg1**, **arg2**, etc., are the arguments required for the evaluation of the function. Arguments must appear in a parenthesised list as shown above and their exact number depends on the function being used. However, some functions, such as **PI**, do not require arguments and are used without parentheses.

There are four types of arguments used with functions: **Numeric** values, **Range** values, **String** values and **Conditions**, the type used being dependent on the type of function. **Numeric** value arguments can be entered either directly as numbers, as a cell address, a cell range name or as a formula. **Range** value arguments can be entered either as a range address or a range name, while **String** value arguments can be entered as an actual value (a string in double quotes), as a cell address, a cell name, or a formula. **Condition** arguments normally use logical operators or refer to an address containing a logic formula.

Excel has many types of functions including financial, logical, text, date and time, lookup and reference, mathematical and trigonometric, statistical, database, engineering and information. Each type requires its own number and type of arguments.

Finally, you can also use the **Formulas** tab to place and work with formulas and functions. As shown in Fig. 9.8 below, the main function types have their own **Ribbon** buttons (to see these as they are displayed here, maximise the **Excel** window). Just tapping or clicking these and pointing to a function on one of their lists, gives you a good overview of what the function does and what parameters it needs.

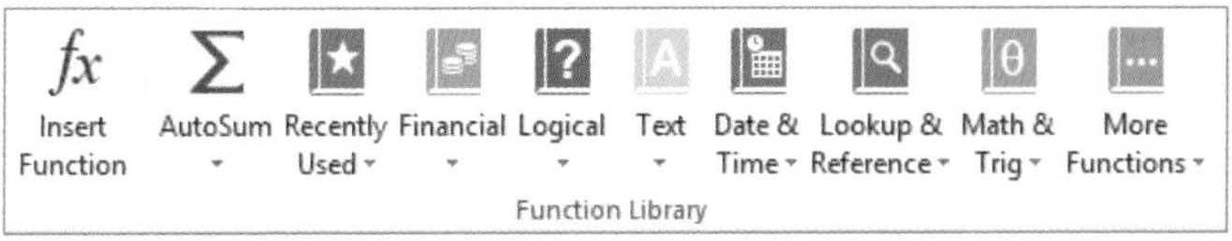

Fig. 9.8 The Formulas Function Library.

Building a Formula

You can enter formulas straight into a selected cell, or into the **Formula** bar, which is re-sizeable. In Fig. 9.9, I will step through the procedure of building a simple formula in cell D3, to average the contents of cells B2 to B4, normally referred to as the range (B2:B4) with explanation given on the next page.

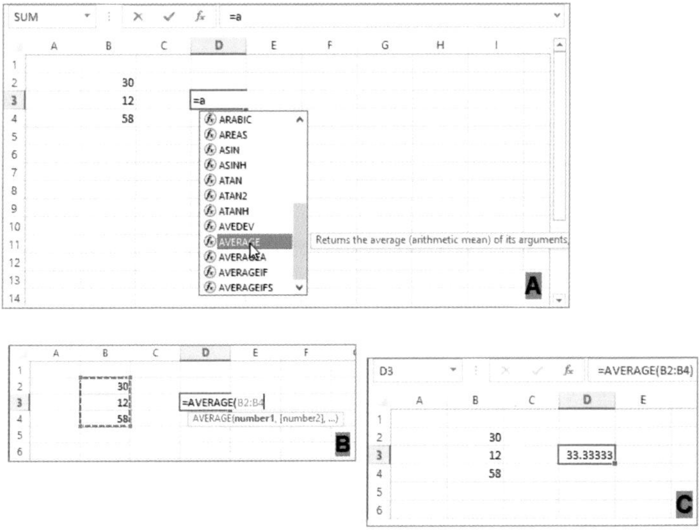

Fig. 9.9 Building a Simple Formula with a Function.

In **A** (see previous page), type **=a** into cell D3. **Excel**, expecting a formula with '**a**' as its first letter and opens the **Formula AutoComplete** feature listing all such formulas.

Next, select **AVERAGE** from the displayed list, then choose the range B2:B4, which (refer to **B** on the previous page), enters the function and the selected range into the formula, with a syntax pop-up below it to help you. Inserting the end bracket and pressing **Enter**, completes the operation.

The result is shown in cell D3 and the completed formula in the **Formula** bar when the cell is selected, as shown in **C** on the previous page. The function use in **Excel** is very intuitive!

Printing a Worksheet

The quickest way of printing your work is to load the worksheet you want to print into **Excel**, say **Project 2**, tap or click the FILE command button, then tap or click the **Print** button to display the screen shown in Fig. 9.10 below.

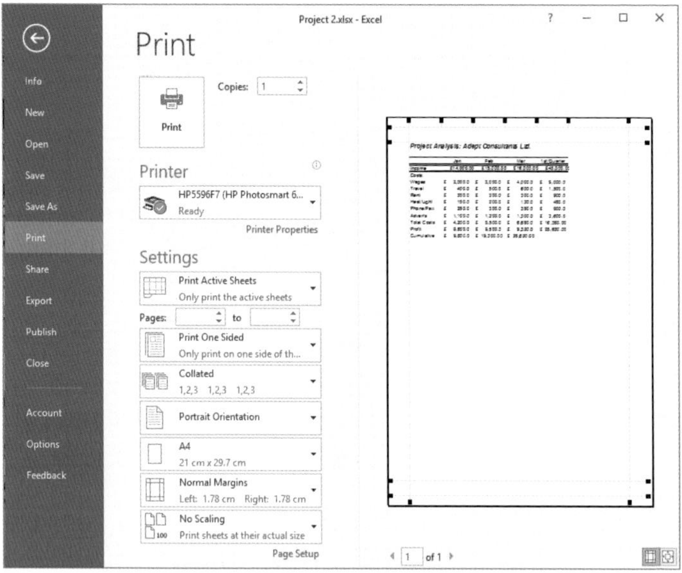

Fig. 9.10 Print Menu Options.

Note the **Preview** pane on the right of the displayed screen. What you see here is dependent on the selected printer. You can also change the number of copies to be printed, the settings, the orientation and paper size. Use the **Zoom to page** button, to be found at the bottom right corner of the **Print** screen, to get the best view of your work and the **Print** button to print it.

Printing a Large Worksheet

As an example of choosing a smaller print area than the current worksheet, open the **Project 2** file, if not already opened, and select the range A1:E12 by highlighting it, then tap or click the **Print Area** command button on the **Page Layout** tab, shown in Fig. 9.11, and choose the **Set Print Area** option on the drop-down menu. Now selecting the **File**, **Print** button, displays only the highlighted area of the worksheet in the **Preview** screen.

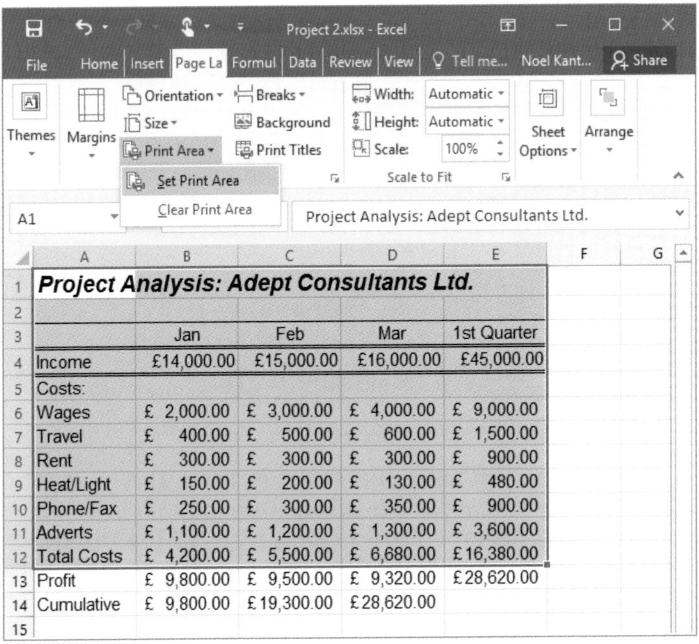

Fig. 9.11 Adjusting Page Settings.

Enhancing a Worksheet

You can make your work look more professional by applying various enhancements, such as single and double line cell borders, shading certain cells and adding meaningful headers and footers as I show later in this chapter.

Formatting Cells

With **Excel** it is easy to enhance cells by colouring them appropriately. To do this, select the range you want to format, say A5:A14, then click the **Format** button on the **Home**, **Cells** group, and select **Format Cells** (you'll have to scroll down) from the displayed drop-down menu, as shown in Fig. 9.12.

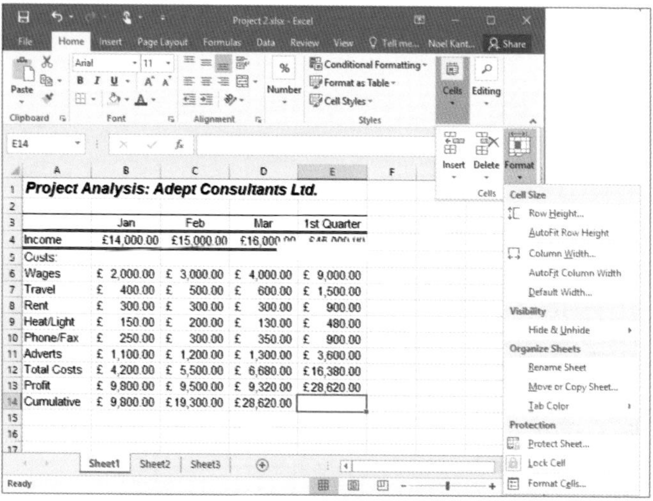

Fig. 9.12 Selecting and Formatting Cells.

This opens the **Format Cells** dialogue box with a number of tabs which can be used to apply different types of formatting to cells. Using the **Fill** tab and clicking the **Fill Effects** button, opens a similarly named dialogue box in which you can select one or two colours, the shading styles and variants of your preference. I gave the **Income** and **Months** labels (A4) and (B3:E3) a bluish tint and repeated the process, but this time gave the **Costs** labels (A5:A14) a pinkish tint.

Below I show the **Format Cells** screen and the result of using the **Fill Effects** screen in a composite in Fig. 9.13.

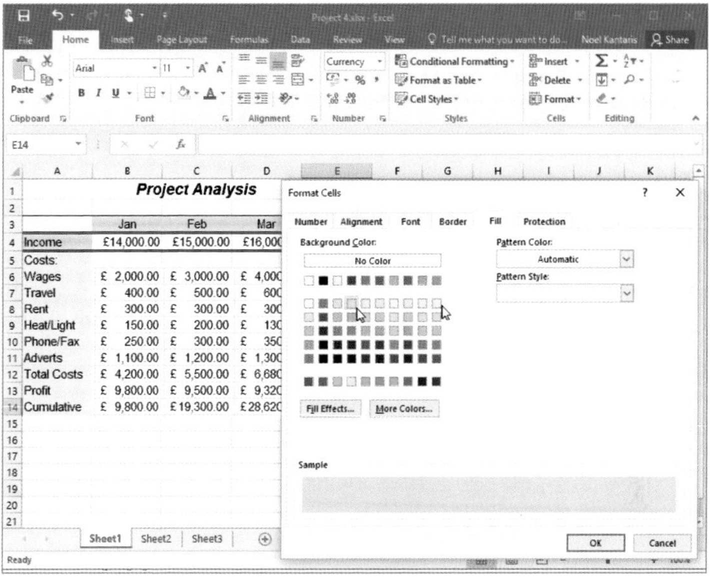

Fig. 9.13 Selecting Fill Effects.

Next, reduce the title of the worksheet to 'Project Analysis', then centre it within the range A1:E1, by first selecting the range, then using the **Home**, **Alignment**, **Merge** button and selecting **Merge and Center**, as shown in the composite in Fig. 9.14. This centres the title within the selected range. Finally, save the worksheet as **Project 3**, before going on.

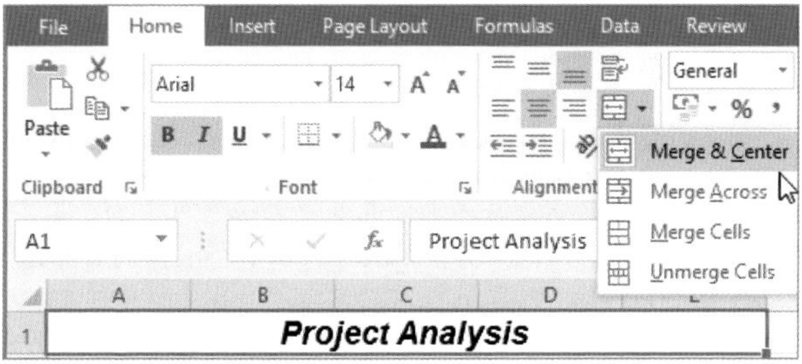

Fig. 9.14 Selecting the Merge & Center Alignment option.

Next, highlight the cell range B6:E14, tap or click the down-arrowhead against **Accounting** in the **Home**, **Number** group and select **Currency** from the drop-down menu, as shown in the composite in Fig. 9.15 below. This places the £ sign infront of each number in the selected range.

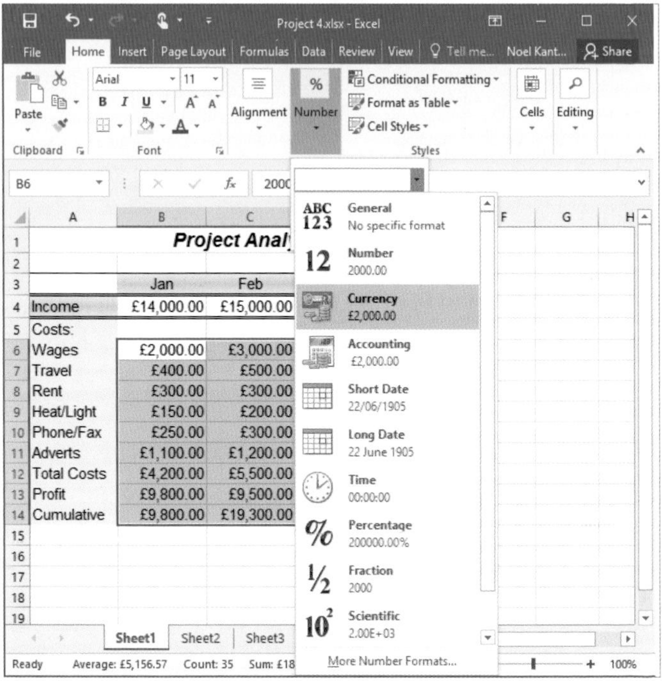

Fig. 9.15 Selecting to Display Numbers in the Currency Format.

When you are satisfied that all is as it should be, tap or click

the **Save** button on the **Quick Access Toolbar** to save your work under the current filename. However, if you are not sure, and want to check later, then you could always use the **Save As** button and give your work a temporary filename (such as **Project 3a**) until you verify that your worksheet is identical to the one above. When that is done, use the **File**, **Info** option, examine the contents of the displayed screen, then tap or click the file location near the top of the screen and select **Open File Location** from the drop-down menu. You can then rename the temporary file.

Page Setup

Before printing a worksheet you should check and, if necessary, change the print settings. Most of the commands for this are in the **Page Layout**, **Page Setup** group shown here in Fig. 9.16 when **Excel** is maximised.

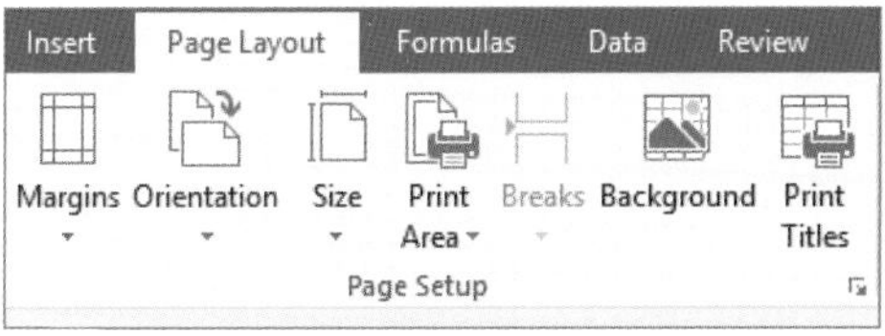

Fig. 9.16 The Page Setup Group.

Next, open **Project 3**, unless already opened, and tap or click the **Dialogue Box Launcher** of the **Page Setup** group to display the screen in Fig. 9.17, with the **Page** tab open.

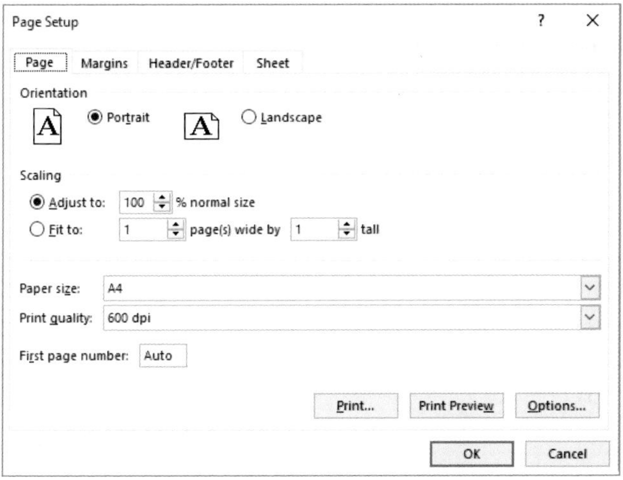

Fig. 9.17 Adjusting Page Settings.

A useful feature of **Excel** is the **Scaling** facility shown in the above dialogue box. Set the **Adjust to % normal size** to 130. Further, you can select to print actual size or a percentage of it, or you can choose to fit your worksheet on to one page which allows **Excel** to scale your work automatically.

In the **Margins** tab, I set the **Center on page** setting to **Horizontally** and clicked the **Header/Footer** tab to display Fig. 9.18.

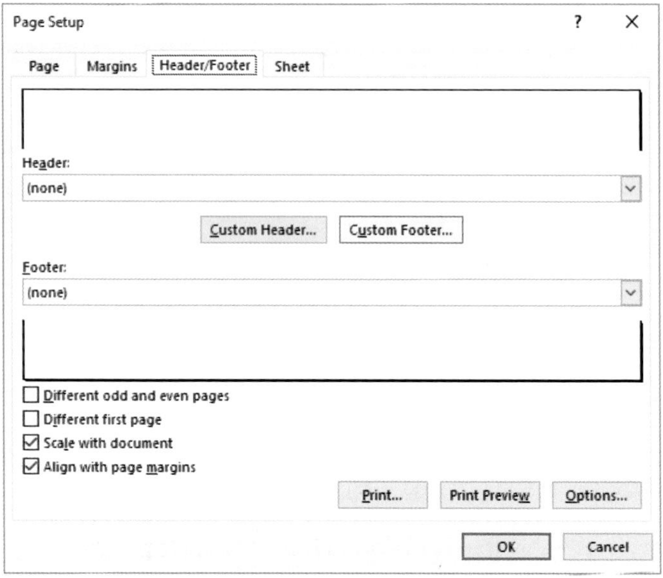

Fig. 9.18 The Header/Footer Tab Settings.

Header and Footer Icons and Codes

Clicking the **Custom Header** button opens the **Header** box shown in Fig. 9.19 on the next page.

You can type text into any of the three boxes, or click on one of the buttons. **Sheet Name**, for example, inserts the **&[Tab]** code which has the effect of inserting the sheet name of the current active sheet at the time of printing. The first icon button displays the **Font** dialogue box, while the others display the following codes:

Code	***Action***
&[Page]	Inserts a page number.
&[Pages]	Inserts the total number of pages.
&[Date]	Inserts the current date.
&[Time]	Inserts the current time.
&[File]	Inserts the filename of the worksheet.

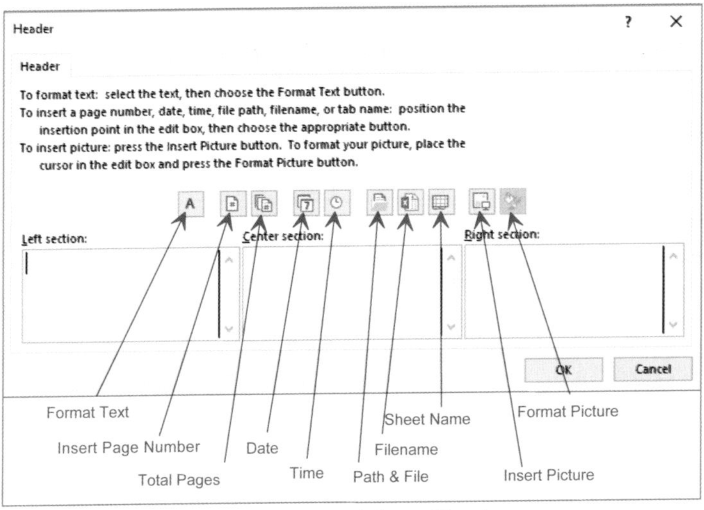

Fig. 9.19 Customising a Header.

On the **Left** and **Right** sections, use the **Format Text** button and type the displayed text in Arial 10 bold, while on the **Center section**, use the **Insert Page Number** button, then tap or click **OK** to return you to the **Page Setup** screen.

Next, use the **Ribbon** command **View**, **Page Layout**, to display the screen in Fig. 9.20.

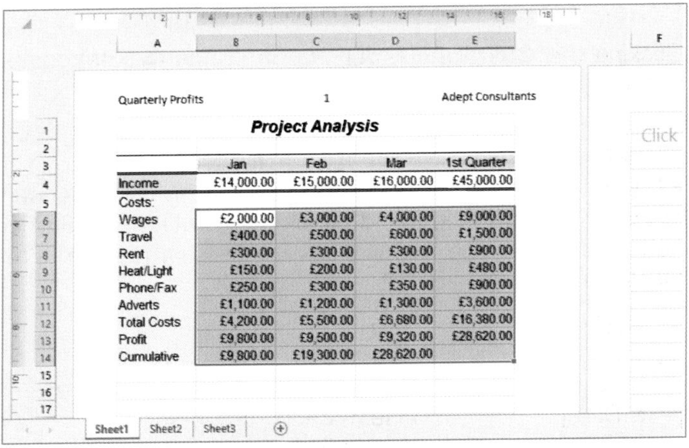

Fig. 9.20 The Page Layout View.

When all is as it should be, save your work under the filename **Project 4** before going on to print it to paper.

* * *

In the next chapter I'll use an example to show you how to link worksheets to create a 3-D workbook, before discussing charts and how to customise and save them.

* * *

10

Excel 3-D Workbooks & Charts

In **Excel**, a **Workbook** is a 3-dimensional file made up with a series of flat 2-dimensional sheets stacked 'on top of each other'. As mentioned previously, each separate sheet in a file has its own **Tab** identifier at the bottom of the screen. Ranges can be set to span several different sheets to build up 3-dimensional blocks of data. These blocks of data can then be manipulated, copied, etc. A cell can reference any other cell in the file, no matter what sheet it is on, and an extended range of functions can be used to process these 3-D ranges.

Creating a Workbook

To demonstrate these ideas, I'll use the **Project 4** worksheet, but make sure that the **View**, **Normal** command buttons is pressed before proceeding with the copying.

I will now fill another three sheets behind the present one, in order to include information about 'ADEPT Consultants' trading during the other three quarters of the year. The easiest way of doing this is by copying the information in Sheet1, including the formatting and all formulas, onto the other three sheets, then edit the numerical information in these appropriately.

Excel has a facility which allows you to copy a sheet into a workbook. There are two ways of doing this: (a) using the **Ribbon** and (b) using a pointer, such as a finger, or a mouse.

With the **Ribbon**, highlight the sheet you want to copy, then use the **Home**, **Clipboard**, **Copy** command, move to a blank sheet and use the **Home**, **Clipboard**, **Paste**, **Keep Source Column Widths** command, as shown in Fig. 10.1 on the next page. This method also retains the formatting.

With your finger or mouse, make the sheet you want to copy the current sheet, then touch and hold or right-click the actual sheet tab (sheet identifier) to display Fig. 10.2. Next, selecting the **Move or Copy** option, displays a further screen as shown in Fig, 10.3.

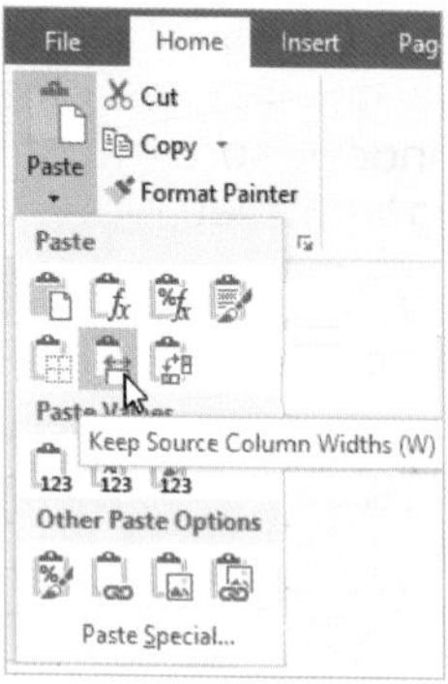

Fig. 10.1 Pasting a Copied Sheet.

Fig. 10.2 Contextual Menu.

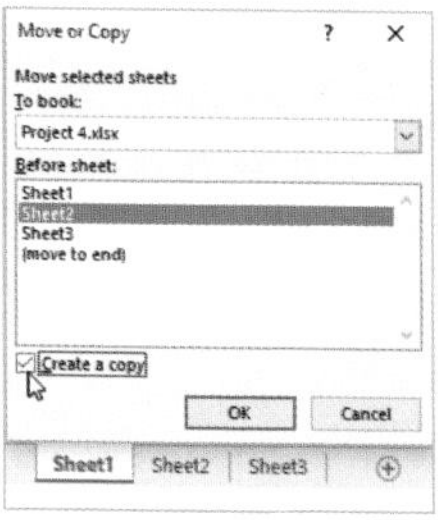

Fig. 10.3 The Move or Copy Box.

Make sure you select to insert the copied sheet before **Sheet 2**, and also tick the **Create a copy** box in Fig. 10.3, before selecting the **OK** button.

When you have three copies placed on your workbook, double-tap or double-click the **Tabs** of **Sheet1** and the three new sheets in succession and rename them '**Quarter 1**', '**Quarter 2**', etc., then change the formatting of cells E4:E14, as well as those of B12:D14, of all the worksheets, so they stand out from the rest, as shown in Fig. 10.4 on the next page.

To achieve the above suggestions, use the **Home**, **Format Cells** command, then the **Fill** and **Border** tabs of the **Format Cells** dialogue box. In addition, use the **Format**, **Format Cells** command and in the **Format Cells** dialogue box use the **Fill Effects** button and select a **Horizontal** shading style variant (with the colours chosen previously) to reproduce what is shown in Fig. 10.4 for all the quarters of the year. I leave it to you to experiment with all these suggestions.

The correct contents of the second sheet should be as shown in Fig. 10.4. Be extra careful, from now on, to check the identification **Tab** at the bottom of the window, so as not to get the sheets mixed up and edit the wrong worksheet!

	A	B	C	D	E
1		***Project Analysis - 2nd Quarter***			
2					
3		Apr	May	Jun	2nd Quarter
4	Income	£15,500.00	£16,000.00	£16,500.00	£48,000.00
5	Costs:				
6	Wages	£3,500.00	£4,000.00	£4,500.00	£12,000.00
7	Travel	£500.00	£550.00	£580.00	£1,630.00
8	Rent	£300.00	£300.00	£300.00	£900.00
9	Heat/Light	£150.00	£120.00	£100.00	£370.00
10	Phone/Fax	£300.00	£350.00	£400.00	£1,050.00
11	Adverts	£1,250.00	£1,300.00	£1,350.00	£3,900.00
12	Total Costs	£6,000.00	£6,620.00	£7,230.00	£19,850.00
13	Profit	£9,500.00	£9,380.00	£9,270.00	£28,150.00
14	Cumulative	£9,500.00	£18,880.00	£28,150.00	
16					

Fig. 10.4 The Data for the Second Quarter.

If you make any mistakes in format shading, you can correct it using the **Home**, **Format Painter** command in the **Clipboard** group. Simply move to a cell whose format you want to copy, then tap or click the **Format Painter** icon and move to the cell or cells you want to paste the selected formatting and tap or click.

Next, build two additional sheets for the last two quarters of the year (see below for details on the 3rd and 4th quarters).

	Jul	Aug	Sep	Oct	Nov	Dec
Income	17,000	17,500	18,000	18,500	19,000	19,500
Costs:						
Wages	4,000	4,500	5,000	4,500	5,000	5,500
Travel	600	650	680	630	670	700
Rent	300	300	300	300	300	300
Heat/Light	50	80	120	160	200	250
Phone/Fax	350	380	420	400	420	450
Adverts	1,400	1,450	1,500	1,480	1,500	1,530

After building up the four worksheets (one for each quarter), save the file as **Project 5**.

Linking Sheets

Use the **Home**, **Cells**, **Insert** command and click **Insert Sheet** to place a worksheet in front of the 'stack' of data sheets to show a full year's results. Next, make a copy of the 1st Quarter sheet (using the **Home**, **Copy** button), and place it in the new front sheet (using the **Home**, **Paste** button) as discussed in page 170 (Fig. 10.1) so as to retain all column widths and formatting of cells. Next, highlight cells B3 to E14 and delete the content, then add an extra column to the newly created sheet, say before column C, to give you enough columns for the four quarters plus a column for **Totals**) as shown in Fig. 10.5 below. Finally, rename the worksheet's **Tab** to **Summary**.

I'll now link the summary sheet to the other quarterly data sheets so that the information contained on them is automatically summarised and updated on it. The quarter totals in each Quarter's worksheet (cells E3 to E14) are selected and copied in turn to column B3, C3, D3 and E3. Use the **Home**, **Clipboard**, **Copy** button, then move to the **Summary** sheet and paste each to the appropriate column by tapping or clicking the **Paste** down-arrowhead button and selecting the **Paste Link** icon pointed to in Fig. 10.5.

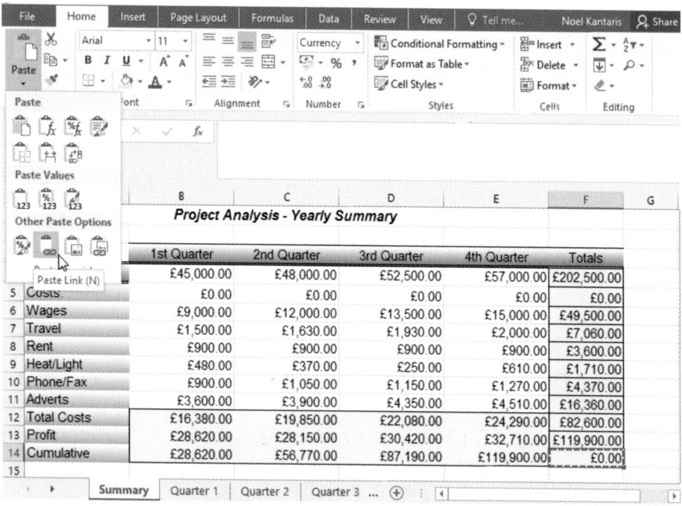

Fig. 10.5 Linked Data in the Summary Sheet.

Do note that empty cells linked with this method, like those in cell row 5 of each quarter, appear as 0 (zero) in the **Summary** sheet. These can be removed with the **Delete** key.

Next, insert appropriate formulas in row 14 to correctly calculate the **Cumulative** values in row 14 and **Totals** in column F of the **Summary** sheet (the total yearly **Profit** should be £119,900 – if not, you have made a mistake). Finally, save the resultant workbook as **Project 6**.

Relative and Absolute Cell Addresses

Entering a mathematical expression into **Excel**, such as the formula in cell C14 which was

=B14+C13

causes **Excel** to interpret it as 'add the contents of the cell one column to the left of the current position, to the contents of the cell one row above the current position'. In this way, when the formula was later copied into cell address D14, the contents of the cell relative to the left position of D14 (i.e. C14) and the contents of the cell one row above it (i.e. D13) were used, instead of the original cell addresses entered in C14. This is relative addressing. To see the effect of relative versus absolute addressing, copy the formula in cell C14 into C16 using the **Copy** and **Paste** buttons. The result is shown in Fig. 10.6.

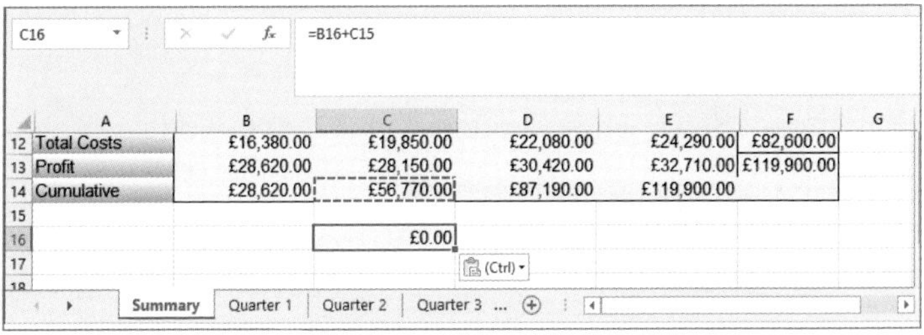

Fig. 10.6 Demonstrating Relative and Absolute Cell Addressing.

Note that in cell C14 the formula was =B14+C13. However, when copied into cell C16 the formula appears as

=B16+C15

This is because it has been interpreted as relative addressing. In this case, no value appears in cell C16 because an attempt is made to add two blank cells. Now change the formula in cell C14 by editing it to

=$B$14+$C$13

which is interpreted as absolute addressing. Copying this formula into cell C16 calculates the correct result. Highlight cell C16 and observe the cell references in its formula; they have not changed from those of cell C14.

When creating a financial model in a spreadsheet it is common practice to put all the control parameters on a sheet of their own. These might be the $/£ exchange rate, or the % rate of inflation for example. Whenever these parameters are needed in a cell formula in the model they should not just be entered straight into the formula, but absolute references should be made to them in the parameter sheet. In this way you can change a parameter in one place on the parameter sheet and see the overall effects when the model is recalculated. The $ sign must prefix both the column reference and the row reference.

Mixed cell addressing is permitted; as for example when a column address reference is needed to be taken as absolute, while a row address reference is not.

Freezing Panes on Screen

With large sheets when you are working in the data area you may not be able to see the label cells associated with that data and it is easy to get very confused.

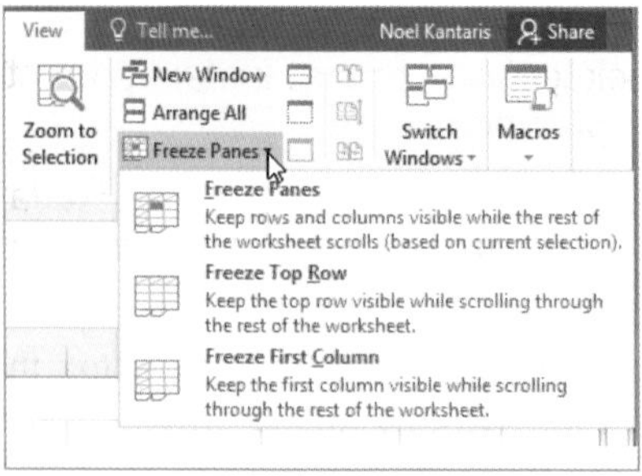

Fig. 10.7 The Freeze Panes Button.

To get over this you can freeze column (or row) labels of a worksheet on screen so that they are always visible. To do this, move the cell pointer to the right of (or below) the column (or row) which you want to freeze and tap or click the **View**, **Window**, **Freeze Panes** command button shown in Fig. 10.7. Selecting **Freeze Panes** from the drop-down menu will place black lines in the sheet to show what is frozen. Then everything to the left of, or above the cell pointer will freeze on the screen when you scroll through the worksheet.

To unfreeze panes, click the **View**, **Window**, **Freeze Panes** button again and select the **Unfreeze Panes** option. This is only available if you have rows or columns frozen.

In **Excel** you cannot use **Page Layout** view with frozen panes in your sheet. If you try, a warning message is displayed as shown in Fig. 10.8. If you click the **OK** button, the sheet will be unfrozen.

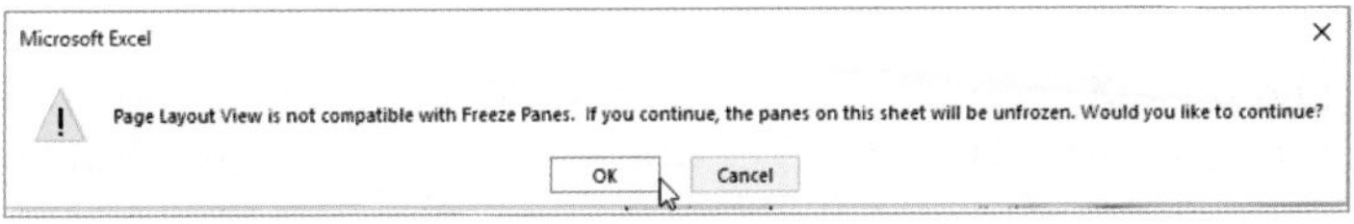

Fig. 10.8 Another Excel Warning Message.

Spreadsheet Charts

Excel makes it very easy to create professional looking charts or graphs from your data. The saying ‘a picture is worth a thousand words’, applies equally well to charts and figures. They allow you to visually see data trends and patterns.

As we shall see, the package can almost instantly create many different chart and graph types:

> Column, Line. Pie, Bar, Area, XY, Stock Surface, Radar, Treemap, Sunburst, Histogram, Boax & Whisker, Waterfall, Combo and several 3-D options of these charts.

These are made available to you once you have selected the data you want to chart from the **Charts** group on the **Insert** tab.

Charts (you can have several per worksheet) can be displayed on screen at the same time as the worksheet from which they were derived, since they are created in their own chart frame and can be embedded anywhere on a worksheet. They can be sent to an appropriate output device, such as a plotter or printer, or copied to another program such as **Word** or **PowerPoint**.

Preparing a Simple Column Chart

To illustrate some of the graphing capabilities of **Excel**, I'll plot the income of the consulting company discussed in the **Project 6** file. If you haven't already done so, you will need to complete the exercise described earlier and have to hand the linked workbook shown in Fig. 10.5, page 172.

Now you need to select the range of the data to be graphed. Such a range does not have to be contiguous for each graph, as with some other spreadsheets. With **Excel**, you select your data from different parts of a sheet with the **Ctrl** key pressed down. This method has the advantage of automatic recalculation should any changes be made to the original data. You could also collect data from different sheets to one 'graphing' sheet by linking them as I showed you earlier with the **Summary** sheet.

If you don't want the chart to be recalculated when you do this, then you must use the **Home**, **Clipboard**, **Copy** and **Paste**, **Paste Special** command buttons and choose the **Values** option from the displayed dialogue box. This copies a selected range to a specified target area of the worksheet and converts formulas to values. This is necessary, as cells containing formulas cannot be pasted directly since it would cause the relative cell addresses to adjust to the new locations; each formula would then recalculate a new value for each cell and end up giving wrong results.

Creating a Column Chart

To obtain a chart of 'Income' versus 'Quarters', select the data in cell range A3:E4, then click the **Insert**, **Charts**, **Column** button, shown in Fig. 10.9 on the next page.

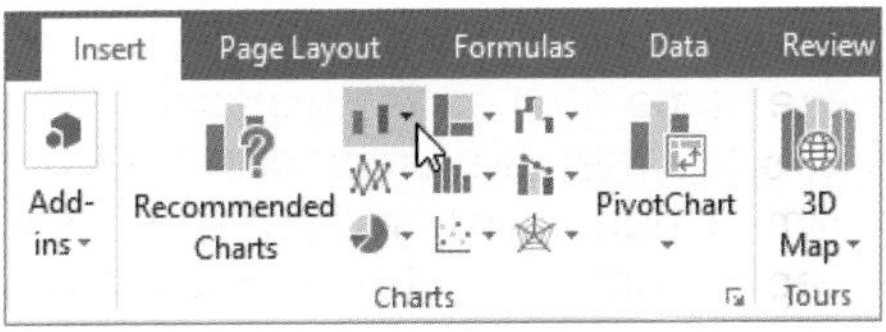

Fig. 10.9 Charting Buttons on the Insert Tab.

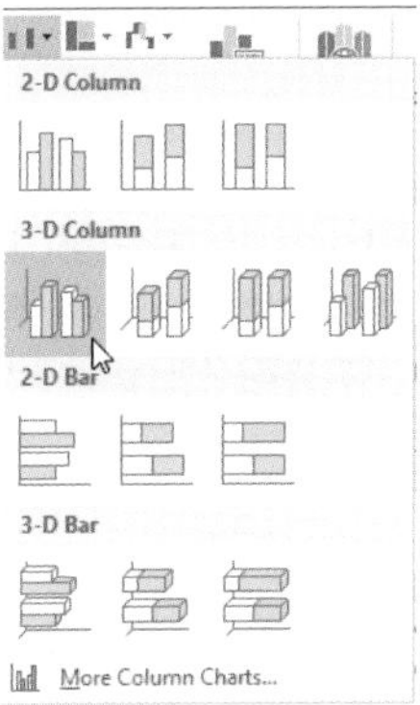

This opens the drop-down gallery of chart options shown in Fig. 10.10. Now select the **3-D Clustered Column** type and just click it to create the chart shown in Fig. 10.11 below. That's all there is to it, just a few clicks!

Fig. 10.10 The Column Charts Gallery.

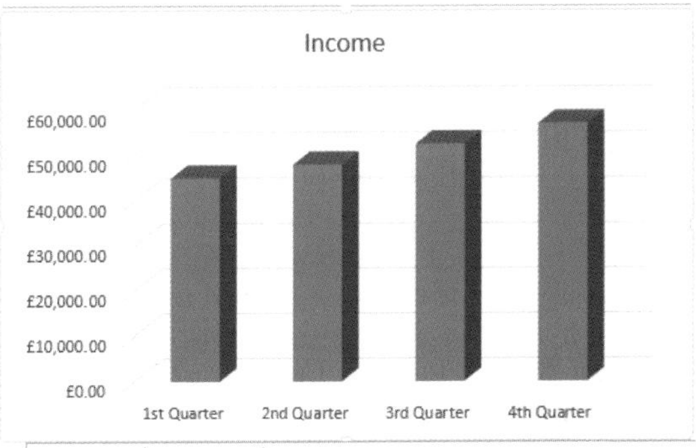

Fig. 10.11 A 3-D Clustered Column Chart.

While the frame containing a chart is selected (you can tell from the presence of the handles around it), you can change its size by dragging the small two-headed  arrow pointer (which appears when the mouse pointer is placed on the handles at the corners or middle of the frame). You can also move the frame and its contents to another position on the worksheet by dragging it to a new position.

The Chart Tools

When you select a chart in **Excel** by clicking it, the **Chart Tools** add the **Design** and **Format** tabs display, as shown below.

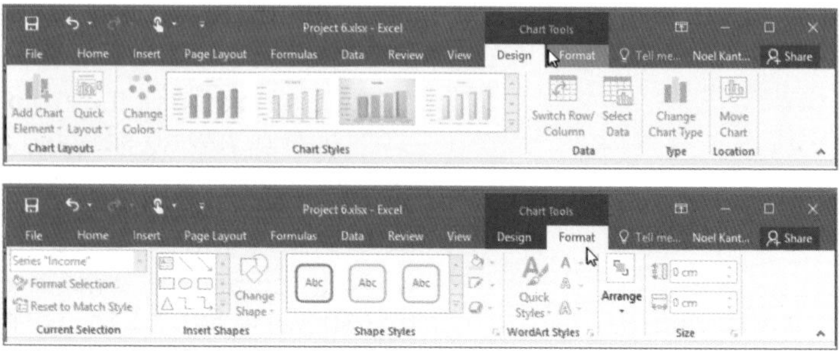

Fig. 10.12 The Design Tab (Top) and the Format Tab (Bottom).

The **Design** tab groups controls for changing **Chart Layouts**, **Chart Styles**, **Data**, **Type** and **Location**, while the **Format** tab groups controls for formatting **Current Selection**, **Insert Shapes**, set **Shape Styles** and **WordArt Styles**, **Arrange** and **Size** objects.

Customising a Chart

Now it is time for you to 'play'. The only way to find out what all the charting controls do is to try them all out. Remember that some options are applied to the chart element that is currently selected, others to the whole chart.

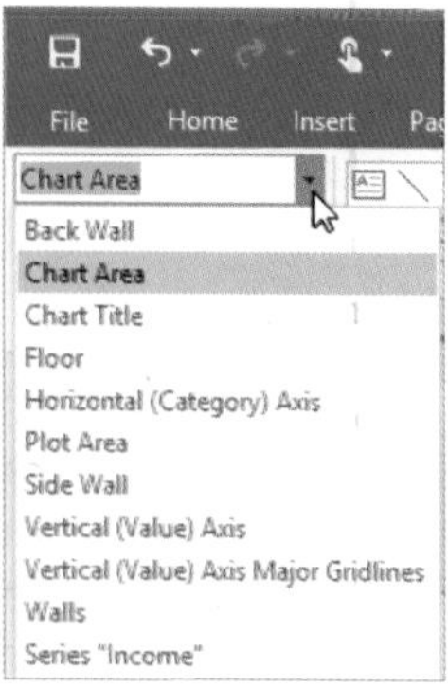

To control what is selected, tap or click the down-arrowhead next to the **Chart Elements** box (below the FILE command button) in the **Current Selection** group of the **Format** tab, and then tap or click the chart element that you want, as shown in Fig. 10.13.

Fig. 10.13 The Chart Elements Box.

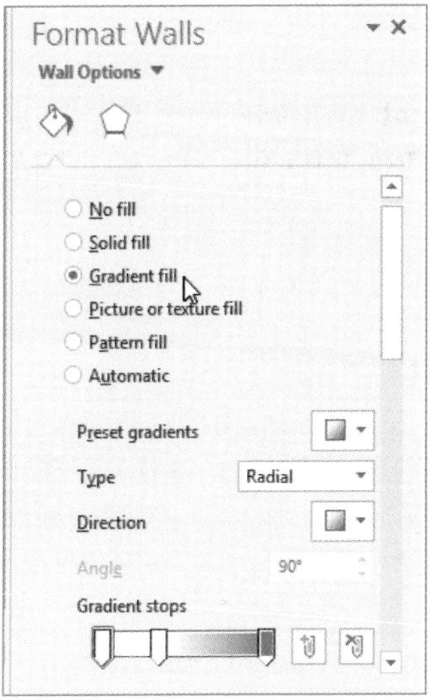

Fig. 10.14 Setting Format Options for Chart Elements.

From the **Chart Elements** box, as you select each element, it opens a **Format** control box on a pane to the right of the screen, shown in Fig. 10.14, in which you select the formatting options you want.

You can also use the **Color** button, having selected a **Gradient fill** option, as shown and use the **Gradient** stops facility to format your chart walls to something similar to that shown in Fig. 10.15. Try it, it can be fun!

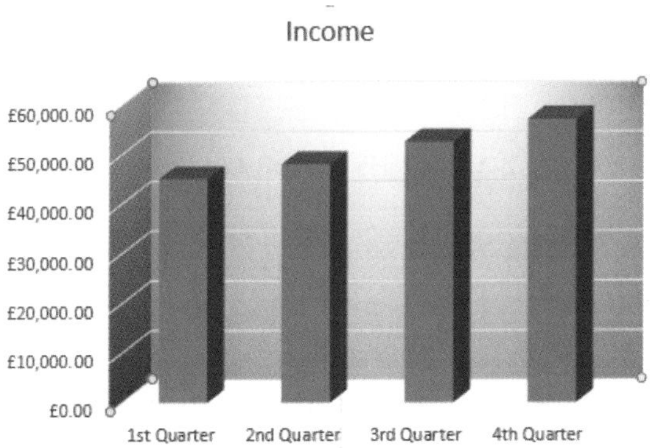

Fig. 10.15 A Gradient 3-D Clustered Column Chart.

You can now change the May income (on the Quarter 2 sheet, Fig. 10.4, page 171) from £16,000 to £26,000, and watch how the change is reflected on the redrawn graph. Finally, revert to the original entry for the May income and then save your work again under the filename **Project 7**.

When Excel creates a chart, it plots each row or column of data in the selected range as a 'data series', such as a group of bars, lines, etc. A chart can contain many data series, but Excel charts data according to the following rules:

1. Selected range contains more rows than columns of data. Excel plots the data series by columns.

   X-axis labels 1st data series 2nd data series 3rd data series

   ↓ ↓ ↓ ↓

2. Selected range contains more columns than rows of data, or the same number of columns and rows. Excel plots the data series by rows.

   Legend labels
   X-axis labels →
   1st data series →
   2nd data series →

If you select a range to chart which includes column and row headings and text above or to the left of the numeric data, then **Excel** uses the text to create the axis labels, legends and title.

Saving Charts

When you save a workbook, the chart or charts you have created are saved with it. However, it is a good idea to locate charts on a separate sheet. To do this, tap or click the **Insert Worksheet** ⊕ tab at the bottom of the screen, move the new sheet in front of the **Summary** tab and rename it **Charts**.

Next, select the chart you want to move and use the **Chart Tools**, **Design**, **Location**, **Move Chart** command to open a dialogue box in which you can specify that the chart should be moved to the **Charts** sheet. Next, go to the **Charts** tab sheet and rename the chart to **Income Column** in the **Name** box and press **Enter**, then save the workbook as **Project 8**

To select a different type of chart, click the **Design**, **Type**, **Change Chart Type** button shown here. **Excel** uses 15 basic chart types plus a variety of 3-D charts as well as templates. With all these, there are more options than you would ever need.

Drawing a Multiple Column Chart

As an exercise, consider a new column chart which deals with the quarterly 'Costs' of Adept Consultants. To achieve this, first choose the **Summary** sheet of workbook **Project 8**, then select the cell range A3:E3, press the **Ctrl** key, and while holding it down, select the costs range A6:E11.

Next, tap or click the **Insert**, **Charts**, **Column** button, select **Clustered Column** from the gallery as pointed to below. The six quarterly costs will be drawn automatically, as displayed in the composite screen dump in Fig. 10.16.

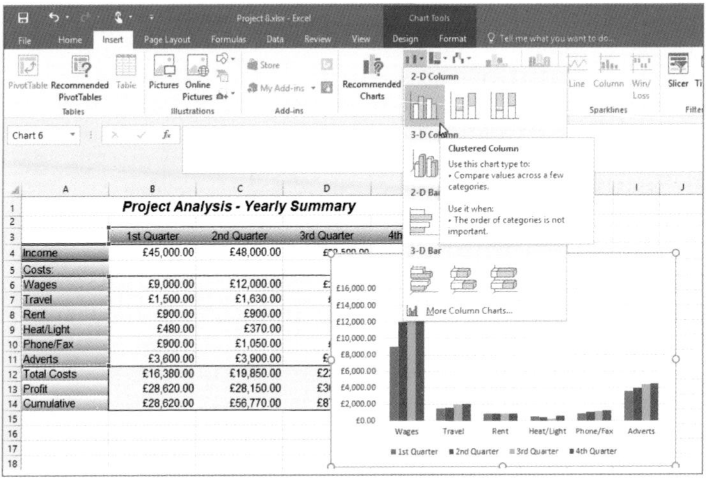

Fig. 10.16 Creating a Costs Column Chart.

Because the selected range contains more rows than columns of data, **Excel** follows the 1st rule of data series selection, which is not really what is expected.

To have the 'quarters' appearing on the x-axis and the 'costs' as the legends, you need to tell **Excel** that your data series is in rows by tapping or clicking the **Design**, **Data**, **Switch Row/Column** button on the **Ribbon**. Immediately this is done the column chart changes to that shown in Fig. 10.17 on the next page.

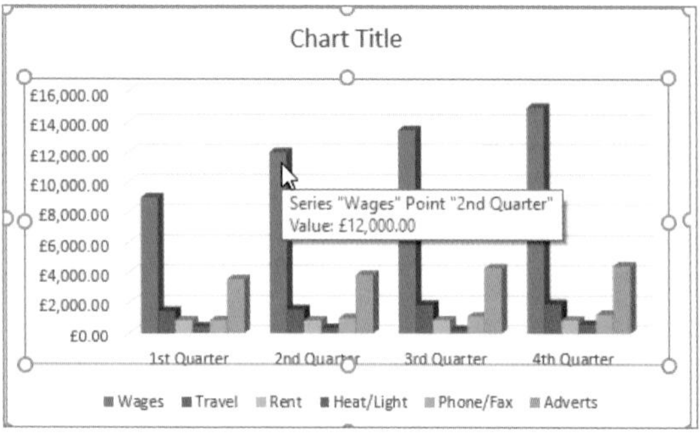

Fig. 10.17 The Costs Column Chart.

Next, change the chart title by over-typing the entry 'Chart Title' in the text box, where it appears in Fig. 10.17, with 'Annual Costs'.

Finally, move the chart to the **Charts** tab sheet, as before, and rename it **Costs Column** and press **Enter**. Finally, save the workbook under the name **Project 8** using the **File**, **Save** command which will overwrite the previous version.

Changing Titles and Labels

To change a title, an axis label or a legend within a chart, tap or click the appropriate area on the chart. This reveals that these are individual objects (they are surrounded by small green circles and squares called 'handles') and you can edit, reposition, or change their font and point size. You can even rotate text within such areas in any direction you like.

To demonstrate some of these options, I'll use the **Costs Column** chart saved in **Project 8**, so get it on screen if you are to follow my suggestions.

To change the font size of a chart title, tap or click in the **Chart Title** area to select it and choose the existing title text (**Annual Costs**). Then simply tap or click the **Home** tab and use any of the **Font** group buttons. In Fig. 10.18, displayed on the next page, you can see what happens when you opt to change the colour of the chart title by tapping or clicking on the **Font Color** A button.

You can also change the colour of the chart title area by tapping or clicking the **Fill Color** button. In this way you can make your chart or axis titles really stand out. There are also options to apply a gradient or a texture to a title.

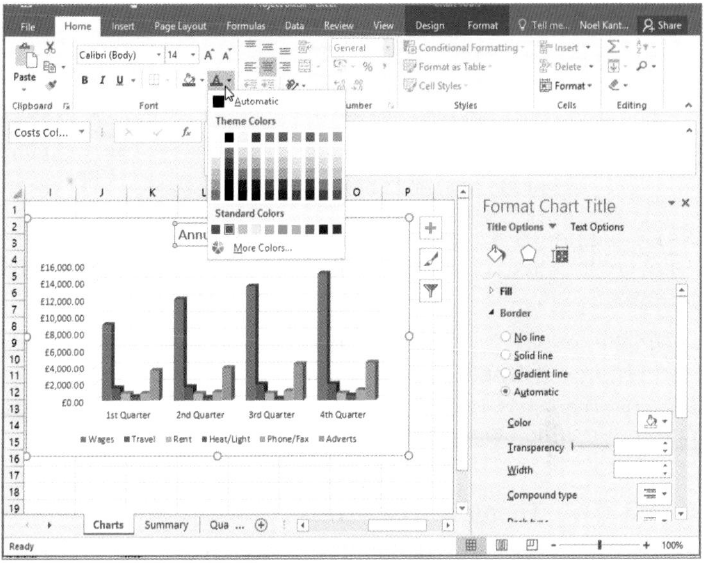

Fig. 10.18 Annotating a Chart.

In the **Chart Tools**, **Format**, **WordArt Styles** group you can also find the **Text Outline** and the **Text Effects** buttons. The latter also includes **Shadow**, **Glow** and **Reflection** effects. The possibilities are almost limitless!

Drawing a Pie Chart

To change the chart type, simply select the chart, click the **Design**, **Type**, **Change Chart Type** button, shown here, and choose from the gallery.

As a last example in chart drawing, I used the data ranges A6:A11 and F6:F11 of the **Summary** worksheet to plot an **Exploded Pie in 3-D** chart, as shown in Fig. 10.19 on the next page.

Next, copy the chart to the **Charts** tab sheet of the workbook, and use the **Chart Tools**, **Design**, **Chart Styles** and select the last option from the displayed list (the one pointed to).

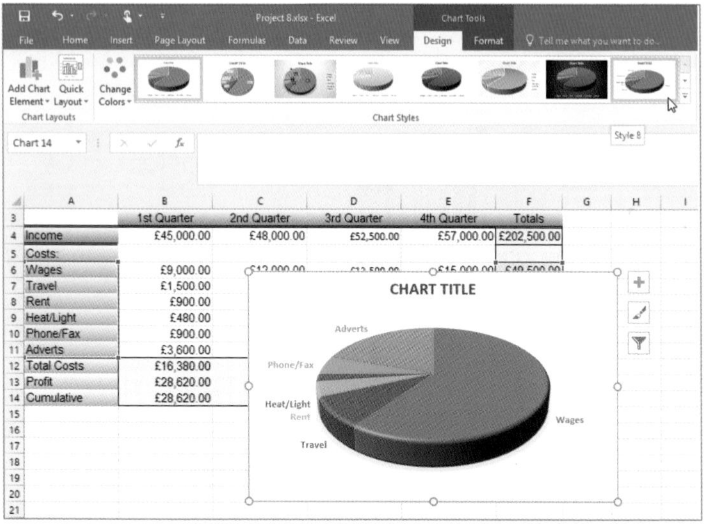

Fig. 10.19 A 3-D Pie Exploded Chart.

Finally, move this pie chart to the **Charts** tap and rename it **Pie Costs**, then drag some slices around and re-size them (you might have to also drag some of the labels), to obtain the pie chart shown in Fig. 10.20 below.

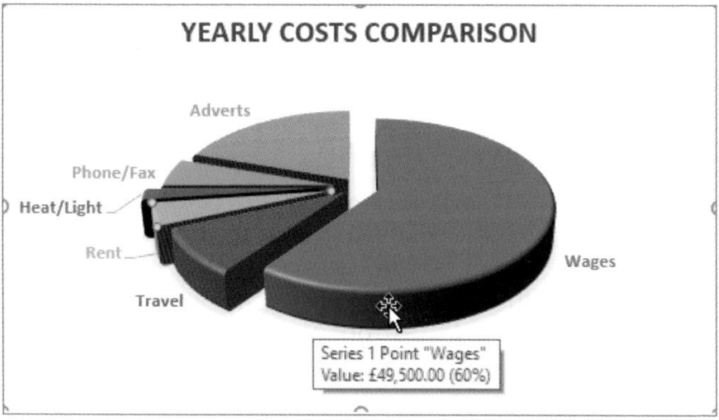

Fig. 10.20 The Final 3-D Pie Exploded Chart.

This chart tells us, for example, that **Wages** for the whole year amount to 60% of the total yearly costs. Other cost categories are also displayed with their appropriate percentages. Pointing to any pie slice, opens a pop-up showing the actual data series, its value and its percentage of the whole.

Sharing & Exporting Excel Workbooks

Just as with **Word** you can share workbooks in a couple of ways. Having opened the workbook in **Excel**, use the **File**, **Share** option to open the screen shown in Fig. 10.21.

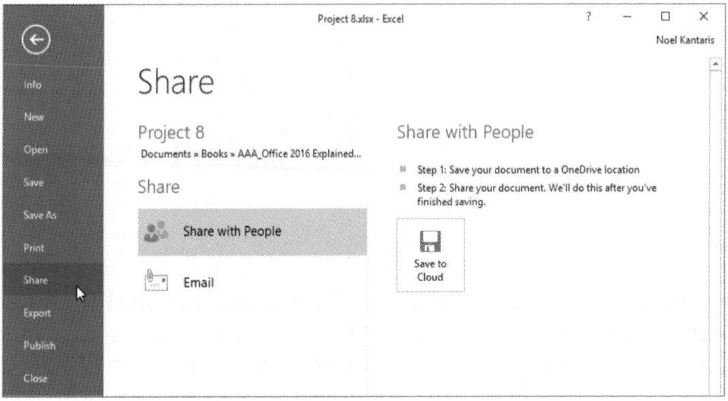

Fig. 10.21 Sharing an Excel Workbook with People.

You can select one of the displayed options which is either to **Invite People** to share it, having first saved your workbook to **OneDrive** location (see page 14), or **Email** the workbook to a friend as an attachment.

The **File**, **Export** option (see Fig. 10.22 on the next page) allows you to create a **PDF/XPS Document** format that you can publish or send to friends in a form that cannot be changed, while the **Change File Type** option, changes the current format of an **Excel** document to an **Excel 97-2003 Workbook**, **OpenDocument Spreadsheet**, **Template**, etc. These facilities are very useful and easy to implement. I leave it to you to explore them further.

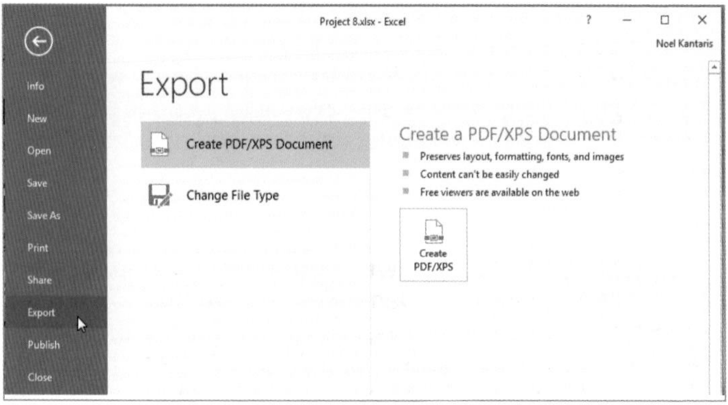

Fig. 10.22 The Excel File Export Screen.

* * *

Excel has many more features than the ones I have introduced here. For example, you could use **Excel**'s database and macro capabilities, and also explore its various tools, such as the **Goal Seek**, **Scenarios**, **Auditing**, and **Solver**. I hope that I have given you sufficient basic knowledge for you to be able to explore these topics by yourself.

* * *

11

The PowerPoint Environment

Microsoft **PowerPoint** provides an easy way to quickly generate powerful, attractive presentations or slide shows, using text, graphics, **SmartArt** graphics, advanced slide layout capabilities and **Style** galleries. With **PowerPoint**, you can save time creating and formatting presentations with **Themes** that give a consistent look and feel across all your **Office** documents.

PowerPoint 2016, just as its predecessors **PowerPoint** 2013 and 2010, takes advantage of the **Ribbon** interface, and includes several other improvements over pre-2010 versions of the program. Some of these, are:

- Using **SmartArt** graphics to create professional visual illustrations of your ideas which are fully editable.
- Use of **Themes**, **Layouts** and **Quick Styles** that offer a wide range of formatting options.
- Manage your **PowerPoint** files from the **Office File Backstage** view.
- Add video, pictures, animation, and make your presentations portable and even turn them easily into a video or slide show.

In addition, **PowerPoint** 2016, just as its predecessor (**PowerPoint** 2013) can be used on tablets and laptops with touch-sensitive screens. The **Presenter View** automatically adapts to your projection set-up. **Themes** come with variations, making it simpler to choose the look you want and collaboration has been improved with the ability to ask questions and get a response.

Starting PowerPoint

I have already discussed in Chapter 1 how to pin shortcuts on the **Taskbar** of all the applications that make up **Office** 2016. This makes it easier to access the individual Applications.

So, to start **PowerPoint**, tap or click its icon on the **Taskbar** shown here on the left, which opens a screen similar to that in Fig. 11.1.

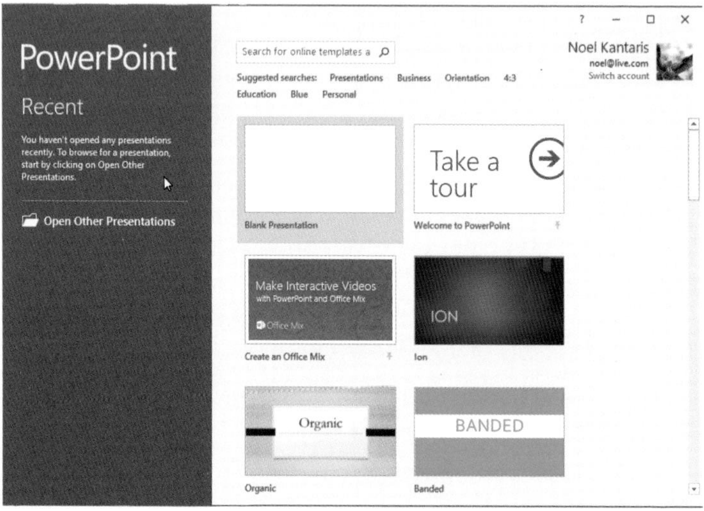

Fig. 11.1 PowerPoint 2016's Opening Screen.

Whether you have used a previous version of **PowerPoint** or not, the first time you use the program, it might be a good idea to **Take a tour** by activating the second tile above.

The PowerPoint Screen

As seen in Fig. 11.1, the opening screen includes a variety of templates, but it is best to open the 'Blank Presentation' screen at this stage, as shown in Fig. 11.2 on the next page.

When **PowerPoint** is loaded and the **Blank Presentation** is opened, a screen displays with a similar File command button, **Quick Access** toolbar, **Title** bar and **Ribbon** to those of **Word** and **Excel**. Obviously there are differences, but that is to be expected as **PowerPoint** serves a different purpose to the other programs.

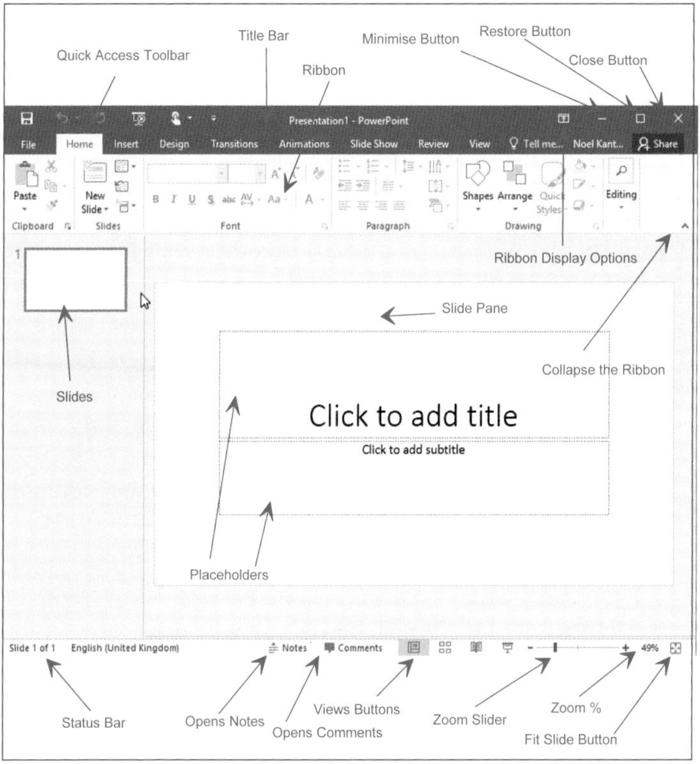

Fig. 11.2 Parts of the Default PowerPoint Opening Screen.

The **Blank Presentation** screen of PowerPoint is shown above. The program follows the usual Microsoft Windows conventions with which you should be very familiar with by now. Scroll bars and scroll buttons only appear when you have more than one slide in your presentation.

The Ribbon

The **PowerPoint** 2016 **Ribbon** has eight tabs, each one with the most used controls grouped on it for the main program actions. For a general description of the **Ribbon**, see Chapter 1, page 5.

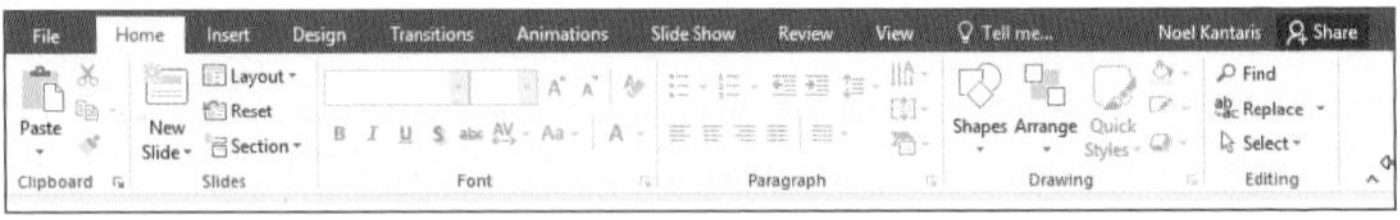

Fig. 11.3 The Home Tab of the PowerPoint 2016 Ribbon.

A quick look at the **Home** tab, displayed in Fig. 11.3, shows that it contains groups for the more common **PowerPoint** activities, such as the **Clipboard**, **Slides**, **Font**, and **Paragraph** groups of commands, together with the **Drawing** and text **Editing** group of commands.

Tapping or clicking a new tab opens a new series of groups, each with its relevant command buttons. The contents of the other tabs allow you to do the following:

- The **Insert** tab enables you to immediately insert Slides, Tables, Images, Illustrations (such as Shapes, SmartArt and Charts), Links, Text based features, Symbols and Media Clips (such as Video and Audio).
- The **Design** tab groups controls for Page Setup, choosing and modifying Themes and controlling the Background of your slides.
- The **Transitions** tab allows you to add and control the Timing and Preview your work.
- The **Animations** tab allows you to add Animation and control its Timing.
- The **Slide Show** tab groups the actions used when Starting a Slide Show, Setting it Up and controlling your Monitors.
- The **Review** tab gives you control for Proofing your presentation and to initiate and track review and approval processes. It lets you add, edit, delete and move between Comments and Notes.

- The **View** tab is where you go to set what you see on the screen. You can choose between Presentation Views, Master Views, Show or Hide screen features, Zoom to different magnifications, change between Color and Grayscale, control the arrangement of windows and run and record Macros.

It is worth spending some time here examining the various **Ribbon** tabs and the commands grouped within them. You could also use the **Tell me** text box on the **Ribbon** to type queries (see next section) to find out specific details.

Getting Help in PowerPoint

Whether you have used a previous version of **PowerPoint** or not, the first time you use the program, it might be a good idea to type a question in the **Tell me** text box, for example, something like 'start presentation', then select an appropriate topic from the drop-down menu, as shown in Fig. 11.4.

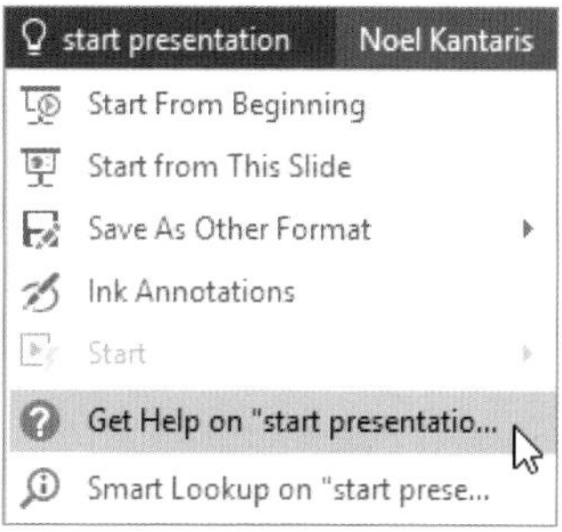

Fig. 11.4 The PowerPoint Help Menu.

After looking at 'Get Help on "start presentation", have a look at the other options listed. I suggest you spend a little time here browsing through the various topics before going on.

In particular, the last option 'Smart Lookup on "start presentation", gives you a list of 'Insights' on how to start a presentation. If anything, it gives you advice on a topic which might be useful to some people!

PowerPoint Templates

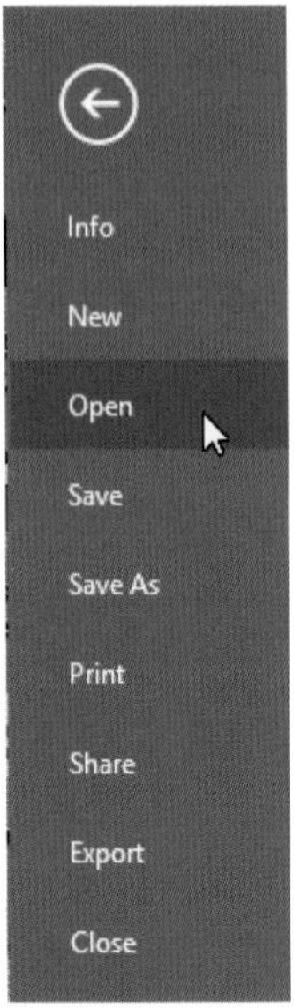

Before we can look at the views of **PowerPoint**'s main working area, we need to have a presentation active in the program. If you have a saved presentation, you can click the File command button and select the **Open** option on the **Backstage** screen, shown here in Fig. 11.5.

If not, press the **New** button to open the **Available Templates and Themes** list, part of which is shown in Fig. 11.6. This lists all the **Templates** that are available to you for creating new presentations, including a large number to be found online.

Fig. 11.5 Part of the Backstage Screen.

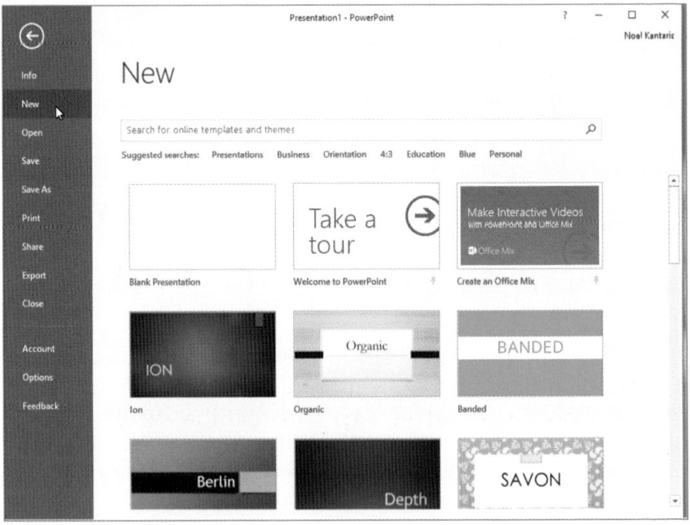

Fig. 11.6 The Available Templates and Themes List.

In addition to the templates displayed in Fig. 11.6, there are seven areas that you can search for specialised templates and themes. These are:

> **Presentations**, **Business**, **Orientation**, **4-3**, **Education**, **Blue**, and **Personal**.

It is worth spending some time looking at what is available here. Some templates contain a full presentation for you to use and practise with. Having examined a group of templates, tap or click the **File**, **New** command button to get back to the **Search** screen.

For now, however, tap or click the **Presentations** menu option and select the **Fresh food presentation** template shown in Fig. 11.7.

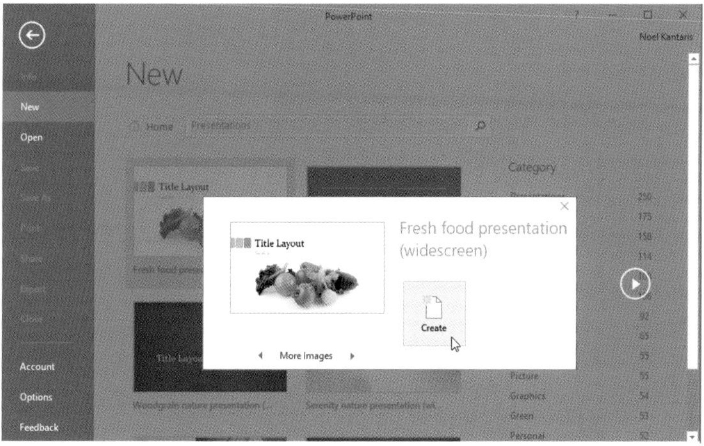

Fig. 11.7 The Fresh Food PowerPoint Presentation.

Next, tap or click the **Create** button on the presentation title, also shown here, to create the presentation displayed in Fig. 11.8 on the next page.

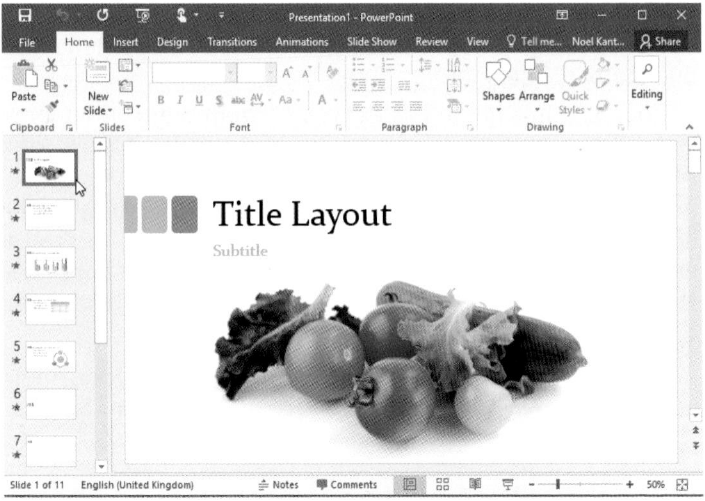

Fig. 11.8 PowerPoint's Window with a Presentation.

You can save the above presentation by tapping or clicking the File command button and selecting the **Save As** option on the **Backstage** screen. In this way, whatever you do to this presentation, you'll still have the original intact.

PowerPoint by default shows a presentation in **Normal** view. If you are following this on your PC, have a look through this presentation. The main pane displays vertical scroll bars which you can use to move through the individual slides, but the current slide will always show completely and be re-scaled if you re-size the program window.

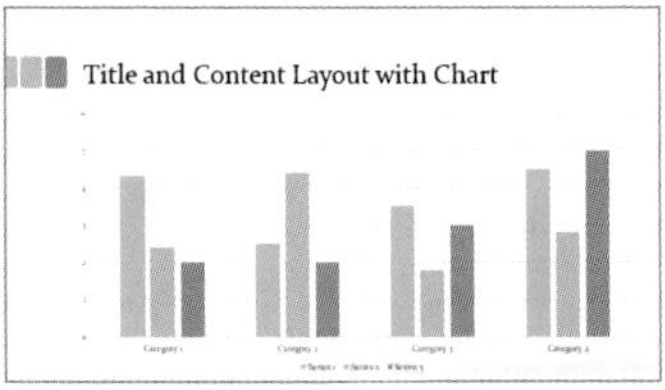

Fig. 11.9 The Contents of a Slide.

The two arrow buttons below the right-hand scroll bar let you step up or down through the slides. The second slide of this example is shown in Fig. 11.9. The word 'slide' refers to each individual page of a presentation which can be formatted for overhead projector acetates, or for electronic presentation on screen.

PowerPoint Views

You need to change your working view often in **PowerPoint**, so Microsoft has made this easy to do from the **Ribbon** in the **View**, **Presentation Views** group of controls. For **Normal**, **Slide Sorter** and **Reading View** the controls are also on the **Status** toolbar. Also on the **Status** toolbar you will find the **Slide Show** control button, as shown in Fig. 11.10 and an additional button that refits the slide to the window after zooming operations.

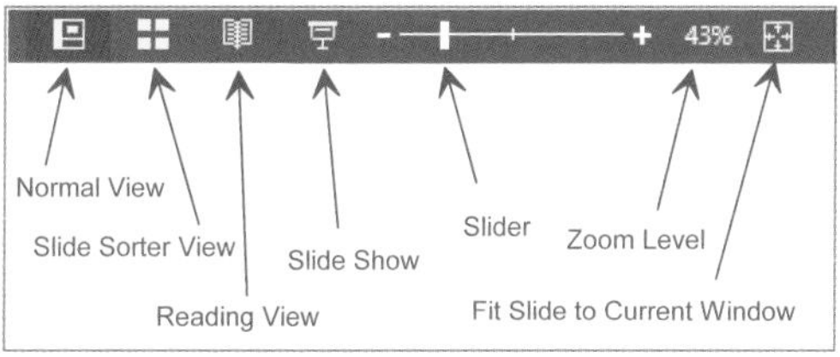

Fig. 11.10 The Views Control Toolbar.

Normal and Outline View

The **Normal** view, shown in Fig. 11.8 on the previous page, shows the slides in your presentation as thumbnails. They make it easy for you to navigate through your presentation and to see the effects of any design changes. You can also easily rearrange, add or delete slides from the **View**, **Presentation Views** group.

The **Normal** view is the main editing view, which is used to write and design a presentation. This view can also be accessed from the **View** tab, in the **Presentation Views** group, as shown in Fig. 11.11 on the next page.

Next to the **Normal** view, from the **View**, **Presentation Views** group, you'll see the **Outline View** of your slide text and on the right of the screen, the slide displays in a large view, as shown in Fig. 11.11 on the next page.

You can use these views to work on all aspects of your presentation, and you can adjust their thumbnail size by dragging the border between the left and right panes.

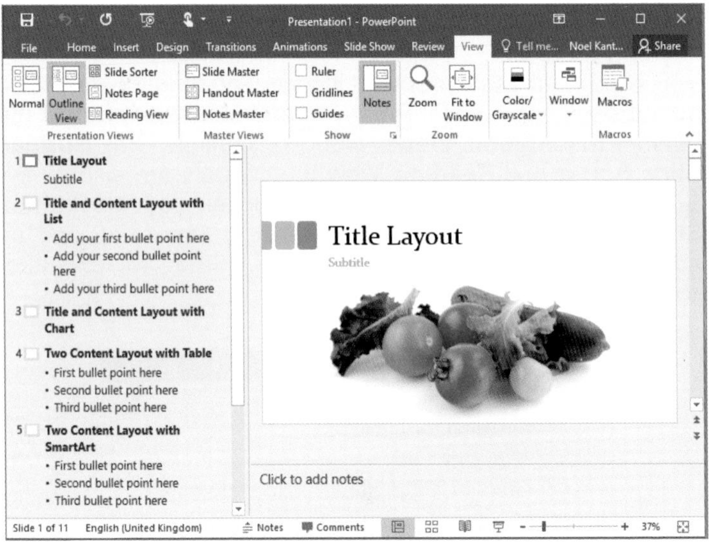

Fig. 11.11 The Outline View.

The **Outline View**, shows your slide text in outline form. This is a good place to enter and edit the text of your presentation.

The **Slide Sorter**, in the **View** tab, displays the whole presentation at once (Fig. 11.12), which allows you to sort your slides in the order you would like them to be. This facility can also be accessed from the **Status** bar.

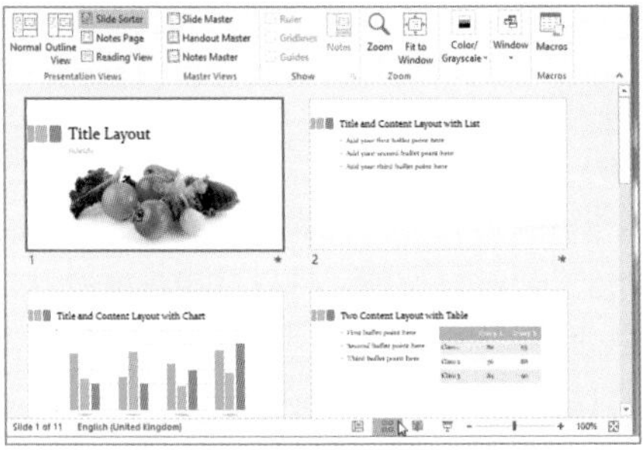

Fig. 11.12 The Slide Sorter View.

You can use the **View**, **Master Views**, **Slide Master** to add a logo or insert a picture to one slide, which will them appear in all your slides.

The **Notes Master**, is used to design and format your notes page. You can also customise how your notes will display when printed out with your presentation.

Notes Page View

If you want to view and work with your slide notes in full-page mode you can use the **Notes Page** view, opened by tapping or clicking the **View**, **Presentation Views**, **Notes Page** button.

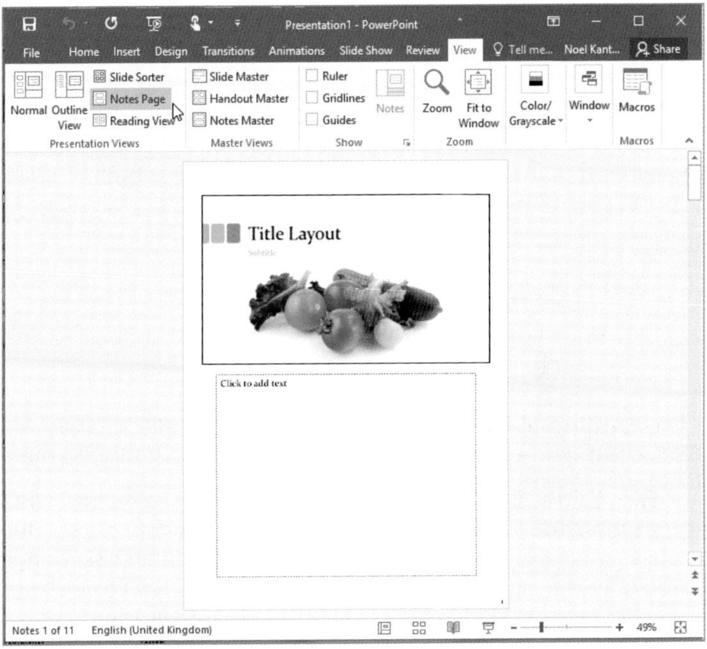

Fig. 11.13 Notes Page View.

As shown in Fig. 11.13 above, the **Notes Page** view has two panes. The upper one showing the current slide, and the lower one to hold your notes. You can add pictures here as well.

Also, as mentioned on the previous page, you can use **Notes Master** to design and format a consistent **Notes Page**. This is a powerful tool indeed.

Slide Show View

The **Slide Show** view which takes up the full computer screen, like an actual presentation, can be started by tapping or clicking the **Slide Show** button on the **Task** bar. In this view, you see your presentation the way an audience will. You can see how your graphics, timings, movies, animated effects and transition effects will look during the actual presentation.

To see the next slide on a touch-sensitive screen, in full-screen view, tap the right-arrowhead button in Fig. 11.14. To return to a previous slide in full-screen view tap the left-arrowhead button. To end the show, tap the last button which returns you to the **Normal** view.

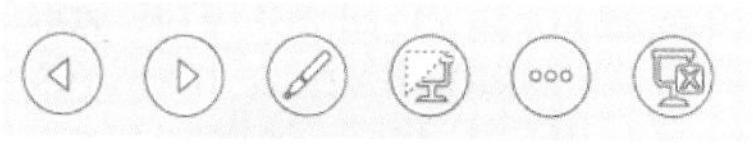

Fig. 11.14 The Navigation Buttons on a Touch-sensitive Screen.

The above buttons are rather faint on the screen as they are almost the same shade as their background. I leave it to you to explore the other buttons.

To navigate a full-screen slide show when using the mouse, start the slide show, then right-click the mouse button to display the contextual menu shown in Fig. 11.15 and use the **Next** and **Previous** menu options. As expected, every time you select such a menu option the actual menu disappears from the screen, so it is best to use the faint arrowheads shown in Fig. 11.14.

To return to the **Normal** view from a full screen slide show, either use the right-click **End Show** menu option or press **Esc**.

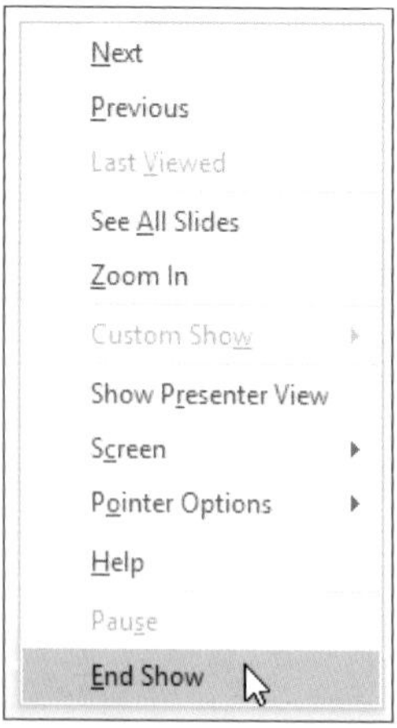

Fig. 11.15 Mouse Right-click Menu.

Setting Animations and Transitions

Your presentation will appear more professional if you set animations and transitions. To provide additional emphasis, or show your information in phases, you can animate or add special visual or sound effects to text or objects in your presentation. For example, you could apply a fly-in animation to all items on a slide or apply the animation to a single paragraph in a bulleted list.

To do this, tap or click the text or object that you want to animate (I chose the text "Title Layout" on the first slide in order to illustrate the process).

On the **Animations** tab, in the **Advanced Animation** group, select the animation effect that you want from the **Animation** styles list shown in a maximised **PowerPoint** screen in Fig. 11.16. If the **PowerPoint** screen is not maximised, then the **Animation** styles appear in an additional window. I chose the **Bounce** effect – you might need to scroll down to see it as pointed in the screen below). Check the effect by clicking the **Preview** button. The screen below has been captured in mid-bounce

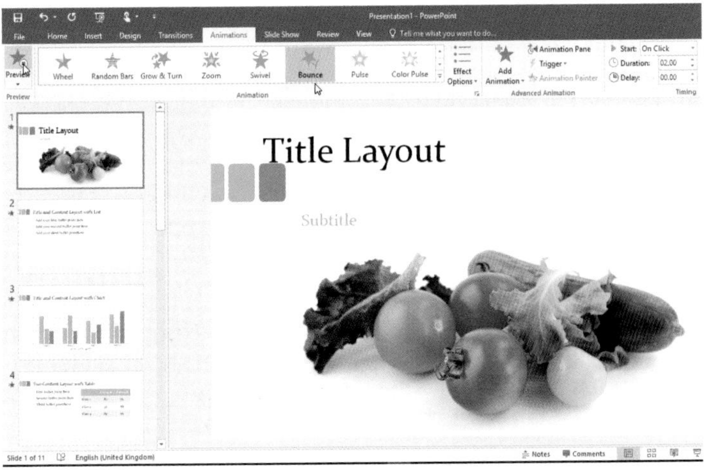

Fig. 11.16 The Animation Styles.

Adding Transitions

Slide transitions are animation-like effects that occur in **Slide Show** view when the show moves from one slide to the next. You can control the speed of each slide transition effect, and you can also add sound.

In **Normal** view select a slide and tap or click the **Transitions** tab, then in the **Transition to This Slide** group, select any of the available slide transitions, such as **Cut**, **Fade**, **Push**, etc., as shown in Fig. 11.17 which was captured while the **Split Transition** was being executed.

Fig. 11.17 The Effect of Adding a Transition.

As you select a different **Transition** the effect is demonstrated on your screen. To set the slide transition speed click the arrowheads next to the **Duration** button, and select the speed you want. When you are happy with your choice click the **Apply To All** command button.

* * * * *

In the next Chapter I'll try to design a presentation from scratch, so that you can apply some of the skills you have gained so far from this chapter.

12

Designing a Presentation

In this chapter I'll use some of **PowerPoint**'s tools to design a simple presentation quickly and effectively. Below, I show the first page of the finished presentation so that you can have an idea of the overall design.

Fig. 12.1 The First Page of My Presentation.

By default, when **PowerPoint** starts it gives you the chance to open **Recovered** files (if any), **Recent** files (if any) or **Open Other Presentations**. Selecting the latter, then **New**, allows you to open a **Blank Presentation** template which is the simplest of the templates to use when you first start, as it is plain and can be adapted to many presentation types.

To create a new presentation based on the **Blank Presentation** template, tap or click its entry on the available list of templates.

Initial Setup

These days, most presentations are probably given electronically, either in person, by e-mail or from a Web site, but the first thing to do is to check the initial slide size for your presentation.

To do this tap or click the **Customize**, **Slide size**, followed by **Custom Slide Size** button, shown here in Fig. 12.2 (left), located on the **Design** tab to open the **Slide Size** box shown in Fig. 12.2 (right).

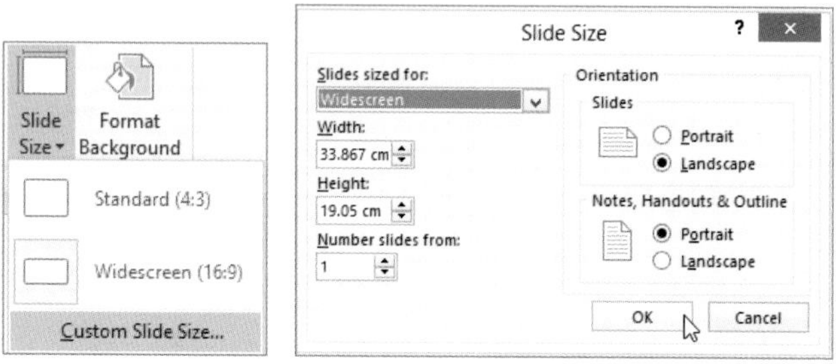

Fig. 12.2 Selecting the Slide Size.

In the **Slides sized for** drop-down list select from several on-screen sizes, your paper size if the presentation is to be printed on paper or acetate, 35 mm slides and others. If necessary, select **Portrait** or **Landscape** orientations.

Applying a Theme

PowerPoint provides a wide variety of design themes that make it easy to change the overall look of your presentation. As discussed earlier, a theme is a set of design elements that provides a specific, unified appearance for all of your **Office** documents by using particular combinations of colours, fonts and effects.

PowerPoint automatically applies the **Office** 2016 theme to presentations that are created with the **Blank Presentation** template, but it is easy to change the look of your presentation at any time by applying a different theme.

If you can choose your theme before you put data on your slides, you will save a lot of time later on. On the **Design** tab, in the **Themes** group, you can select how your slide will look with a particular theme. Next, you can go to the **Variants** group to choose a variation to the theme, then use the **Color** down-arrowhead to display the background colours available to you, as shown in the composite of Fig. 12.3.

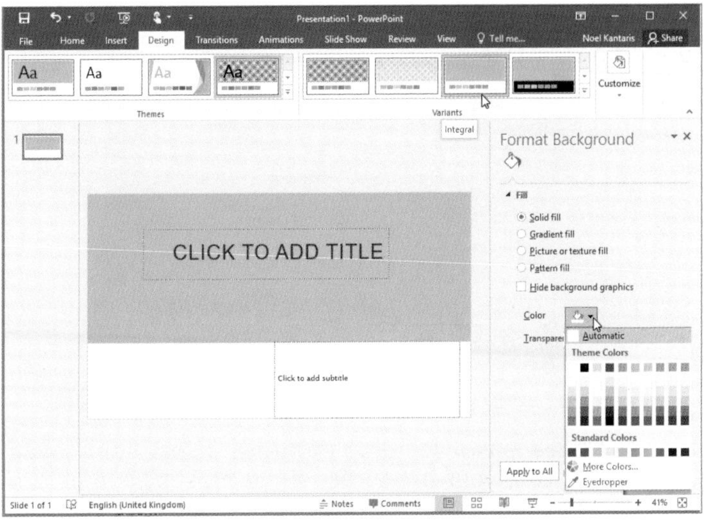

Fig. 12.3 Selecting a Theme for the Presentation.

Above, I chose the first theme displayed at the top left corner (you might have to scroll down the **Themes** to see it), then I chose the **Integral** variation from the **Variants** (again, you might have to scroll down to select it) and moved the **Title** text box within the coloured section of the slide.

By default, **PowerPoint** applies themes to the entire presentation, but not the background colour selection. To apply this to all the slides, tap of click the **Apply to All** button situated to the left of the **Color** options screen. If you only want to change a few slides, select them on the **Slides** pane, right-click or touch and hold the theme that you want to apply to them, and then select **Apply to Selected Slides** on the context menu that displays on screen.

Adding Text to a Slide

The single opening slide that is provided automatically in your presentation has two place-holders, one formatted for a title and the other formatted for a subtitle. This arrangement of place-holders on a slide is called a layout.

Click the place-holder where you want to add the text, and type in, or paste, the text that you want to add.

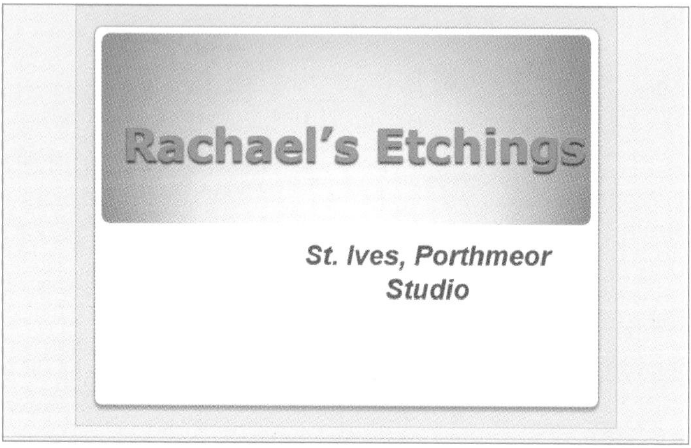

Fig. 12.4 Entering and Formatting Text into a Place-holder.

Here I have typed in the presentation title and formatted the text, increased its size and changed its colour. The subtitle was similarly changed to what is shown above.

Formatting Text

Hopefully the theme formatting will be fine, but if not, you can apply any changes of your own to any text you enter. There are many ways to change the appearance of text on a slide, ranging from the basic buttons on the **Home** tab or the **Mini** toolbar for formatting font, style, size, colour, alignment and other paragraph characteristics, to **WorldArt** styles on the **Text** group – you might need to increase the **PowerPoint** screen to see these features clearer.

Bulleted Lists

Some place-holders automatically format your text as a bulleted list, but you can control this. Tapping or clicking the **Home**, **Paragraph**, **Bullets** button will switch the text selected between a bulleted list and unbulleted text.

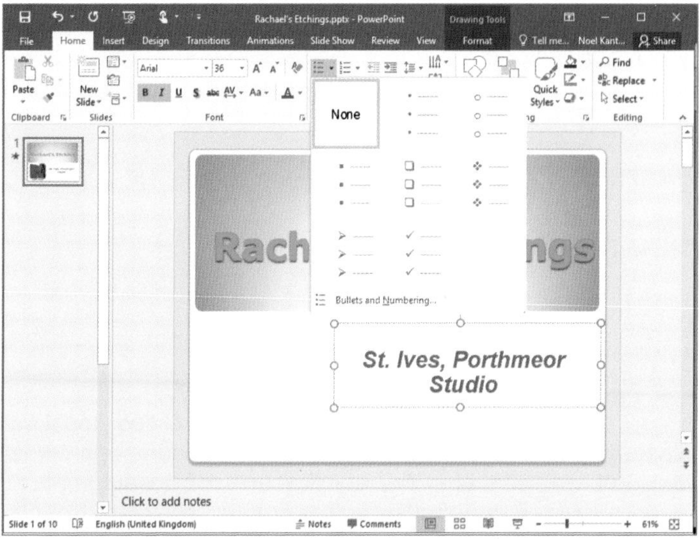

Fig. 12.5 Changing the Type of Bullets Used.

To change the style of the bullet characters in a bulleted list, tap or click the down-arrowhead next to **Bullets**, and then select the bullet style that you want, as shown in Fig. 12.5. You can also make these changes with the **Mini** toolbar.

Adding Slides

To add a slide to your presentation, you first choose a layout for the new slide, if it is to be different from your first slide, as described earlier. To do this, tap or click the arrowhead next to the **Insert**, **Slides**, **New Slide** button to open the gallery displayed in Fig. 12.6 on the next page, showing thumbnails of the various slide layouts that are available.

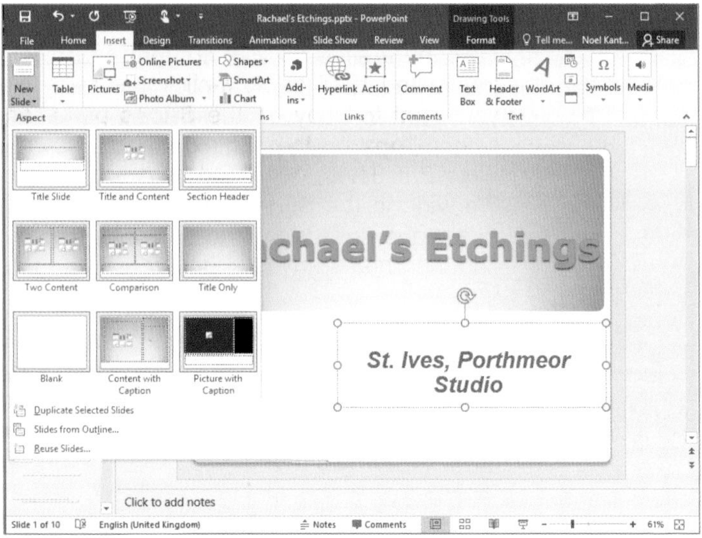

Fig. 12.6 The New Slide Gallery.

There are layout options for most types of slides, most with place-holders. Those that display coloured icons can contain text, but you can also tap or click an icon to automatically insert a table, a chart, a **SmartArt** graphic, a picture from file, a clip art or a media clip, as shown in Fig. 12.7 below.

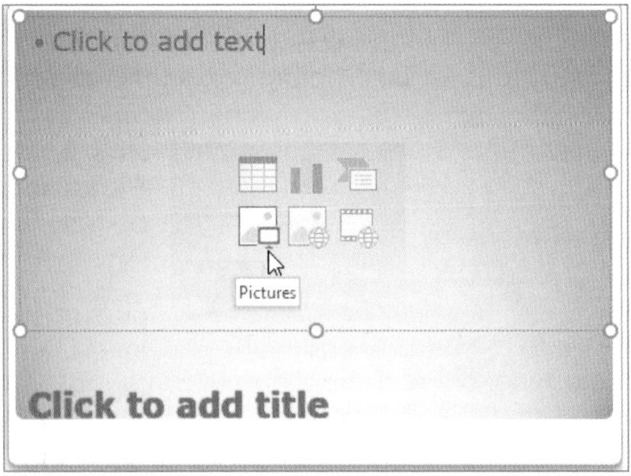

Fig. 12.7 The Content with Caption Layout for a New Slide.

Manipulating Slides

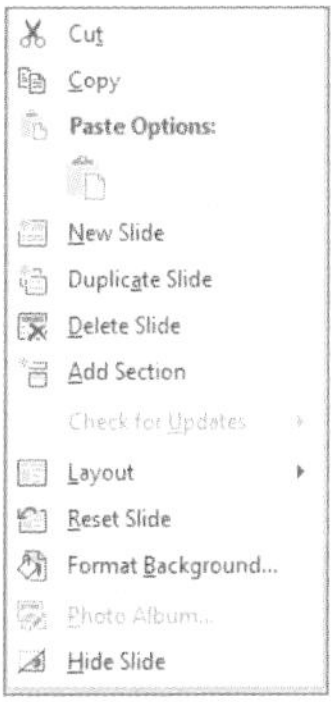

Fig. 12.8 Slide Context Menu.

To copy a slide with its content and layout, touch and hold or right-click the slide that you want to copy on the **Slides** pane, and select **Copy** on the context menu, shown in Fig. 12.8. Then touch and hold or right-click the slide in the **Slide** pane where you want to add the new copy, and select **Paste**. You can then make any changes you want to the new slide.

While you are in the **Slides** pane, you can drag slides up and down the list to rearrange them in the presentation. To delete a slide, select it and choose the **Delete Slide** option from the context menu.

Adding Pictures

You can insert or copy pictures and clip art into a **PowerPoint** presentation from commercial suppliers, Web pages, or files on your computer. You can also use pictures and clip art as backgrounds for your slides.

Inserting a Picture from a File

To insert a picture, tap or click where you want to insert it on the slide, either in a place-holder, or on the slide itself, then tap or click the **Insert**, **Images**, **Pictures** command button.

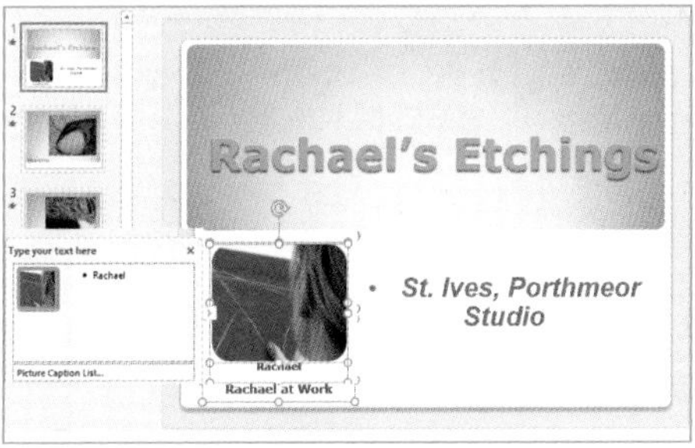

Fig. 12.9 Selecting and Inserting a Picture into a Slide.

Next, locate the picture you want to insert, and double-tap or double-click it. The result of such an action is shown here in Fig. 12.9.

Pictures that you insert from a file are embedded in a presentation. You can reduce the size of a presentation file by linking a picture instead. In the **Insert Picture** dialogue box, shown in Fig. 12.10 below, select the picture that you want to insert, click the arrowhead next to the **Insert** button, and then click **Link to File**.

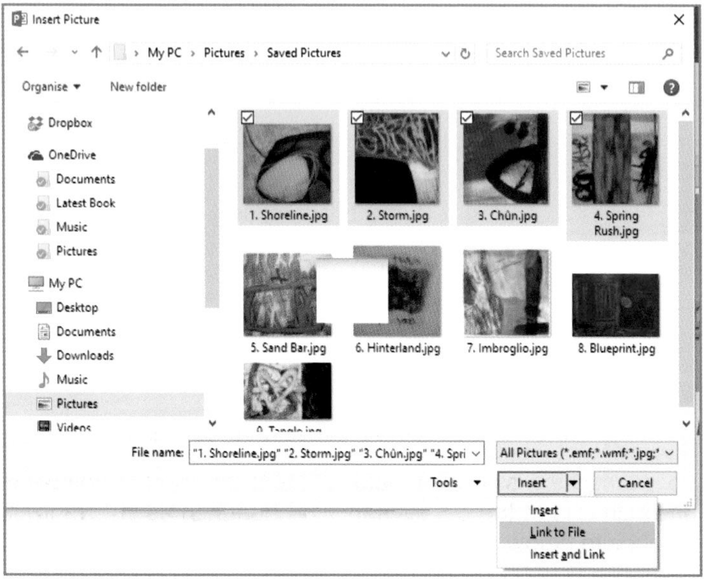

Fig. 12.10 Selecting and Linking Four Pictures into a Slide.

To copy a picture from a Web page, touch and hold or right-click the picture and select **Copy** on the shortcut menu. In your presentation, touch and hold or right-click where you want to insert the picture, and tap or click **Paste**.

If you don't select a place-holder for the picture, or if you select a place-holder that can't contain an image, the picture is inserted at the centre of the slide. You can now move it, re-size it, rotate it, add text to it, or even delete it from a touch and hold or right- click menu.

When you select a picture or other type of graphic in **PowerPoint** the **Picture Tools** commands become available in the **Format** tab as shown in Fig. 12.11 on the next page.

The **Picture Tools** commands let you add effects to images such as a shadow, glow, crop, compress, re-size and remove image background. The latter does not always work for all images, perhaps because of image reflections.

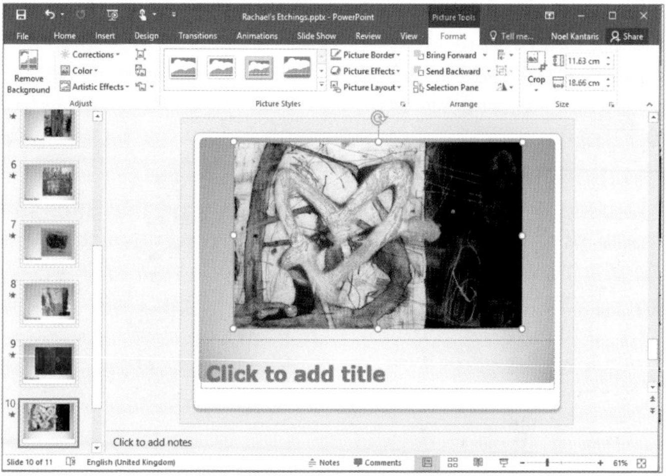

Fig. 12.11 Removing a Picture Background.

To change the size of a picture, place the mouse pointer on or touch one of the corner selection handles, as shown in the composite below, and drag the image to the size you want.

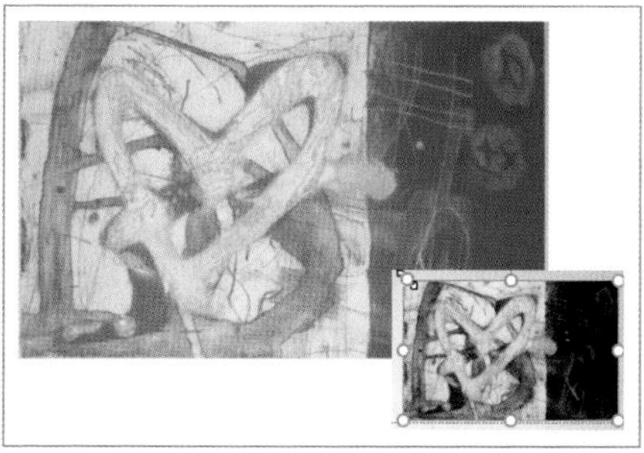

Fig. 12.12 The Re-sizing Operation.

To move the picture, just drag it with the ✥ pointer to wherever you want on the slide.

Saving a Presentation

As with any software program, it is a good idea to name and save your presentation right away and to remember to save your changes frequently while you work. That way you won't lose your hard-earned work. The quickest way to save a document to disc is to tap or click the **Save** button on the **Quick Access** toolbar. The usual way however is from the File command button, which gives you more control over the saving operation.

Tapping or clicking the **Save As** option on the **Backstage** screen, opens the **Save As** dialogue box from which you can navigate to where you want to save your work. Clicking the down-arrowhead against the **Save as type** box opens a menu of options as shown in Fig. 12.13.

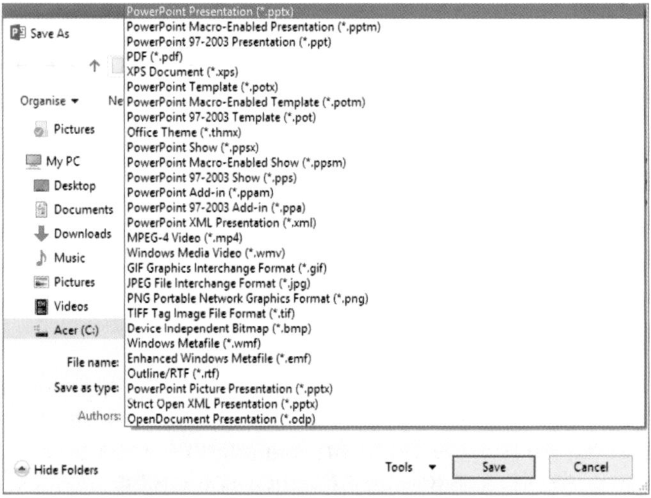

Fig. 12.13 The PowerPoint Save As Type Options.

Select **PowerPoint Presentation** if it will only be used for versions of **PowerPoint** from 2007-2016. For a presentation that can be opened in either **PowerPoint** 2003, or earlier versions, click the **PowerPoint 97-2003 Presentation** option, but you will not be able to use any of the new features available in **PowerPoint** 2007-2016.

Adding Transitions and Animation

It is easy to add transitions and animation to your presentation to make it more interesting. For example, select the first slide, then tap or click the **Transitions** tab on the **Ribbon**, tap or click the **More** down-arrowhead button pointed to in Fig. 12.14, and select the **Rotate** effect to be applied during the transition between the previous slide and the current slide.

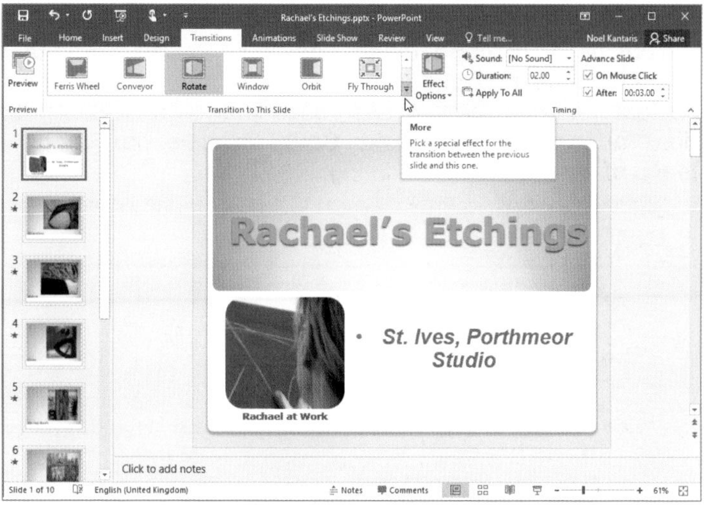

Fig. 12.14 Applying a Transition to a Presentation.

Next, click the **Apply To All** button in the **Timing** group, to apply the selected transition to all the slides of the presentation, set the **Duration** (the length of the transition) to 2 seconds, then check the **After** box and set the timing of the **Advance Slide** to 3 seconds, as shown above.

Finally, include some animation by tapping or clicking the **Animations** tab, selecting the top place-holder (the one that holds the title), then click the **Add Animation** button on the **Advanced Animation** group and select the **Fly in** option from the displayed menu shown in Fig. 12.15 on the next page.

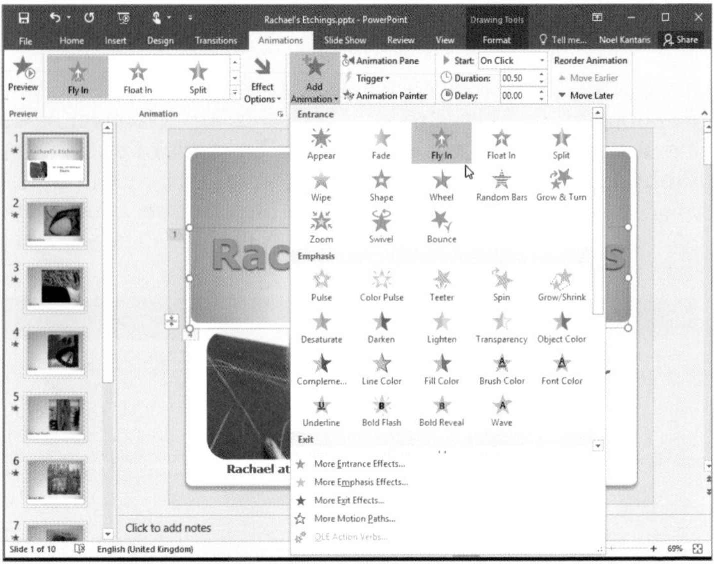

Fig. 12.15 Applying an Animation to a Presentation.

Next, set the **Duration** (which is the length of the animation) in the **Timing** group to 3 seconds, then click the **Effect Options** button in the **Animation** group and select an appropriate direction from which your animation is to appear.

Finally, repeat the process for the subtitle, and give it a different direction for its appearance. You are now ready to test your efforts by clicking the **Slide Show**, **Start Slide Show**, **From Beginning** command button and enjoy your creation! Do try it using your own pictures. It is the only way to learn!

In my example, the title flies in from the top left corner of the screen, the subtitle from the bottom right corner, while the picture bounces in from the left.

Fig. 12.16 Selecting an Effect Option.

SmartArt Graphics

When you want to illustrate a process, or the relationship between hierarchical elements, you can create a dynamic, visually appealing diagram using **SmartArt** graphics. This is a powerful tool available in **PowerPoint**, **Word** and **Excel**. By using predefined sets of formatting, you can easily create the following diagrams:

Process Visually describe the ordered set of steps required to complete a task.

Hierarchy Illustrate the structure of an organisation.

Cycle Represent a circular sequence of steps, tasks or events; or the relationship of a set of steps, tasks or events to a central core element.

Relationship Show convergent, divergent, overlapping or merging elements.

To see some of the many **SmartArt** layouts, tap or click the place holder that contains text, then tap or click **Insert**, **Illustrations**, **SmartArt**, as shown in Fig. 12.17.

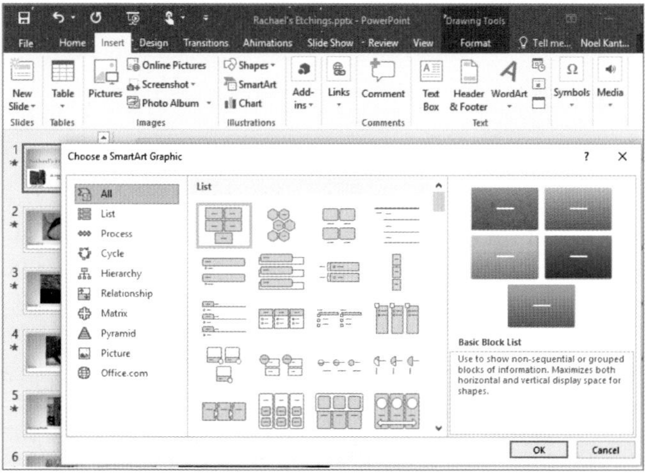

Fig. 12.17 Some of the Many SmartArt Graphics Layouts.

Converting Pictures to a SmartArt Graphic

Apart from converting text to a graphic (see next section), **PowerPoint** allows you to convert pictures on your presentation slide into a **SmartArt** graphic, using one of the photo-centric **SmartArt** graphic layouts.

To illustrate the above point, you can tap or click on the picture of the second slide of your presentation to display the **Picture Tools** tab on the **Ribbon**, then select **Format**, **Picture Layout**, **Convert to SmartArt Graphic** button pointed to in Fig. 12.18.

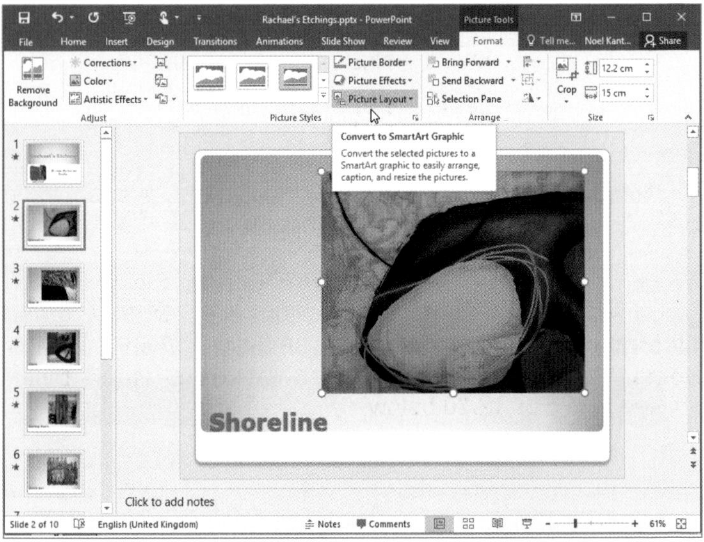

Fig. 12.18 Converting a Picture to a SmartArt Graphic.

Next, select an option from the list. As you place the mouse pointer on an option, the picture changes to show you how it will look if you choose that option. Touching an option with your finger changes the look of your work to that selection.

Once the **SmartArt** graphic is created you can move it, re-size it, rotate it, add text to it and change its font and colour. You can also apply animation to it, as you can with all the graphics. This really is an easy process, and the results can be excellent.

Converting Text to a SmartArt Graphic

Below, I list the steps needed for designing a presentation, by inserting bulleted information on a slide, before converting it to a **SmartArt** graphic. First, insert an extra slide at the end of the presentation, then type in the information given below. Obviously, if you are using a different presentation example, you should use your own appropriate list.

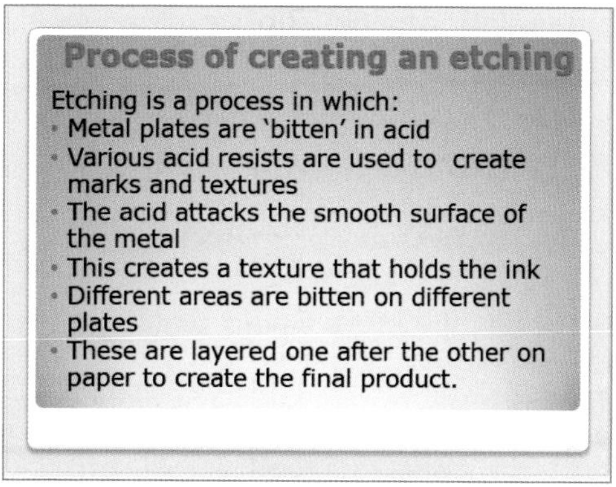

Fig. 12.19 Necessary Steps to Designing a Presentation.

To convert the above text into a **SmartArt** graphic, use the **Home**, **Paragraph**, **Convert to SmartArt Graphic** button pointed to in Fig. 12.20 below.

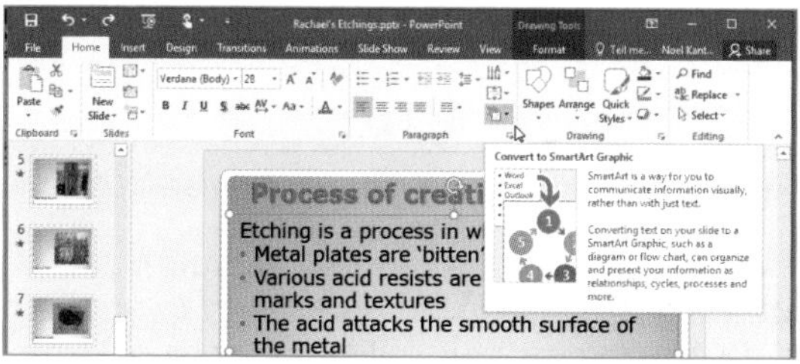

Fig. 12.20 The Convert to SmartArt Graphic Button.

Note that for the **Convert to SmartArt Graphic** button to appear in the **Paragraph** group, the place holder of the entered text must have been selected, as shown above. Tapping or clicking this button displays all the **SmartArt** graphics available, as shown in Fig. 12.21 on the next page.

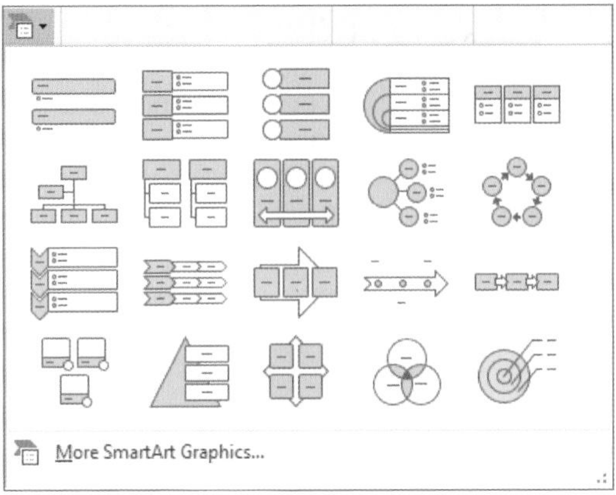

Fig. 12.21 The Available SmartArt Graphics.

Tapping or clicking the **More Smart Graphics** link opens the screen shown in Fig. 12.22 below.

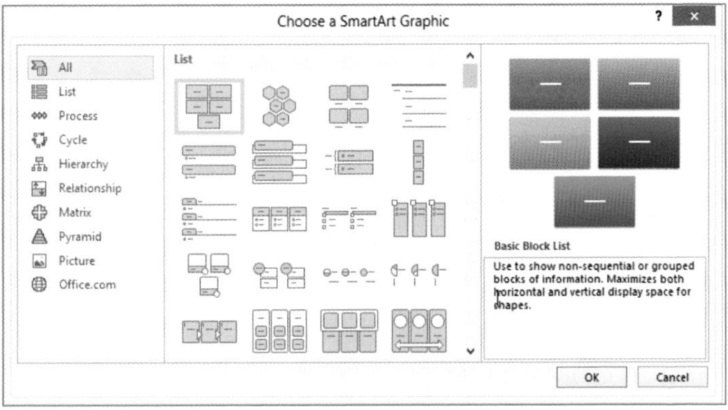

Fig. 12.22 More SmartArt Graphics.

As usual, you can see how a **SmartArt** graphic looks with your text by hovering the mouse pointer over the thumbnail. Using your finger, however, tends to convert the text immediately to the graphic you are touching.

I leave it to you to experiment with this type of conversion and to see which **SmartArt** graphic you prefer.

Sharing & Exporting Presentations

Just as with **Word** and **Excel**, you can share **PowerPoint** presentations in several different ways. Having opened the presentation in **PowerPoint**, use the **File**, **Share** option to open the screen shown in Fig. 12.23 below.

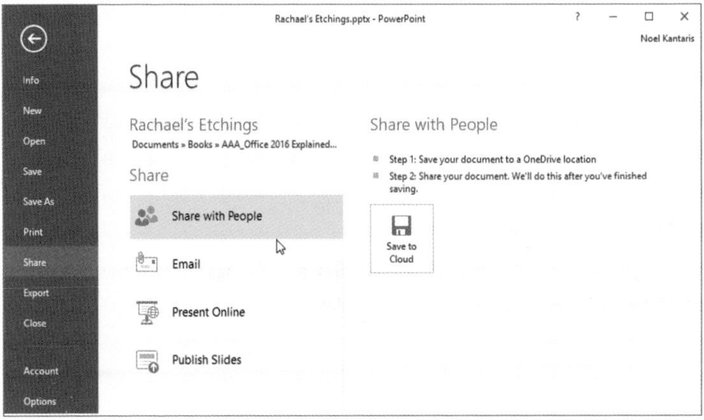

Fig. 12.23 Sharing a PowerPoint Presentation with People.

You can select one of the displayed options to **Invite People** to share it, having first saved your document to a **OneDrive** location (see page 14), **Email** a document as an attachment, **Present Online** by creating a link to share with selected individuals. Anyone using the link can see the document while being presented online. Finally, you can use the **Publish Slides** option to store slides in a shared location so that others can access them.

The **File**, **Export** option allows you to create a **PDF/XPS Document** format that you can publish or send to friends in a form that cannot be changed, while the **Create a Video** option can be used to burn a presentation to disc, upload to the Web or e-mail it as an attachment.

In addition, you can use the **Package Presentation for CD** to create a CD that other people can watch on their computer, while the **Create Handouts** option allows you to use **Word** to create and edit handouts.

Finally, the **Change File Type** option can create **PowerPoint** 97-2003 presentations for people who don't have a version of **PowerPoint** 2007-2016, create a **PowerPoint** template or a **PowerPoint** show, to mention but a few of the available options.

* * *

PowerPoint 2016 is obviously capable of a lot more than I have introduced here, but you should now be happy to create your own presentations and to explore more of the package by yourself.

* * *

13

Microsoft OneNote 2016

OneNote is a digital notebook that allows you to gather information in the form of text, Web pages, images, digital handwriting, audio or video recordings.

OneNote 2016, just as its predecessors **OneNote** 2007, 2010 and 2013, takes advantage of the **Ribbon** interface, and includes several other improvements over pre-2007 versions of the program. If you have upgraded from **OneNote** 2013, you'll notice that although all the features you are used to are still here, there is a more colourful border and some additional features. Some of these, include:

- Better integration with other Office Applications and services.
- The possibility to embed videos from Office mix, Vimeo and YouTube into a OneNote page.
- With Windows 10's new Edge browser, you can now scribble or highlight information on a Web page which is then shared with OneNote.
- You can also send information to OneNote via the me@onenote.com address which is a great way of storing important information in OneNote. Such information can then be searched and found easily.
- The adoption of the OneNote Clipper allows you to quickly clip part or an entire Web page so you know where to find it later. Clipper is a free App that you can get from onenote.com/clipper which will then sit in you browser's Favorites bar, so it is easily accessible when you need it.

Starting OneNote

I have already discussed in Chapter 1 how to pin shortcuts on the **Taskbar** of all the applications that make up **Office** 2016. This makes it easier to access the individual Applications.

So, to start **OneNote**, tap or click its icon on the **Taskbar** shown here on the left, which opens a clean screen similar to that in Fig. 13.1.

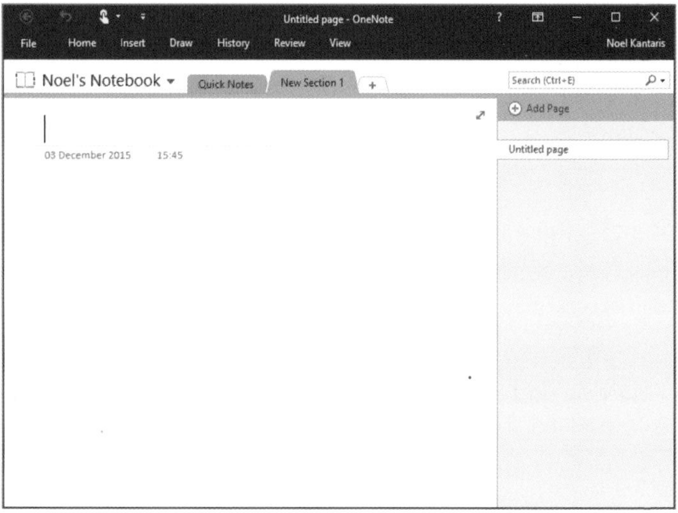

Fig. 13.1 OneNote 2016 Opening Screen.

If you have upgraded to **OneNote** 2016 from one of the previous two versions (2010 or 2013) of the program in which you had used it to take notes, you can find such notes or links to them by tapping or clicking the File command button to display them on a screen similar to the one shown in Fig. 13.2 on the next page.

If, however, you have already started an example in **OneNote** 2016, then that example is opened on a screen similar to that of Fig. 13.1 above.

For now, have a look at the constituent parts of **OneNote**'s screen, as shown for an earlier example in Fig. 3.3 also shown on the next page.

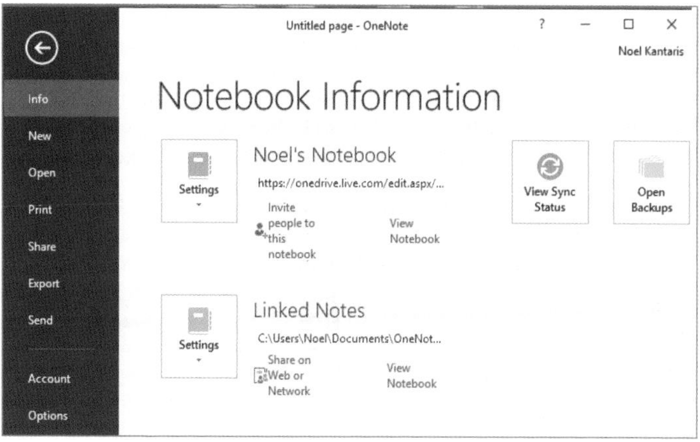

Fig. 13.2 The OneNote 2016 Information Screen.

The OneNote Screen

The OneNote screen below, displays some sample notes.

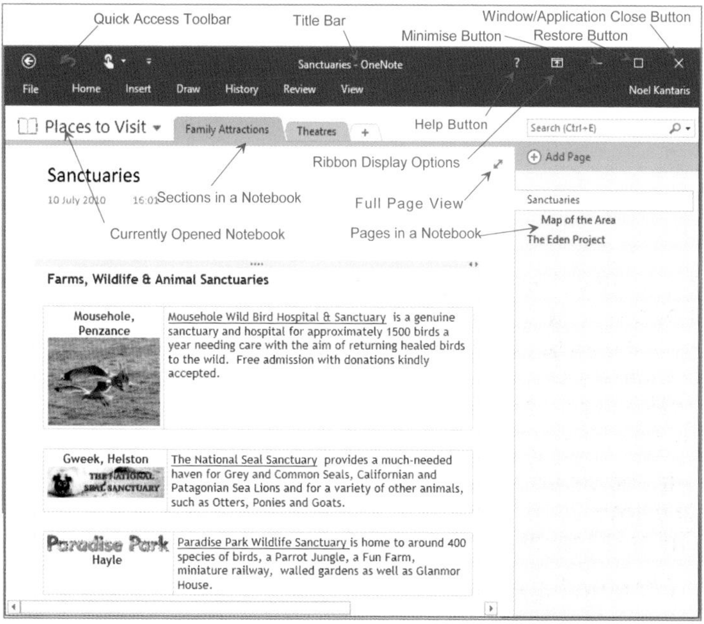

Fig. 13.3 Displaying OneNote 2016 Sample Notes.

On the displayed screen of the example shown in Fig. 13.3, you see all the various elements that make up **OneNote**. These are:

- **Notebooks** that display on the left of the screen. In Fig. 13.3, the **Sanctuaries** notebook is shown opened – you can create more than one notebook, but only one can be opened at a time.
- **Sections** that display at the top of the screen as tabs which stretch to accommodate the length of their description. Each notebook can have several Sections.
- **Pages** and **Sub-pages** that display on the right of the screen. Each section can have as many pages and sub-pages as required.

The Ribbon

When you first start **OneNote**, the **Ribbon** displays minimised as shown in Fig. 13.3, which gives you more space for your note-taking. However, as soon as you tap or click one of its tabs it displays in the normal way. In Fig. 13.4, the **Home** tab of the **Ribbon** is shown.

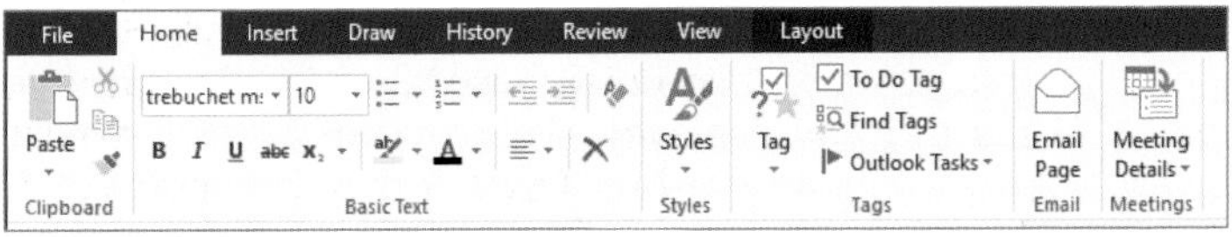

Fig. 13.4 The Home Tab of the OneNote 2016 Ribbon.

As usual, the **Home** tab contains all the things you use most often, such as the **Cut** and **Paste** commands, **Basic Text** formatting, using **Styles**, **Tags**, **E-mail a Page**, etc.

Tapping or clicking a new tab opens a new series of groups, each with its relevant command buttons. The content of the other tabs allow you to do the following:

- The **Insert** tab, displays groupings to enable you to immediately insert Space, Tables, Images, Links, Files, Recordings, Time Stamps, Page Templates and Symbols.

- The **Draw** tab allows the selection of various tools, including drawing pens, the ability to insert shapes and change their colour.
- The **History** tab allows you to keep track of Unread pages, Recent Edits, Find or Hide Authors, look at Page Versions or the Notebook Recycle Bin.
- The **Review** tab groups controls for checking the spelling of your documents and for opening the research pane to search through reference materials, translate a page or select a different language and take linked notes in a docked window.
- The **View** tab allows you to change what you see on the screen. You can choose between Normal View, Full Page View, or Docked to Desktop View, select different Page Setups, Zoom to different magnifications and control document windows.
- The **Layout** tab allows you to Create or Delete Tables, Insert tables into your notes, Format them or Convert them to an Excel spreadsheet.

Do note that when you dock **OneNote** to the **Desktop** by selecting to do so from the **View** tab, you can only see the page you are using to take notes – **Notebooks**, **Sections**, or other **Pages** are not displayed. This type of display persists even when you change to **Full Page View**. To return to the view shown in Fig. 13.3 (page 221), you must use the **Normal View** button that displays on the docked notebook.

To make the **Ribbon** visible all the time, click the **Pin the Ribbon** button, situated above the **Pages** pane, but only if the **Ribbon** is active. To minimise the **Ribbon**, click the **Collapse the Ribbon** button.

That is all the content of the fixed **Ribbon** tabs, but there are still others that only appear when they are actually needed. These contextual tabs contain tools that are only active when an object such as a picture, chart or equation is selected in the document. These will be covered later as and when they crop up.

Quick Access Toolbar

The **Quick Access Toolbar** is the small area to the upper left of the **Ribbon**, as shown in Fig. 13.3 and enlarged here. This feature displays buttons for the things that you use over and over every day, such as **Back**, **Undo**, **Touch/Mouse Mode**, and the **Customize Quick Access Toolbar** button. The bar is always available, whatever you are doing in a program, and it is very easy to add buttons for your most used commands.

Tapping or clicking the **Customize Quick Access Toolbar**  button, displays a menu of options as shown in Fig. 13.5.

You can select the **More Commands** option in Fig. 13.5, to add others, such as the **Redo** command which is to be found under **Popular commands**.

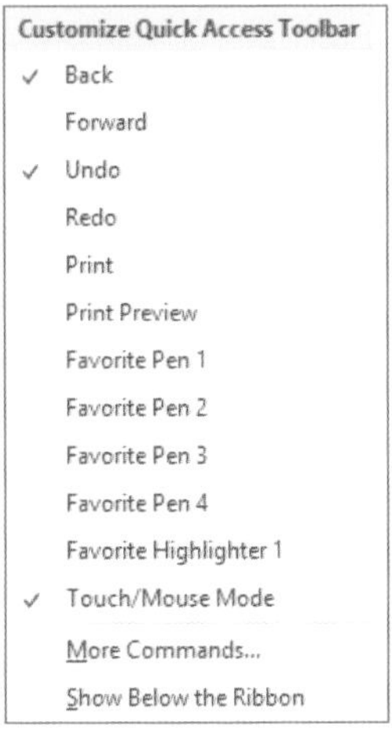

Fig. 13.5 Quick Access Options.

Context-Sensitive Menus

Almost everything you can do with the **Ribbon**, you can also do with context-sensitive menus. For example, touching and holding or right-clicking a **Section** tab, displays Fig. 8.6.

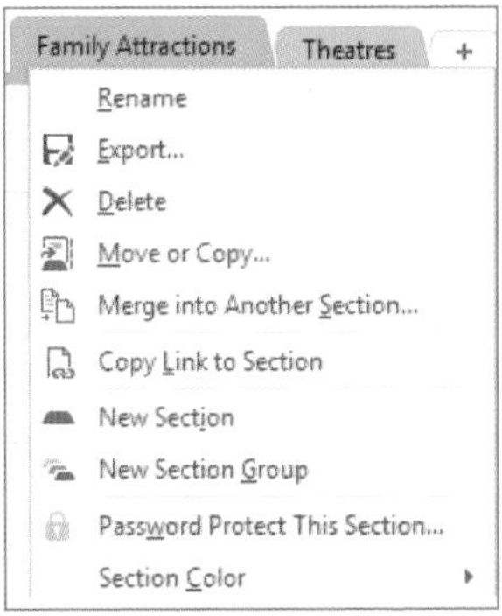

Fig. 13.6 A Section Context-Sensitive Menu.

The OneNote Backstage View

In common with all the other **Office** applications, **OneNote** also uses the File command button to display the **Office Backstage** view where you can access all the options relating to **OneNote** and the current document in your notebook. For example, you can get information on the current document, open an existing document, create a new document, save and print documents.

Creating a New Notebook

To create a new notebook, tap or click the File command button, then click the **New** button to display the screen shown in Fig. 13.7.

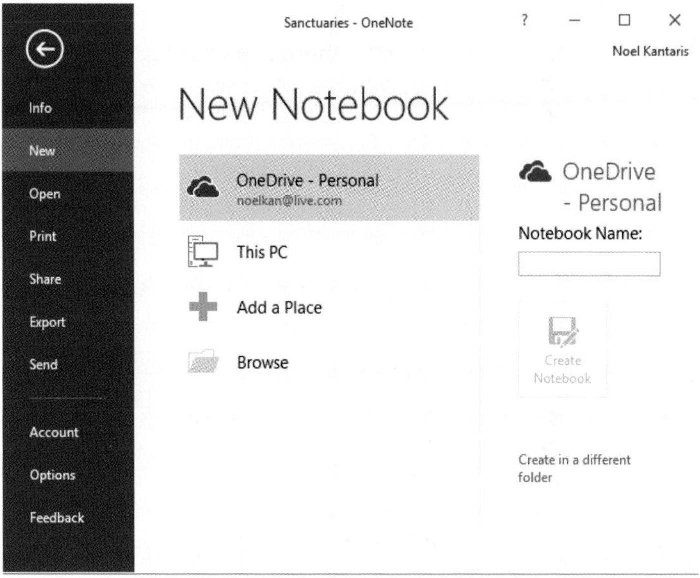

Fig. 13.7 Creating a New Notebook in OneNote.

Note that you must select where you want your new **Notebook** to be created; on the Web (on **OneDrive**), on **This PC** or a different place.

I chose the **This PC** option, then gave it a name and location, and selected the **Create Notebook** button shown in Fig. 13.7 on the previous page.

The project I'm undertaking here is to find new places, using the **Internet**, to take summer visitors near where I live in South West Cornwall. You can create a similar **Notebook** near where you live. So let's start.

I used **Google** and typed 'Places to visit in Cornwall UK'. Each section of this **Notebook** will include different places, such as beaches, heritage sites, gardens, galleries, family attractions and museums. This might be rather ambitious, as I have already found, on one Web site alone, 155 beaches, 23 heritage sites, 23 gardens, 38 galleries, 45 family attractions and 21 museums, most of them near me! So, I'll limit this example to only two sections and include a couple of pages per section. It is an example, after all!

When you create a new **Notebook**, what displays in **OneNote** is shown in Fig. 13.8 below, with the name of the new **Notebook** on the left (shown open), and one section named **New Section 1**. To give the latter a meaningful name, double-tap or double-click it to highlight it and type a new name. I chose to call this section 'Guide to West Cornwall'. Also note that this first section has one 'Untitled page' associated with it (you can have many pages per section), which can also be renamed by typing a new name at the insertion cursor position above the date.

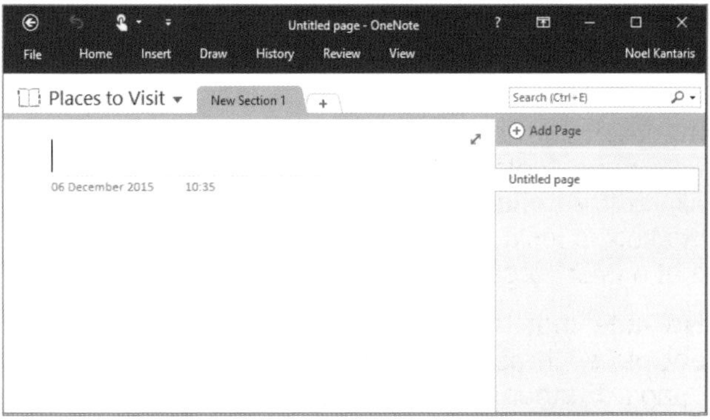

Fig. 13.8 Renaming a Section and a Page.

When you find something on a Website that interests you, select it by highlighting the portion you want, touch and hold or right-click it and select the **Send to OneNote** option from the displayed shortcut menu, as shown in Fig. 13.9.

Fig. 13.9 Selecting Information on a Web Site.

If you do not select what you want prior to sending information to **OneNote**, the whole page of that Website will be transferred over, which perhaps is not your intention. However, you can edit the transferred content in **OneNote** and only retain what you want.

What appears now in **OneNote** is shown in Fig. 13.10 on the next page. Note that at the bottom of the **OneNote** page, a link to the original site from which you obtained the information is included, so that you can go back to the Web page at a later stage.

Also note that later you can add more sections to your **Notebook**, such as 'Gardens' as shown in Fig. 13.10 on the next page. Further, sections can be rearranged to a different order, as will be discussed later.

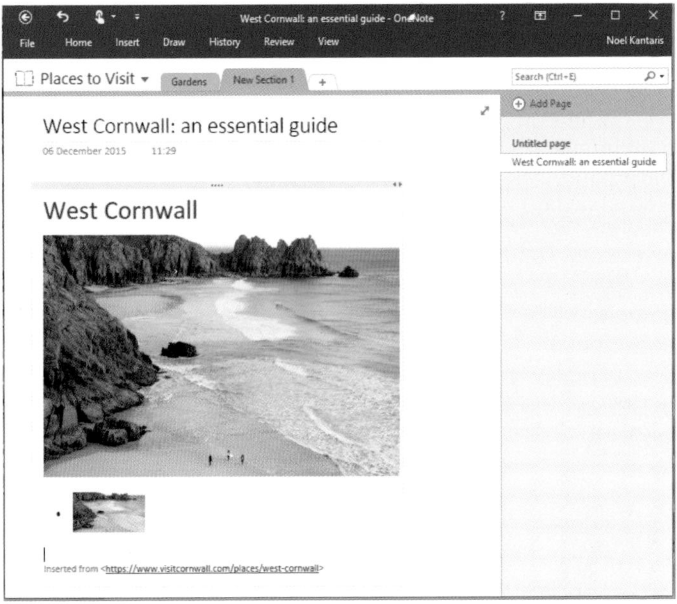

Fig. 13.10 Transferred Information into OneNote.

You can change the order in which pages appear in **OneNote** by dragging a page up or down to a desired position, as shown here in Fig. 13.11.

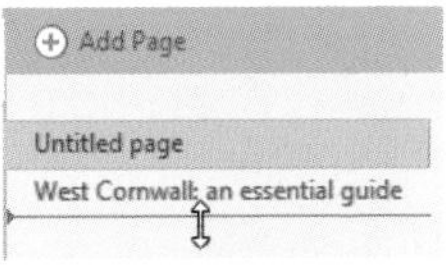

Fig. 13.11 Moving a Page.

You can also move sections in the same way. Here I illustrate the process by first creating a new section, as shown in Fig. 13.12, and naming it **Gardens**, then selecting the **Guide to West Cornwall** section and starting to drag it to the left of the **Gardens** section to change the order of appearance of the sections. As you start dragging, a small, solid arrowhead (see Fig. 13.13), indicates the place where the section you are moving will be placed.

Fig. 13.12 Creating a New Section.

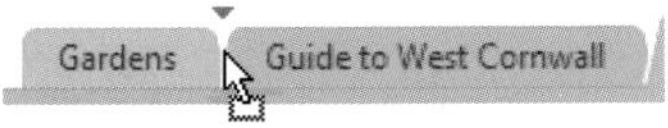

Fig. 13.13 Moving a Selected Section Left or Right.

Saving a Notebook

Unlike in other **Office** applications, there's no **Save** or **Save As** command in **OneNote**. The program automatically and continually saves everything you do, including typing, editing, formatting, searching and sharing your notes. **OneNote** saves and retrieves everything automatically.

To show you that these commands do not exist, tap or click the File command button to open the **Backstage** view as shown in Fig. 8.14 below, where you'll notice the lack of such commands.

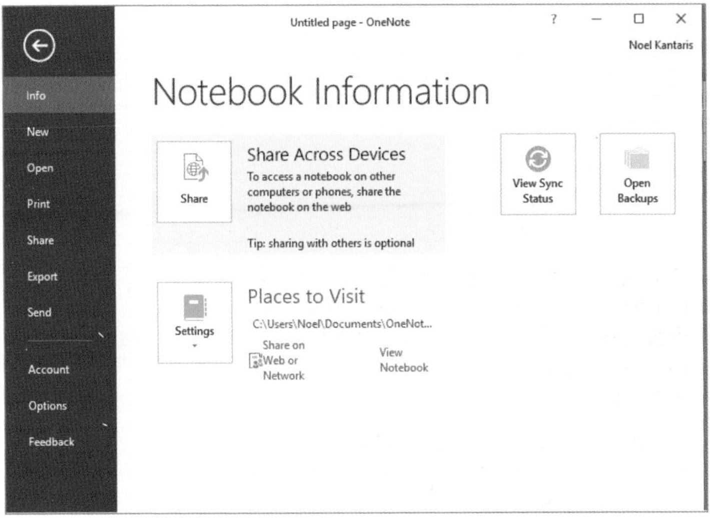

Fig. 13.14 The File Backstage View Available Options.

However, you can choose to save a **OneNote** notebook in a **PDF** or **XPS** file format. Such files can't be changed by others, but are ideal for sharing or printing. To do this, you'll have to **Export** your current creation to one of the file formats available, as shown in Fig. 13.15 on the next page.

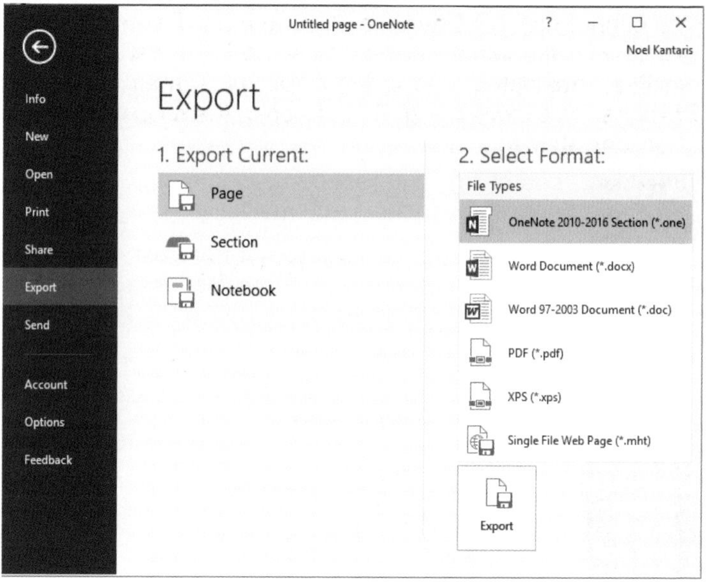

Fig. 13.15 The Export File Options.

File Formats in OneNote

OneNote 2016 uses a type of file format with the extension **.one**, first introduced in **OneNote** 2010. However, saving a **OneNote** notebook in this format has the following advantages and implications:

The new file format to all versions between 2010 to 2016 is required for many of the new **OneNote** features, such as linked note taking, use of mathematical equations, multilevel sub-pages, versioning and Web sharing.

OneNote version 2010 through to version 2016 can read and edit **OneNote** 2007 format notebooks which are opened in 'Compatibility Mode'. When you save such notebooks, they will be saved in **OneNote** 2007 format so that you can continue to collaborate with colleagues who have not upgraded to one of the last three versions of **OneNote**, namely 2016, 2013 or 2010.

You cannot convert **OneNote** 2016 to a 2007 version so that friends with the latter can read your work. To verify this, use the **File**, **Info** option and in the displayed screen tap or click **Settings**, as shown in Fig. 8.16, to open the drop-down menu of options shown.

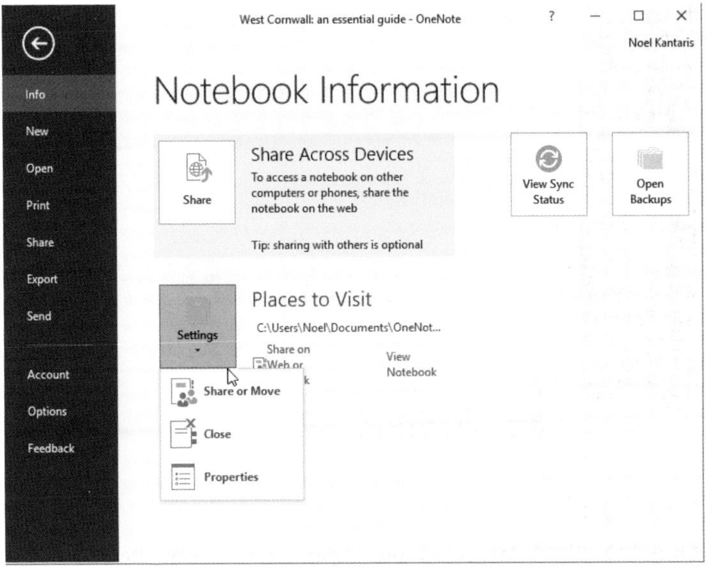

Fig. 13.16 The Notebook Information Screen.

Tapping or clicking the **Properties** option, displays the dialogue box in Fig. 13.17, where you can see for yourself that you can only convert to versions 2010-2016.

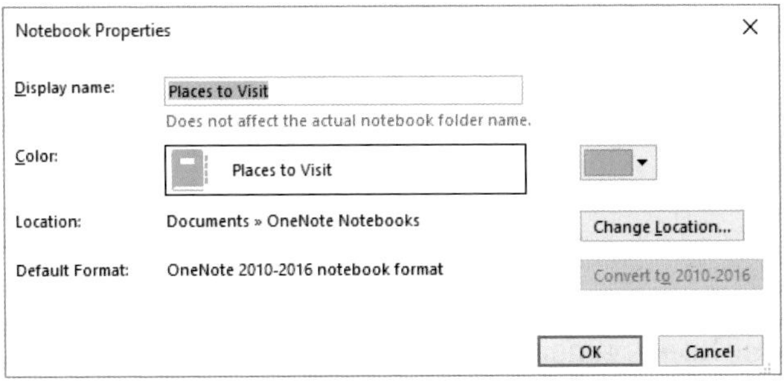

Fig. 13.17 The Notebook Properties Dialogue Box.

Using Templates in OneNote

OneNote 2016 allows you to apply built-in templates to the design of new pages, or apply your own custom templates. To find such templates, open a notebook and use the **Insert**, **Page Templates** command on the **Ribbon** to display Fig. 13.18.

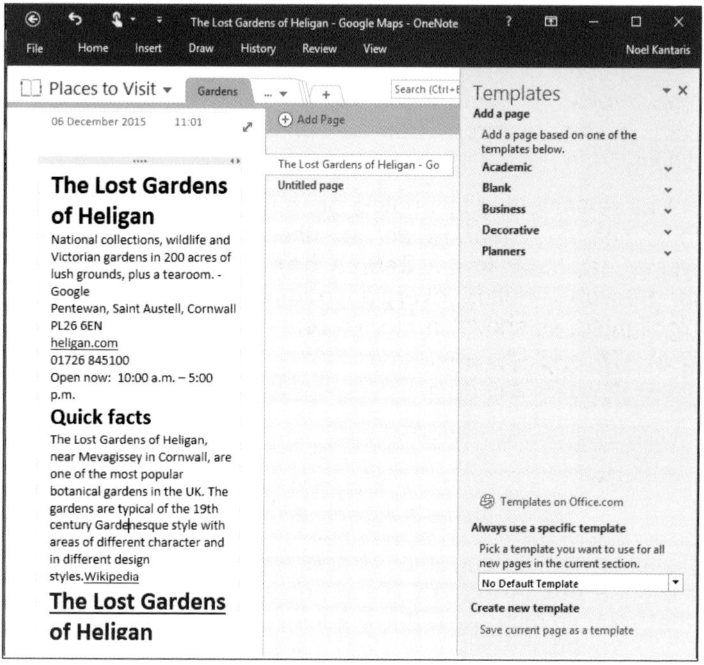

Fig. 13.18 Selecting a Page Template.

You could use any of the **Templates** under, say, **Academic** (for simple or detailed lecture notes, maths/science class notes or history notes), **Business** templates, etc. Also you could find additional templates on **Office.com** by tapping or clicking the **Templates on Office.com** link, then selecting a template category. Alternatively, you could create your own template by using the **Save the current page as a template** link at the bottom of the list displayed on the right in Fig. 13.18.

Searching Notebooks

One of the biggest advantages of an electronic notebook over a paper one, is the ability to search for information quickly and easily. Not only can you search one specified notebook, but you can also choose to search all your notebooks, or restrict your search to sections, or pages.

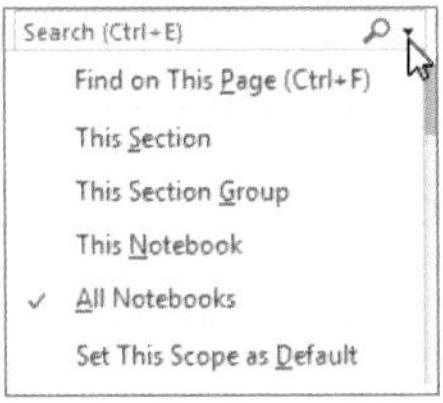

Fig. 13.19 Where to Search.

By default **OneNote** searches **All Notebooks**, as shown here by the tick in the **Search** box options displayed in Fig. 13.19, but it can be changed.

Before searching this notebook, I added two more sections to it; one on **Theatres** and another on **Sanctuaries**. Now typing, say 'seal' in the **Search box** and tapping or clicking the **Search** button, every appearance of that word displays highlighted, as shown in Fig. 13.20.

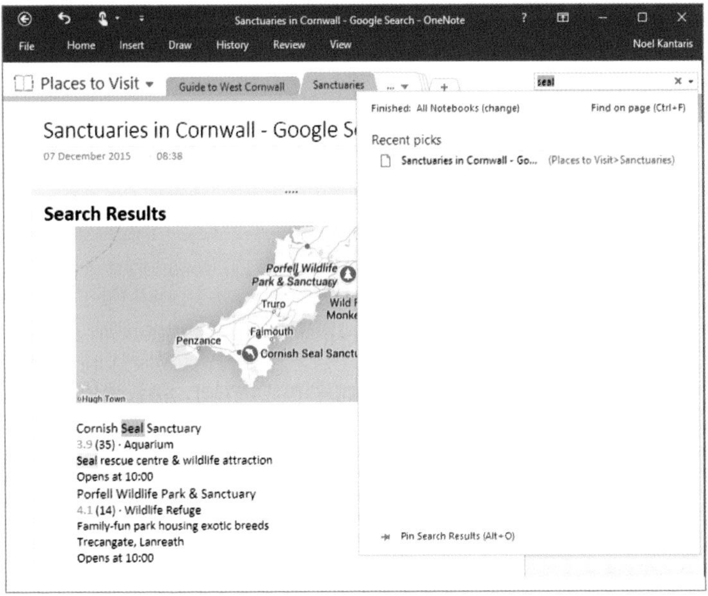

Fig. 13.20 Search Results.

Taking Linked Notes

Sometimes it is useful to make notes while you are working with other **Office** applications or **Internet Explorer**. **OneNote** allows you to do that by letting you take notes in a docked **OneNote** window. While taking notes in this way, **OneNote** stores with each paragraph, picture or Web page, a link to the original document or site so that you can return to it later.

As an illustration, you might like to take linked notes on a newly created **OneNote** notebook (call it "Several Links"), then do the following:

Use the **View**, **Dock to Desktop** command on **OneNote**'s **Ribbon**, **Views** group, to dock the newly created notebook to the desktop.

Start **Word** and on its **Ribbon** use the **Linked Notes** button on the **Review** tab, then open a document in Word (say PC User Group) and type 'PC User Group' in the docked **OneNote** notebook.

Repeat the process of first starting **PowerPoint** then **Internet Explorer** and while each displays a screen, type a relevant note in the **OneNote** docked notebook, as shown in the top half of the composite in Fig. 13.21. As each note is typed, a small graphic appears on the left margin indicating the application being used.

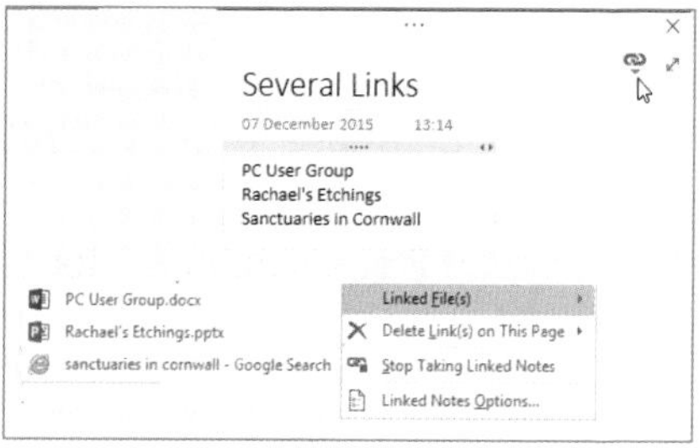

Fig. 13.21 Linked Notes.

Finally, tap or click the **Link Note Taking** button (pointed to at the top-right corner in Fig. 13.21) and select the **Linked File(s)** entry drop-down menu to display all the **Linked Notes** as shown on the left in Fig. 13.21. Tap a graphic and see what happens!

Sharing OneNote Notebooks

Just as with **Word**, **Excel**, and **PowerPoint** you can share **OneNote** notebooks in several different ways. Having opened a particular **OneNote** notebook, use the **File**, **Share** option to open the screen shown in Fig. 13.22 below.

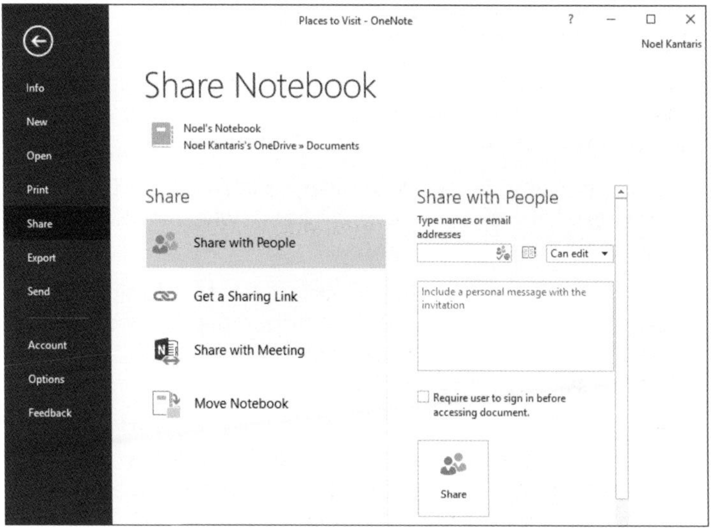

Fig. 13.22 Sharing a Notebook with People.

You can select one of the displayed options to **Invite People** to share it, having first saved your document to a **OneDrive** location (see page 14), **Email** a link to selected friends or colleagues or **Share with an Online Meeting** with selected individuals.

When you first select the notebook you want to send to the **OneDrive**, you are asked to specify the drive and folder where it is to be sent, after which it is synchronised with the original **Notebook**.

To have a look at a **Notebook** on **OneDrive**, use **Internet Explorer** and go to www.live.com, sign in with your **Live ID** and **Password**, and select the folder that contains it.

In Fig. 13.23 below, I show the 'Places to Visit' notebook with the section **Theatres** opened in **OneNote**

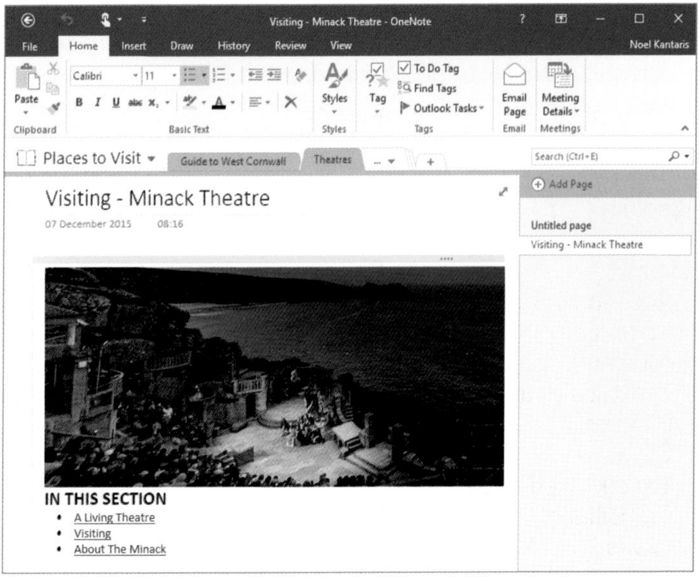

Fig. 13.23 A Link to the Minack Theatre.

This is an additional Section I created in the 'Places to Visit' notebook. The **Minack Theatre** Website is worth visiting. You can find out its history, what plays are on in the Summer and the times of the performances. This is an experience that should not be missed if you ever happened to visit Cornwall!

* * *

OneNote is obviously capable of a lot more than I have discussed here, but you should now be happy and able to create your own notebooks and to explore more of the package by yourself.

* * *

Index

W

Z